Toward the Recovery of Unity

"... the desire for Unity and the search after Unity both in the nation and the Church has haunted me all my days."

—F. D. Maurice

TOWARD THE RECOVERY OF UNITY

> The Thought of
> Frederick Denison Maurice

EDITED FROM HIS LETTERS, WITH AN INTRODUCTION, BY JOHN F. PORTER AND WILLIAM J. WOLF

NEW YORK
1964

Copyright © 1964 by The Seabury Press, Incorporated
Library of Congress Catalog Card Number: 64-12942
449-264-C-3
Design by Nancy H. Dale
Printed in the United States of America

Acknowledgments

Grateful acknowledgment is made to the following authors and publishers for permission to use material from the titles listed:

Cambridge University Press, England—Herbert G. Wood, *Frederick Denison Maurice*

The Macmillan Company, New York—R. H. Hutton, *Guides of English Thought in Matters of Faith*

Newman Press, Westminster, Maryland—L. Bouyer, *The Spirit and Forms of Protestantism*

Charles Scribner's Sons, New York—Frederick Maurice, *The Life of Frederick Denison Maurice, Chiefly Told in his Own Letters* (1884); Alec Vidler, *Witness to the Light*

C. W. Stubbs, *Charles Kingsley* (1899)

Preface

In Frederick Denison Maurice life and thought are intertwined with rare integrity. Students of Maurice have long profited from the massive two-volume *Life* written by his son chiefly from his father's letters. These volumes, however, are almost unobtainable. The present volume of selections from Maurice's letters is another step in the growing revival of interest in him.

Despite passages of great power in his published works, for most readers Maurice's style is a barrier. In his letters, however, his expression is easy and his germinal ideas are simply and movingly set forth. The letters are by far the best introduction we have to the thought of *The Kingdom of Christ* and the *Theological Essays*, two of his better known and recently republished books.

The introductory essay has been written: (1) to acquaint the reader who comes to Maurice for the first time with the events of his life; (2) to discuss Maurice's leading themes as they are exhibited in his books; (3) to serve as background for the selections that follow; and finally (4) to evaluate his contribution for today, particularly in Christian ecumenism. We predict a growing influence for Maurice's principles in the coming decades.

We want to express our gratitude to the Archbishop of Canterbury, Arthur Michael Ramsey, for pointing us to a little known letter of Maurice's in the works of F. J. A. Hort. Our thanks also are due Principal Alec Vidler, the Reverend David Patton, Frederick B. Maurice (a great-grandson), and Mr. W. J. Evans, the Warden of the Working Men's College, London. We had hoped to secure access to the autograph copies of the letters used by the son in his biography, but they have apparently been lost. Numerous letters not found in the son's biography have been consulted and some have been included, with identification in footnotes. The chronological order of the selections makes it easy for the reader, if he wishes, to consult the larger context in the *Life*. At times phrases in foreign languages have been translated and editorial information inserted, within brackets, into the letters. We hope these selections will lead many readers into the excitement and edification of coming to know Frederick Denison Maurice.

J.F.P.
W.J.W.

Heath, Massachusetts
August, 1963

Contents

The Thought of Frederick Denison Maurice

Introduction: The Life and Influence of Frederick Denison Maurice

The ministry of Frederick Denison Maurice has had a profound influence on English Christianity and has helped to shape the pattern of its thought to a greater degree than is commonly recognized.

Positing Christology as the starting point of all Christian theology and ethics—a radical departure in his day—F. D. Maurice helped to establish a principle that has become a commonplace in ours. Likewise, he insisted that the Gospel be heard in terms of its universal message, an insistence which sounded dangerous to his contemporaries. Indeed, he was constantly accused of being a Universalist by those who prided themselves on their orthodoxy. Today this is the accepted context in which the Gospel is viewed.

Maurice's social concern gave rise to the Christian Socialist movement and the tradition in which William Temple stood. His polemics against a sectarian approach to the Church embodied the earliest dawning of an ecumenical theology, and his thought about this was later to guide many of the early leaders of the ecumenical movement.

Thus it was that a quarter of a century after Maurice's death, Bishop Collins could observe:

Many elements in his [Maurice's] teaching have been so generally assimilated among us that this very fact stands in the way of our realizing our debt to him; we neither know whence we derived them nor who it was who brought them forth, but assume that our fathers were as familiar with them as we are.

3

He then wisely added: ". . . it may be doubted whether we have yet begun to assimilate some of the most essential elements of his teachings." [1]

Maurice's continuing influence has been due to the fact that Maurice was not only the greatest Anglican thinker of the nineteenth century, but also one of the clearest examples to be found anywhere of a Christian prophet. He was extraordinarily sensitive to the unbelief that lay hidden beneath the conventional religion and popular orthodoxies of his day, and that had even insinuated itself into theological method.

His period was one of upheaval when the notorious injustices of early capitalism had yet to be challenged by a Christian voice. Like a true prophet, Maurice saw that this social breakdown was rooted in a theological breakdown; and it was the latter which became his real target. Hence, simply to give leadership to the Christian Socialists was in his judgment not enough. He felt it necessary also to challenge the popular notions of heaven and hell, which were considered by most churchmen of that day a necessary part of the apparatus of social control. Although his daring resulted in his dismissal from his professorship at King's College, London, he did succeed in making men realize that "eternity was not time extended."

Maurice was also an educator, very much aware that the seeds of a new era were being sown and that the narrow sectarianism then typical of Christianity was not adequate to meet the crisis. Few men in his day were as sensitive as he to all that was going on in the hearts and minds of their contemporaries; and he alone had the theological power to interpret these intellectual and social developments from a Christian point of view and to reconcile their truths with the Gospel. Nothing seemed to him to expose the bankruptcy of contemporary orthodoxies more than the constant vilification by the religious press of those whose opinions deviated from the editors'. Nothing seemed more calculated to drive all the important movements of the century into anti-Christian channels than the shallow dogmatism with which Christians resisted new

---

[1] W. E. Collins, *Typical English Churchmen from Parker to Maurice* (New York: E. & J. B. Young & Co., 1902), p. 328. Quoted by Alec Vidler, *Witness to the Light* (New York: Charles Scribner's Sons, 1948), p. 17.

4

truth. "The orthodoxy which covers our atheism must be broken through" was his own statement of his purpose.

He approached the task not by joining the modernist or Liberal abandonment of traditional Christianity; rather, he reasserted its forgotten depths. His Christological orientation made it possible for him to recover biblical theology in a day when both Catholic and Protestant thought had obscured it with systems of dogmatic theology. "In reading Maurice," complained one of his most unsympathetic contemporaries, "one has to learn not so much a new set of facts as a new way of thinking."

Undoubtedly this explains why Maurice's own generation had such difficulty evaluating him. There were those, like Julius Hare, who spoke extravagantly of him as the "greatest mind since Plato." A good many more agreed with J. A. Froude, the Tractarian leader, who wrote, "As thinkers, Maurice, and still more the Mauricians, appear to be the most hideously imbecile that any section of mankind has been driven to believe in."

Foresight of what was to come might have given Froude pause. For among his "Mauricians" were to be eventually listed such diverse figures as Congregationalists P. T. Forsyth, H. A. Wood, and H. Richard Niebuhr and Presbyterians John and Donald Baillie, as well as Anglicans like Henry Scott-Holland, F. J. A. Hort, William Temple, Alec Vidler, and the present Archbishop of Canterbury, Michael Ramsey. One may not properly call these men "Mauricians," for it would violate the spirit of Maurice's theology to make him the father of a school of thought. The fact nonetheless stands that Maurice contributed greatly to their thinking and that he clearly paved the way for the post-liberal revival of theology, as well as for the development of the ecumenical movement itself.

▶ His Life and Influence

John Frederick Denison Maurice, as he was christened, was born at Normanstone on the coast of Suffolk, England, on August 29, 1805. His father, Michael Maurice, was a Unitarian minister of the old English variety rather than of the modern anti-Trinitarian persuasion. He did not object to the doctrines of the creeds so much as to their use, at least as a test for Church membership. The simple assertions of the Fatherhood of God found in the Bible were adequate for him. He had been a younger colleague of Joseph Priestley during the time a fanatical mob had burned Priestley's house. As a young man, Michael Maurice had given up a fortune rather than forsake his religious beliefs, and later in order to support his family he boarded pupils. Frederick, the only boy to survive infancy, had three older sisters (Elizabeth, Mary, and Anne) and four younger ones (Emma, Priscilla, Esther, and Lucilla).

The family was tightly knit and affectionate until serious religious dissensions began to disturb its unity. Elizabeth became a member of the Church of England. Two other sisters and finally the mother joined Baptist fellowships with strict Calvinistic theologies. Young Frederick was bewildered at the quarrels these religious changes occasioned. Forbidden by their father to engage in religious discussions at home, members of the family wrote long letters to each other to explain their stands. Maurice's later drive to realize unity and to bring reconciliation to warring factions may have been rooted psychologically in these family confrontations that were so painful to the growing boy. Later he was to write: "I not only believe in the Trinity in Unity but I find in it the center of all my beliefs: the rest of my spirit, when I contemplate myself or mankind. But, strange as it may seem, I owe the depth of this belief in great measure to my training in my home. The very name that was used to describe the denial of this doctrine is the one which expresses to me the end that I have been compelled, even in spite of myself, to seek." [2]

When he was not yet fifteen Frederick and a boyhood friend drew up and signed this resolution: "We pledge each other to endeavor to distinguish ourselves in after life, and to promote as far as lies in our power the good of mankind." To prepare himself for the study of law Frederick lived for some time in London with a family closely allied to the Wilberforces and to evangelical circles in the Church of England. There is some indication from a letter that the sense of religious depression that he experienced at that

---

[2] Frederick Maurice, *The Life of Frederick Denison Maurice* (New York: Charles Scribner's Sons, 1884), I, 41. Referred to hereinafter as *Life*.

time was much helped when a woman of his acquaintance introduced him to the writings of Erskine of Linlathen. Later a warm friendship developed between these men. Maurice was undoubtedly influenced by Erskine's conception of Christ as dying not only for the elect, but for all men, thus making Christ the Head of all mankind.

In 1823 Maurice entered Cambridge University, where he became a member of the Apostles' Club and developed skill in literary criticism. His tutor, Julius Hare, introduced him to Plato and to German thought. Hare later became his close friend and married his sister Esther. His most intimate friend was John Sterling, who has been described so colorfully in Thomas Carlyle's biography of him as "the noble Sterling, a radiant child of the empyrean, clad in bright auroral hues in the memory of all that knew him." Sterling shared Maurice's enthusiasm for Coleridge and helped him to overcome the great shyness that prevented him from participating in university life. Maurice took a First in civil law, but could not receive his degree because he would not subscribe to the Thirty-nine Articles. With Sterling he moved to London in 1827 to write for literary journals and finally to edit one, the *Athenaeum*.

The dissatisfaction with Unitarianism that Maurice had been feeling since boyhood was resolved when he became a member of the Church of England. His affectionate letters to his father during this period articulate tenderly, but with great conviction, his joy in knowing God as the Holy Trinity. He returned to university study in 1830, this time to Exeter College, Oxford, to prepare for ordination. During this period he finished a long novel, *Eustace Conway*, with his mother transcribing the copy and reading the chapters at the deathbed of his sister Emma. He was ordained in 1834.

From a country curacy in Bubbenhall, Warwickshire, he wrote *Subscription No Bondage*, a defense of the Articles as requirements at the universities. This first theological book drew considerable praise from members of the Oxford Movement. His growing estrangement from them may be traced to his disagreement with a tract of Pusey's on Baptism, which Maurice thought undercut the scope of Christ's redemption by seemingly limiting it to a special infusion of grace given to the newly baptized and capable of being

7

blotted out by subsequent sin. For Maurice baptism was the sacrament of constant union that declared Christ had redeemed all men. It was not the Catholicism of the Tractarians that offended him, but their exclusiveness and utter failure to comprehend Protestantism. In 1843 he wrote to Hare about W. G. Ward's inability to understand Luther. "The notion of Luther believing that the Gospel required a lower form of righteousness than the law! What havoc we must have made with his teaching before an intelligent and pious man could have produced such a conception of it. I am afraid we have to learn Protestantism again as well as Catholicism." [3]

Maurice's *Subscription No Bondage* deserves study today, quite apart from its dated controversy, as a thoughtful analysis of the theological foundations of education and culture. In 1870, as he drew near the end of his life, he indicated its importance in his own understanding of his work. "No book which I have written expresses more strongly what then were, and what still are, my deepest convictions." [4]

At the request of an editor preparing an encyclopedia, Maurice began an article on *Moral and Metaphysical Philosophy* which continued to grow over the years until it ripened into two volumes with that title. He was called in 1836 to become chaplain of Guy's Hospital in the Southwark slums of London, where his ministry to the ill brought out his pastoral warmth. Medical students were impressed with his lectures to them. From this time also dates his friendship with Sir Edward Strachey, who became a pupil in his household. Maurice's letters to Strachey were fortunately preserved and are some of the most valuable.

Maurice married Anna Barton, sister-in-law of John Sterling, in 1837. Two sons, Frederick and Edmund, were born. Frederick, who was to become a major general in the British Army and a military writer, deserves the gratitude of all students for the wonderfully understanding and balanced two-volume biography of his father and collection of his letters, which he published in 1883 and 1884.

In his mid-thirties Maurice wrote his theological masterpiece, *The Kingdom of Christ* (1838), which began as a series of letters

[3] *Ibid.*, I, 357.
[4] *Ibid.*, I, 174.

to a Quaker "concerning the Principles, Constitution, and Ordinances of the Catholic Church"; he revised it in 1842.[5] The first half consists of an analysis of Quakerism, Pure Protestantism (Lutheranism, Calvinism, Zwinglianism, and Arminianism), Unitarianism, Roman Catholicism, and contemporary religious, philosophical, and political movements. His basic conclusion is that nearly every one of these movements is right and truthful in its positive assertions, but wrong in its negations. These negations are compounded into systems that further divide men and shatter the unity of Christ's Church. Rarely has a man been able to live and think himself more imaginatively and appreciatively into the beliefs of others. Maurice is a Christian Socrates meeting other Christians on their own ground.

The second half of *The Kingdom of Christ* describes the "hidden hunger" of the previous systems and interprets the Bible as the progressive manifestation of covenantal relations between God and man in terms of family, then nation, and finally the Church as the kingdom of Christ. The Catholic Church is for Maurice not just a theological idea, but a concrete, historical reality, unfortunately obscured by systems that have been forced upon it. The "signs of a spiritual society" are then analyzed in the usual order in which men are drawn into communion with Christ: baptism, the creeds, forms of worship, the Eucharist, the ministry, and undergirding them all, the Bible. Relations between Church and nation are described and the Church of England, particularly its party structure, is analyzed with respect to the previous problems and concerns. This book is commonly misunderstood as simply an apology for the Church of England. *The Kingdom of Christ* sets forth theological principles which have yet to come into their own in Christian ecumenism. Maurice states his intention in these words:

I am not ignorant, also, that the hints which I have offered in opposition to systems may, themselves, be turned by myself or by others into a system. . . . On the other hand, if there be anything here which may help to raise men above their own narrow conceptions and mine,

---

[5] Edited by Alec Vidler in 1958 (London: SCM Press, 1958; New York: Seabury Press). All references to *The Kingdom of Christ*, unless otherwise noted, are to this edition.

may lead them to believe that there is a way to that truth which is living and universal, and above us all, and that He who is Truth will guide them in that way—this which is from Him and not from me, I pray that He will bless.[6]

John Sterling's wife died suddenly on Easter Tuesday in 1843, leaving him with six small children for whom the Maurices assumed much responsibility. Then Sterling himself began a losing battle with tuberculosis. Mrs. Maurice took Sterling into their home and nursed him, with her husband's help, until his death in September, 1844. In the process she too contracted the disease, and her devoted husband watched beside her bedside until the end in 1845. Four years later he married Georgiana Hare, half-sister of his friend Julius Hare who had married Esther Maurice. Maurice gave up the chaplaincy at Guy's Hospital to become chaplain of Lincoln's Inn, a center for law students. Earlier he had been appointed professor of English literature and of modern history at King's College, London. In 1846 he accepted the chair of divinity in its newly established theological college.

Scholarly recognition came to him in 1845 with his appointment by the Archbishop of York and the Bishop of London to the Boyle Lectureship. The lectures developed into *The Religions of the World*, a pioneer work in the field and one that enjoyed immediate popularity. So much more is now known about the world's religions, and Maurice so frequently employs an inadmissible style of asserting what the Buddhist or Hindu "will have thought" (Leslie Stephen called this tense "the conjectural preterite" in Maurice), that little attention is usually paid to the book today. It has, however, a surprising relevance for the recent debate by William Ernest Hocking, Hendrik Kraemer, and Arnold Toynbee on the Christian attitude toward the world's religions. Professor H. G. Wood has caught the highly dialectical method of Maurice.

His task . . . is to discover the element of truth in other religions, to show how Christianity, rightly understood, can do justice to them, to admit that in actual fact Christianity has needed the corrective contained in the insights of other faiths, to suggest that Christianity, again rightly understood, can supply what is lacking in other faiths. Throughout he has in mind the theory that the religions of the world

[6] F. D. Maurice, *The Kingdom of Christ*, II, 346-47.

are but so many products of man's wishful thinking, and also that kind of speculation about religions which blurs all the distinctions between them and so misses their true significance.[7]

In 1845 the Archbishop of Canterbury invited Maurice to give the Warburton Lectures. These were to develop into his *Epistle to the Hebrews*, which contains an important preface that is longer than the book itself. It is a careful reply to *Essay on the Development of Christian Doctrine*, written by John Henry Newman as he entered the Roman Church. With the growing contemporary interest in Newman in Roman Catholicism it would greatly enrich the current ecumenical dialogue to have Maurice's sympathetic, but also critical evaluation of Newman's seven tests of development republished. Maurice agreed with Newman about the need for authoritative guidance on the part of the contemporary Church, but he denied that an infallible authority had been given. What was given was the historical actuality of Christ and the abiding presence of his Spirit in the entire Christian community. God's judgments were more to be heard in historical events than in oracular ecclesiastical authority.

Maurice is often described as the founder of Christian Socialism. This description may actually be the source of more confusion than light because Maurice's Socialism bears no resemblance to the modern, post-Marxian variety. He was not interested in government ownership of the means of production, but in producers' co-operatives, a radical innovation in his day. More important to him than a specific set of social goals for which legislation should be sought, was the theological analysis of political and economic reform. He wanted to challenge his theological students to a concern for the social implications of the Gospel; and he was as concerned with providing educational opportunities for working men and women by founding colleges for them as he was in improving social conditions. If Christ had redeemed all men, then all of man's life must express this redemption.

Further, the real founder of the Christian Socialist movement was J. M. Ludlow, an English social critic, who had been born in India and educated in France. It was he who interested Maurice

<hr>

[7] Herbert G. Wood, *Frederick Denison Maurice* (Cambridge: Cambridge University Press, 1950), pp. 77-78.

in the cooperative movement and who originally proposed the formation of an association dedicated to the reform of English society along Christian lines. A group of outstanding young men gathered around Maurice and Ludlow after the revolutionary events of 1848, meeting weekly for Bible study. They promoted producers' cooperatives, conducted classes in a slum section of London, and published *Tracts on Christian Socialism*.

The name had been seized upon by Maurice because, as he put it, "It will commit us at once to the conflict we must engage in sooner or later with unsocial Christians and unChristian socialists." [8] "Competition is put forth as the law of the universe. That is a lie. The time is coming for us to declare it is a lie by word and deed. I see no way but by associating for work instead of for strikes . . . This is my notion of a Tailors' association." [9]

Though it made a great impact on English society, the movement did not achieve all that Ludlow envisaged for it, largely because of dissension among the members. Maurice quickly became the real head of the movement and dominated it according to his own understanding that society was already constituted in Christ. His interest was not in social revolution, but in the regeneration of English society by reasserting its foundation in Christ. This involved, in Maurice's eyes, raising the laboring classes up to take their rightful place in the social order, but it did not involve the formation of a new society. Consequently, he ultimately turned the energies of the Christian Socialists from producers' co-operatives to Workingman's College, founded in 1855.

The history of these developments has been painstakingly reexamined by the Danish scholar, Torben Christensen, and fascinatingly told in his *Origin and History of Christian Socialism, 1848-54*.[10] Christensen reveals that there were tragic depths in the conflict between Maurice and Ludlow of which neither were fully cognizant. Of the two, Maurice sounded the more prophetic note. In a sermon for Advent in the turbulent year 1848, he asked the question, "Do you really think the invasion of Palestine by

[8] *Life*, II, 35.
[9] *Ibid.*, II, 32.
[10] Torben Christensen, *The Origin and History of Christian Socialism, 1848-54* (Universitetsforlaget I Aarhus: 1962).

Sennacherib was a more wonderful event than the overthrowing of nearly all the greatest powers, civil and ecclesiastical, in Christendom?" [10a] His repeated references to current events seen under a Christian prophetic interpretation of history bring to mind Reinhold Niebuhr's similar message to our age.

Thus, Maurice is one of the sources of that concern for social redemption that has characterized Anglican theology in the modern period and which, through men like Headlam and Temple, has been a tributary stream to the Life and Work Movement of modern ecumenism. Some sixty years ago Bishop Stubbs wrote of Maurice what would become even more true as time went on:

It was the doctrine of Maurice which . . . kept the whole forward movement in the social and political life of the English people in union with God and identified with religion, a doctrine which, idealized and transfigured in the two great poets of the century, Tennyson and Browning, dominant in the teaching of the Cambridge schools of Lightfoot and Westcott and Hort, assimilated almost unconsciously by the younger Oxford theologians of the *Lux Mundi* school, has during this decade turned the current of our English Christianity to the consideration of the great social problems of the age. . . .[11]

Maurice held the religious press responsible for exacerbating party strife. It seemed as if the press had only to attack someone to have Maurice rise to that person's defense. Sanders writes, "Maurice was undoubtedly one of the most important forces which caused English journalism in the last half of the nineteenth century to insist more and more on the use of the signed article." [12]

Attacked on all sides by the politically conservative papers of both low and high churchmanship, Maurice gave his enemies the opportunity they were seeking to impugn his orthodoxy when he published in 1853 his *Theological Essays*.[13] In this book he criticized the popular equation of eternity with endlessness in reference to future punishment. His own understanding of the word "eternal" was drawn from such Johannine texts as "This is life

[10a] *Ibid.*, I, 484.

[11] C. W. Stubbs, *Charles Kingsley* (Chicago: Stone, 1899), p. 16.

[12] C. R. Sanders, *Coleridge and the Broad Church Movement* (Durham, N. C.: Duke University Press, 1942), p. 238.

[13] Reprinted by Harper & Row (New York: 1957).

eternal that they might know thee the only true God and Jesus Christ whom thou hast sent." He denied that he was a Universalist, but to the self-consciously orthodox of his generation any weakening of the traditional picture of hell seemed to subvert the sanctions for morality.

After much controversy he was dismissed by the Council of King's College for somewhat undefined opinions "of a dangerous tendency . . . calculated to unsettle the minds of the theological students." Four years before his dismissal he had taken time to write a long answer to a letter from F. J. A. Hort (then a student unknown to him), who was troubled by the conventional picture of eternal punishment. This letter remains his clearest statement on the issue.

His earlier writing on education and his conviction that the Church had a primary responsibility to educate the nation led to the foundation of Queen's College, London, in 1848. Started at first as a school for governesses, it quickly became a pioneering agency for the higher education of women. From 1848 to 1854 Maurice served as its principal. After his expulsion from King's he founded the Working Men's College, giving a set of six subscription lectures to raise funds for it. These were published later as *Learning and Working*. It is interesting that his grandson, Major General Sir Frederick Barton Maurice, who was Director of Military Operations, Imperial General Staff, 1915-1918, later served as principal of the Working Men's College.

Maurice made the Gospel the foundation of his educational philosophy. Unfortunately his prophetic role in this field, carried to a depth unparalleled by other writers, still goes largely unrecognized. His lectures in defense of Britain's system of ecclesiastical education were published in 1839 under the title: *Has the Church, or the State, the Power to Educate the Nation?* Three major types of education, he finds, have emerged in Western culture: the Spartan system cultivated discipline; the Athenian encouraged self-expression; and the modern type disseminates scientific information. Each type, he notes, becomes a failure when it is made the sole guide to educational practice. Self-expression alone destroys discipline. Discipline alone stultifies self-expression. The mere dissemination of information loses any central meaning in

14

life. The Gospel, however, furnishes a foundation for the creative combination of all three. Because it brings information of the highest kind, knowledge that men are made sons of God in Christ, it can furnish a productive foundation for the pursuit of scientific information. Yet this higher revelation also reveals a self-centeredness in man at war with his true standing, which must be disciplined if he is to realize sonship. Finally, because the Gospel reveals the ground of man's being in Christ, the Gospel reveals to man his true self and offers him the grace of God to bring this true self to expression. Hence only the Church as the custodian of the Gospel has within itself the foundation for the true education of man. The Church, in other words, is the schoolmistress God has appointed for the race.

The critical question Maurice puts to state education is whether it can ever have the universality to call forth the highest potentialities of its students. "The maxim of a state education must always be, how much nobler a thing it is to make shoes than seek for principles." Since the state must of necessity concern itself with vocational training Maurice did not believe it could ever offer any corrective to the commercial spirit which he believed the ruin of any nation. Compartmentalization would so fragment the educational system that it must fail to impart any sense of meaning to the whole of life or to elicit any universal loyalty. It could teach theology only as another specialty among the various specialties, rather than as the ground of unity for the whole universe. Thus Maurice believed that the true life of man's intellect would be dried up under a state system. Accordingly, the curriculum, under such a system, would treat all subjects only as preparation for a vocation, never as calling forth the specifically human sympathies of man. Consequently the professions (by which Maurice means the occupations dealing specifically with man as man, such as law, medicine, teaching, and the ministry) must inevitably be lowered to the level of trades, by which Maurice means those occupations dealing with man's material wants. What the nation requires, however, is the exact opposite—that the tradesman and the laborer discover in their callings the same dignity as originally attached to the professions. To this end he proposes specific courses of subjects for each. Much of this theory was tested at the Working Men's

College in interesting experiments in adult education. Many of the questions he raised about the adequacy of state-conducted schools have become burning issues today.

Maurice fiercely attacked Dean Mansel's Bampton Lectures on *The Limits of Religious Thought* in a volume written in 1859 and entitled *What Is Revelation?* He returned for a second round in *The Sequel to What Is Revelation.* Mansel was skeptical about our ability to know God. In some ways he anticipates the approach of linguistic analysis and has been defended in modern times as an "incomparable theologian and philosopher . . . shamelessly misrepresented by F. D. Maurice." [14] The asperity of Maurice's attack upon Mansel is surprising, considering his usual ability to see much truth in positions opposed to his own. The explanation is that Mansel's "Christian Agnosticism" cut to the very root of Maurice's faith and actual relationship to God.

Mansel was a gifted logician and witty lecturer who pulled down the opposition with such irreverent mirth that Maurice considered him a baleful influence on the Oxford undergraduate mind. Mansel argued that there could be no philosophically certain knowledge of God and that men must accept the Bible as a divinely given but purely arbitrary authority for the regulation of their thought and conduct. Christianity was commended to men precisely because it was impossible to know God. The Bible was a substitute for any real knowledge of God. Maurice saw in this the essence of all that he opposed in the religion of his day, for to him the Bible was treasured for the opposite reason. It offered a genuine relationship to the living God in intimate union with his Son. Professor A. V. G. Allen, in *The Continuity of Christian Thought*, described the conflict between Mansel and Maurice as "perhaps the most significant one in the whole history of the Church since Athanasius stood up to resist the Arians on a similar, if not the same identical issue." [15]

Maurice was appointed to St. Peter's, Vere Street, London, in 1860. The Colenso controversy brought to a head the question of biblical criticism in England. Bishop Colenso published his *Com-*

[14] G. L. Phillips, in *Theology*, April, 1957, p. 167.
[15] A. V. G. Allen, *The Continuity of Christian Thought* (Boston, New York: Houghton Mifflin & Co., 1893), p. 422.

mentary on the Pentateuch in 1862, just two years after the appearance of *Essays and Reviews*. The situation was particularly difficult for Maurice because he abhorred the outcry and the proceedings against Colenso, yet he could not sympathize with his point of view. Colenso represented the first negative phase of biblical criticism. He seemed to delight in exposing mathematical inconsistencies in the text and believed that this somehow wholly discredited the Pentateuch as history. He proposed the reorganization of religion along rationalist lines. Yet Colenso was a friend who had dedicated a book to Maurice during the controversy over eternal damnation in order to demonstrate his support. It was painful to write against him.

At the same time, Maurice found that the defenders of the Bible did not express his convictions either. He never called the Bible the Word of God as such. It was always the history of God's Word, by which the Word was to be discerned in life. *The Claims of the Bible and Science,* published in 1863, is Maurice's contribution to the issue.

One can only lament Maurice's lack of training in historical methodology, because his approach to the Bible is genuinely prophetic and is dependent upon regarding it as the actual history of the people of God. He was prevented, unfortunately, from giving great leadership in his time by his naïveté in the exegesis of questionable passages. Before the insights of Maurice could come into their own, purged from their precritical limitations, the battle for the freedom of scientific and historical exegesis had to be won.

In 1866 he became Knightbridge Professor of Moral Theology and Moral Philosophy at Cambridge. His book *The Conscience* is the result of his Cambridge lectures. The remainder of his life was spent in these university surroundings, where he also had the unpaid cure of souls at St. Edward's Church. Maurice died on Easter Monday, 1872, as he prepared on his sickbed to receive the Holy Communion. His last words were the Trinitarian Blessing.

Most of Maurice's books were developed from sermons he delivered on the Scriptures. Some of his outstanding books on biblical theology are: *The Prophets and Kings of the Old Testament, The Patriarchs and Law Givers of the Old Testament, The Doctrine of Sacrifice, The Unity of the New Testament, The Gospel of the*

17

Kingdom of Heaven, The Gospel of St. John, The Epistles of St. John, The Acts of the Apostles, and *The Apocalypse.* The liturgical revival today would be enriched by the reprinting of his biblically oriented sermons on *The Prayer Book and the Lord's Prayer* and *The Church a Family,* twelve discourses on the occasional services of the Book of Common Prayer. The extent of his writing throughout an active life is amazing. One estimate runs to more than 16,300 octavo pages.

▶ Maurice as a Man in Christ

Two things about Maurice seem to have attracted men to him wherever he went and to have given him a certain fame. One was his encyclopedic mind and the other his Christ-like character. Even his enemies, once they met him face to face, admitted that they had never known so good a man. He knew how to reach out to other men in deepest sympathy, and he constantly chose to work with the ignorant, the sufferers, and the poor of English society. Yet he was a shy person at the beginning of his life and was always filled with self-doubt and self-reproach. The sense of unworthiness and sin displayed in his correspondence strikes the modern reader as morbid. Apparently it did not so strike those who knew him best. R. H. Hutton attributes it to his intense sympathy with others, claiming that Maurice literally felt the sins and the shame in others as his own, yet constantly accused himself of not having entered more generously into their doubts and feelings. He felt himself implicated in the sins of the age. Hutton, considering this the secret of his sense of inferiority, made this comment:

His confessions must be taken as the outpourings of the conscience of a race rather than as the outpourings of the conscience of an individual, or they will seem artificial and unreal. Once catch the perfect simplicity with which he pours the humiliation of the heart of man, rather than the humiliation of the heart of an individual man—though, of course, it is the experience of the individual man which justifies him in that confession—and you see how truthful and genuine it is, how wonderful was the ardour with which Maurice entered into the social tendencies of his day.[16]

[16] R. H. Hutton, *Modern Guides of English Thought in Matters of Faith* (London, New York: Macmillan & Co., 1887), p. 312.

In theological discussion his aim was not to defeat, but to find the point of reconciliation between various truths. In this he lived out personally his understanding of the vocation of Anglicanism, which was "to hold together things which were never meant to be separated."

All this, however, grew out of his understanding of the Christian life. It was a life of repentance, if repentance is meant as constant dependence upon God-in-Christ. He was a living embodiment of the righteousness which he felt the Scriptures revealed. He trusted in a Deliverer. Though it is fashionable to call him a Johannine thinker, the principle of his life was Pauline. He trusted in a Justifier. His understanding of John opened his eyes to the meaning of Paul's phrase, "Christ in you." He considered Christ both the Word which confronted him and the Person at work in his life, actually giving him all sympathy with others, all strength in temptation, all true thought and good intention. These things, he believed, were first found in Christ, then distributed to men. Christ united each individual and all mankind to the Father. Christ gave each individual and all mankind truth and righteousness. The Christian life was trust and nothing but trust; yet the trust produced certain fruits—sympathy, understanding, the sense of oneness with others, and self-control—all that Paul calls the fruit of the Spirit. Trust, if it was real, involved obedience. Thus faith in Christ enabled him to overcome his shyness and to enter into genuine relationships with other men despite his sense of sin. Maurice put it this way:

That truth, of Christ being in us the hope of glory . . . I have found most necessary to sustain my own spirit when it has been sinking with the sense of its own unworthiness; for it shows that we can have no goodness apart from Him, that all our goodness must be by union with Him who is perfectly good.[17]

▶ *His Method and Style*

There is an inner consistency in Maurice's thought from the time he sought ordination in the Church of England until his

[17] *Life*, I, 230.

death; very few changes are to be recorded. He remained loyal to the basic principle of Christ as King, which he had established very early. He found, however, ever more fascinating ways of illuminating man's cultural task in its light.

Many times Maurice made clear his opposition to system-building. While he modestly described his vocation as "metaphysical and theological grubbing," this phrase really expressed his deliberate choice of the method of laying bare the theological presuppositions of culture and of dogma. In *The Kingdom of Christ* he observed:

Now to me these words [*system* and *method*] seem not only not synonymous, but the greatest contraries imaginable: the one indicating that which is most opposed to life, freedom, variety; and the other that without which they cannot exist.[18]

Behind this opposition to the system is something of Kierkegaard's existentialist protest. The note of struggle in finding "the truth-for-him" can be discerned in one of his letters: "I can say, I did not receive this of man, neither was I taught it. Every glimpse I have of it has come to me through great confusions and darkness." [19] His chief opposition to systems of doctrine, however, was founded on his respect for the facts of historical existence. In this Maurice expresses both the Englishman's empiricism against the conceptualism of Continental thinkers and the Anglican's respect for historical institutions as points of departure for theological analysis.

"When once a man begins to build a system the very gifts and qualities which might serve in the investigation of truth, become the greatest hindrances to it. He must make the different parts of the scheme fit into each other: his dexterity is shown, not in detecting facts, but in cutting them square." [20]

One of his letters provides this insight into his understanding of the theologian's task:

[18] *The Kingdom of Christ*, I, 236.
[19] *Life*, II, 16.
[20] *Ecclesiastical History*, p. 222.

20

. . . Theology is not (as the schoolmen have represented it) the climax of all studies, the Corinthian capital of a magnificent edifice, composed of physics, politics, economics, and connecting them as parts of a great system with each other—but is the foundation upon which they all stand. And even that language would have left my meaning open to a very great, almost an entire, misunderstanding, unless I could exchange the name theology for the name *God*, and say that He Himself is the root from which all human life, and human society, and ultimately, through man, nature itself, are derived.[21]

Maurice's style presents an unfortunate hurdle for the reader. It is often opaque, gristly, and confusing. Partly, this is the result of Maurice's extensive use of the Socratic method of inquiry in which it is not always clear whether Maurice is stating his own argument or that of his imaginary interlocutor. Partly, the difficulty stems from the fact that most of his writing was dictated. One of his biographers has described him at work, sitting on a window seat, hugging a pillow, as his thoughts poured forth. At climactic moments he might rise and take up the poker, punctuating his points with vigorous stirring of the fire. In spite of all this he frequently exhibits a gift for epigrammatic utterance that more than compensates for the difficult task that reading him can be. On the other hand, because of their directness and conversational style, his letters serve as an admirable introduction to his thought.

▶ The Basic Christological Principle

Though it may be said of any theologian that Christology is central to his thought, with Maurice Christology furnishes in a unique way the underlying principle for all that he said and did. It is the element that gives unity and coherence to his thought, yet saves him from constructing a system. He saw the unifying power of Christology more clearly, perhaps, than any other Christian thinker.

In a letter to his son he wrote: "I was sent into the world that I might persuade men to recognize Christ as the center of their fellowship with each other, that so they might be united in their families, their countries, and as men. . . ." [22]

[21] *Life*, II, 136.
[22] *Life*, I, 240.

The basic principle of Maurice's theology is that God has created and redeemed the whole race in Christ. The heart of the Gospel, as he understood it, was that Christ, the Eternal Son of God, is "the Head and the King of our entire race." He believed this to be the witness of the creeds and behind them of the entire biblical revelation. He interpreted every Christian doctrine, and the human situation as well, in the light of the doctrines of the Incarnation and Atonement, placed in a Trinitarian setting:

My desire is to ground all theology upon the name of God the Father, the Son, and the Holy Ghost; not to begin from ourselves and our sins; not to measure the straight line by the crooked one. This is the method which I have learned from the Bible. There everything proceeds from God; He is revealing Himself; He is acting, speaking, ruling.[23]

Maurice felt that the theology of his day, whether Roman Catholic or Protestant, whether Anglo-Catholic or Anglican Evangelical, had wrongly oriented itself around the sinfulness of man as the actual (even if not the explicit) starting point. He proposed instead the early divinity of the creeds, which do not mention the fall of man. Although he took a literalistic view of Genesis and thus believed the fall as historical fact, he maintained that we know Adam and man through Christ, and not *vice versa*, as this statement demonstrates:

Protestants and Romanists, even while they denounce and excommunicate each other, yet appear to recognize the fact of depravity, of Evil, as the fundamental fact of divinity. The fall of Adam—not the union of the Father and the Son, not the creation of the world in Christ— is set before men in both divisions of Christendom as practically the ground of their creed.[24]

Such a passage reveals to us what Maurice meant when he called himself a theological digger. Using the revelation of God in Christ, the union of all men in the Head of the race, he probed into every problem and every area of human life, tracing every abuse or evil in Christendom to an inadequate faith in Christ. This is why, in his book *Christ and Culture,* H. Richard Niebuhr cites Maurice

[23] *Doctrine of Sacrifice,* p. xli.
[24] *Conflict of Good and Evil,* p. 170.

as expressing more clearly than "any other modern Christian thinker and leader" the position that Christ is the transformer and converter of culture.

However, Maurice never leaves in isolation the principle that Christ is the Head of all mankind. It is always correlated with the nature of the Church and its function in the world. To Miss Williams Wynn he wrote in 1858:

I do . . . anticipate a very deep and searching reformation, one which cannot be attended with less trials, one which I trust is to issue in greater blessings than the Reformation of the sixteenth century. . . . I feel very strongly that the ascension of our Lord into the heavens, and the glorification of our nature in Him with the corresponding truth that the Church exists to witness of Him, not only as her Head, but as the Head of every man, will be the battle-cry that will rally Protestants and Romanists, hungry seekers after wisdom, lonely tatterdemalions without bread, about the one standard. . . .[25]

Maurice held his understanding of the concept *Christus Consummator* in close association with that which Archbishop Ramsey has called *Ecclesia Consummatrix*. It remains to underline the significance of this fundamental Christological principle for such other doctrines as revelation, man and sin, the Church and sacraments, and the principle of ecumenism.

▶ Revelation and Scripture

In spite of his precritical attitude toward biblical study, Maurice anticipated many of the theological commonplaces today about revelation and its modes. For Maurice revelation is not a set of dictated propositions, but is given in events, particularly in relationship to the Person of Christ: ". . . The revelation which the reason demands, cannot be one of merely moral principles or axioms—it must be the revelation of a living Being. It cannot therefore be one in which events are merely accidents that can be separated from some idea which has tried to embody itself in them." [26]

[25] *Life*, II, 317.
[26] *The Kingdom of Christ*, I, 177.

He distrusted the scholastic distinction between natural and revealed theology on at least two grounds. He could not accept the notion that there were two distinct pathways to the knowledge of God, especially that there could be one initiated from the side of man by something called "unaided reason." In today's terminology we should say that he believed in general revelation: "I hold that *all* our knowledge may be traced ultimately to Revelation from God." [27] In the second place, he refused to class the Gospel as a religion among the religions of the world. The Bible is not about religion, but about the acts of the living God: ". . . We have been dosing our people with religion when what they want is not this but the living God." [28]

Maurice's use of the Bible has sometimes been criticized as "Platonizing eisegesis." There is no question about the impact of Plato on his thought. Yet the influence is more in terms of a method of inquiry than in substantive propositions. Maurice's method in *The Kingdom of Christ* will remind the reader at once of Socrates' method when seeking the definition of justice by questioning conflicting schools of opinion. Maurice, of course, is leading his respondents on to the admission that there actually is a Catholic Church in their midst and to it each bears a partial witness. Probably the criticism of Platonism is rooted in the recognition that for Maurice the Johannine writings are very much the clue to his understanding of the Bible as a whole. It might even be permissible further to limit the field by saying that within the Fourth Gospel it is the prologue which is the key. Careful study, however, reveals that Maurice integrated Pauline and Johannine Christianity. What may explain the persistent charge of "Platonism" is more the form than the substance of his exposition. Maurice asserts that what God has intended things to be and has made them through redemption is the real, though unseen, world. What the world has become through rebellion is the false, though seen, world.

The Bible is the witness to the kingdom of Christ, and that kingdom is the real theme of the Old Testament and the source of half-truths in other religions and philosophies. In interpreting

[27] *Sequel to What Is Revelation,* p. 97.
[28] *Life,* I, 369.

24

any passage, Maurice tried to understand its simplest and historical context. Then he sought to show how the historical facts therein narrated also were pointers to God's universal kingdom and, in particular, to the constitution of all men in Christ. He believed that the Holy Spirit would reveal the relevance between these insights and the situation of the preacher or reader of the Bible. He believed deeply in the self-authenticating character of revelation. In his own words he states it thus:

I use them [the Scriptures] because I conceive they set forth Christ as the Son of God and the Lord of every man. I do not use them because I think they set forth some standard which is good for a set of men called Christians, who are different from other men, and who have not the same God with other men. I use the Scriptures to show us what I believe is the law and the life for all of us, that law and life of which men in the old world had only a partial glimpse. I should not use them if I thought them less universal and more partial than the books of heathens or of later moralists.[29]

For Maurice the Bible is not a solitary fact. He seeks to lay bare the organic connection that actually exists between Church, creeds, and Bible. His Anglican heritage with its respect for Bible, tradition, and reason received a creative reinterpretation in depth. The following passage of his about these relationships is genuinely illuminating—and indeed relevant in view of the discussion at the Second Vatican Council:

He who dwells with us and governs us, the Ever-blessed Word, has formed us to be one in Him; He seeks to make us one by bringing us to a knowledge of Himself; for this end He has revealed Himself to us, and has preserved the revelation in a book; this revelation He has entrusted to His Church, that she may impart it to men, and train men to apprehend its contents; the Church, in the exercise of her functions, has from Scripture formed a creed which is the first step in her scheme of education; when men were awakened by this creed, it became her duty to use the Bible, that they might know the certainty of those things wherein they have been catechized; with this Bible, she is able to cultivate the reason, which is the organ wherewith we apprehend spiritual matters; the Church tried what she could do without the Bible, and she became weak; the Bible has been set up against the Church, and has been dishonored; the Reason has been set up against both Church and Bible, and has become partial, inconsistent, self-

[29] *Epistles of St. John*, p. 14.

contradictory. Finally, bitter experience must lead us at last to a conviction, that God's ways are higher than our ways; that a universal Church, constituted in His Son, and endowed with His Spirit, is the proper instrument for using His universal book; and this book the instrument for educating the universal reason.[30]

▶ Man and Sin

From his basic Christological principle Maurice's method in evaluating the human situation flows quite logically. Christ precedes Adam in the order of being. When it is written in Genesis that man has been created in the image of God, Maurice at once understands that man has been created by the Eternal Son and that this image can therefore not be destroyed by sin. We are "not to think that the world was created in Adam, or stood in his obedience; for the Scriptures of the New Testament, illustrating those of the Old, teach us that it stood and stands in the obedience of God's well-beloved Son; the real image of the Father, the real bond of human society and of the whole universe, who was to be manifested in the fullness of time, as that which He had always been." [31]

This means that when Christ comes he comes not as an alien intruder into the world and to men, but as the Redeemer of his own creation. While Christ brings us the utterly new gift of redemption he does not extricate us from the race, but restores us to our true life as men created in his image.

It is clear that such a premise will entail a different understanding of sin than the traditional one which speaks either of a total loss of the image of God or only of certain aspects of the image. Maurice does not understand sin prospectively as the prelude to redemption. He sees it retrospectively, in the sense that we are now members of a race that has been redeemed by the incarnation of the Word, by Christ's bearing the sins of the whole world, and by his resurrection from the dead on the plane of our history.

There is no minimizing of the Atonement in Maurice. Indeed, the opposite is the case, for his firm convictions about the work of

[30] *The Kingdom of Christ* (edition of 1838), II, 87ff.
[31] *Patriarchs and Law Givers*, p. 66.

Christ in overcoming sin lead him to demote the doctrine of sin from its too dominant place in popular theologies. Maurice's view of the Atonement, as set forth in his *Theological Essays*, has been characterized as one close to the moral-influence theory. This is only a partial description, although perhaps justified because of the obscurity of expression in that work. His own view of the Atonement is best set forth in *The Doctrine of Sacrifice*, one of the clearest of his writings. Tracing the sacrifices of the Old Testament in a way that would need correction today from newer historical perspectives, Maurice holds, helpfully, that the New Testament asserts sacrifice as the great principle of the divine obedience of the Son before the world existed. What is new here is the careful linking of the Trinity and the idea of creation with the concept of Atonement. Here is his statement:

. . . We see beneath all evil, beneath the universe itself, that eternal and original union of the Father and the Son . . . which was never fully manifested till the Only Begotten by the eternal Spirit offered Himself to God. The revelation of that primal unity is the revelation of the ground on which all things stand, both things in heaven and things in earth. It is the revelation of an order which sustains all the intercourse and society of men. It is the revelation of that which sin has ever been seeking to destroy, and which at last has overcome sin. It is the revelation of that perfect harmony to which we look forward when all things are gathered up in Christ . . . when the law of sacrifice shall be the acknowledged law of all creation.[32]

In terms of Christ's accomplished work, Maurice does not underestimate the power of sin, as he has often been accused of doing. Sin, for him, is defined as self-willed isolation from the true constitution of man as created and redeemed by Christ. Sin is man's refusal to acknowledge his true center in Christ and the desperate effort to establish a false independence. Since Maurice took the fall as a historical event, his interpretation that it must not be the base for theology seems all the more remarkable to us in that this interpretation when put forward today is based on the view that the Genesis account of the fall is a myth with deep insights into the human situation. Maurice also accepted the

[32] *Doctrine of Sacrifice*, p. 194.

reality of the devil, but refused to grant that the world was properly his possession.

Maurice criticized Calvinism for misinterpreting God's election and predestination in a narrowly individualistic and exclusivistic way. It made a travesty of the biblical witness that Christ was himself the elect and predestinated One and that the whole race, not just a favored few, was included in him. This perspective is quite close to Barth's criticism of Calvin. Maurice claimed that the constitution of the race in Christ was the proper background for appreciating the power of Luther's concern for justification by faith and of keeping that cardinal insight uncorrupted. But Protestantism found it almost impossible to submit its doctrine of justification by faith to the experience of justification by faith, with the result that, as Maurice shrewdly observed, "when assent to the doctrine of justification was substituted for belief in the Justifier, Protestantism went into the lean, sickly and yet contentious stage of its existence, only to emerge from that into indifference—a mere denial of Romanism." [33]

▶ The Church and Its Six Signs

For Maurice the Church was organic to the Gospel. The Church is the Body of Christ, given life by its Head, and exists to show the world its true center and to support, by articulating the law of mutual sacrifice, the unity of both nations and families. Maurice held that the Church was really the world when the Christological principle was rightly understood:

The world contains the elements of which the Church is composed. In the Church, these elements are penetrated by a uniting, reconciling power. The Church is, therefore, human society in its normal state; the World, that same society irregular and abnormal. The world is the Church without God: the Church is the world restored to its relation with God, taken back by Him into the state for which He created it. Deprive the Church of its center and you make it into a world.[34]

[33] *Life*, II, 615.
[34] *Theological Essays* (edition of 1957), pp. 276-77.

It was not customary in Maurice's time to develop the idea of the Church as the Israel of God. With a thoroughly scriptural analysis he traced a series of covenants between God and Abraham and the Israelite nation to show that family and nation are preliminary manifestations of church structure. *The Church a Family* continued consideration of this theme. The ultimate pattern of unity is God Himself, who as the Blessed Trinity expresses the ground of the family principle. He described his fundamental position in *The Kingdom of Christ* as follows:

. . . there rose up before me the idea of a *Church Universal,* not built upon human inventions or human faith, but upon the very nature of God Himself, and upon the union which He has formed with His creatures; a Church revealed to man as a fixed and eternal reality by means which infinite wisdom had itself devised.[35]

Just as the Church had a history in Israel and in the New Testament period, so it has today. It is to be recognized by concrete facts of historical existence, not just in theological ideas. The theologian does well to accept the historical givenness of the signs of the Church. As facts of history they are more impressive in their witness to the "Universal Society" than in the views men have entertained about them.

The fundamental sign of church life is baptism, whereby men are forgiven their sins, are incorporated into Christ, and realize their status as sons of God because of the objective and racial atonement effected by Christ. Maurice liked to call baptism "the sacrament of constant union." He stressed the importance of sacraments as demonstrations of the free grace of God in Christ and as salutary checks to any excessive preoccupation of man with his own feelings or faith:

Outward signs and tokens have a great worth. They attest the reality and the universality of God's gifts, as in the case of the water in Baptism and the bread and wine in the Lord's Supper. They prevent men from fancying that their thoughts, and impressions, and beliefs, create the blessings which are bestowed upon us by God's free grace.[36]

[35] *The Kingdom of Christ,* II, 363.
[36] *Acts of the Apostles,* p. 188.

Baptism interprets to man the human situation. Maurice has a way of bringing all his previous insights together when he seeks the depth of his next point. Notice the themes, hitherto separately developed, now focused on baptism:

> I have maintained that Christ, by whom, and for whom all things were created, and in whom all things consist, has made reconciliation for mankind; that on the ground of this atonement for mankind, God has built His church, declaring men one family in Christ. . . . And [we believing] that the mark of that universal body or fellowship, appointed by God Himself is Baptism, do, without fear or scruple, asseverate of ourselves, and of all others who will come to this holy Baptism, of all who bear the marks and impress of that nature which Christ took, in His birth, of the blessed Virgin; that they are admitted into these high and glorious privileges; that they are brought into a state of salvation; that they are made sons of God and heirs of everlasting life. . . . And in saying this, we contend that we give faith . . . a ground upon which to stand, and which otherwise it cannot have.[37]

The second sign, which he elaborated in *The Kingdom of Christ*, is the two creeds which confess the tri-form name into which we are baptized. The creeds are not digests of doctrines; they are our protection against theological systems. To say the creed is to confess the Name, to make an act of allegiance to a person. Baptism is the sign that we are saved by grace; the creed that we are saved by faith.

The third sign of the Church is the existence of set forms of worship, such as are collected in the Book of Common Prayer. Maurice is among the profound interpreters of liturgics. He rejoiced that the ordinary Englishman expressed his worship in forms derived from the Hebrews, the Greeks, and the Latins. It was evidence to him that the Church transcended space and time. Like most engaged today in the Liturgical Movement he held the prayers written in the first ages of Christianity to be "in general more free, more reverent, more universal, than those which have been poured forth since." [38]

The Eucharist is the fourth sign. It testifies that because of Christ's sacrifice once and for all perfected on Calvary a "living

[37] *The Kingdom of Christ* (edition of 1838), I, 88ff.
[38] *The Kingdom of Christ*, II, 45.

and perpetual communion" has been established between God and man. It expresses Christ's "continual presence with His universal family." More significant than the debates over the manner of Christ's presence, Maurice maintained, was the reality of that presence as sheer fact. There was social meaning to the Eucharist and an eschatological anticipation of the new age. Maurice felt personally that the Eucharist expressed a depth and a practicality that man could not find elsewhere, not even in the Bible. "Ask yourself then solemnly and seriously—'Can I find Christianity for men of all countries and periods, all tastes and endowments, all temperaments and necessities so exhibited as I find it in this Sacrament?' " [39]

The ordained ministry is the fifth sign of the Catholic Church. It testifies that there is a permanent structure in the life of the Church, a representative office of sacrificial service. Unless it serves faithfully it may congeal into a hierarchy of power and become only another expression of the world. Maurice wrote that the Four Gospels might be described as "The Institution of a Christian Ministry." The historic episcopate, he believed, expressed the reality of universal communion in the Church and was the order that stood in essential succession to the apostolate. He expresses the idea in these words:

I believe that He meant His Church to stand in certain permanent and universal institutions . . . in a permanent ministry through which He should declare His will, and dispense His blessings to the whole body, and the main office in which should be that apostolic office which belongs characteristically to the new dispensation, seeing that it expresses the general oversight of Him, who no longer confines Himself to any particular nation, but has ascended upon high that He might fill all things.[40]

Although he considered the episcopate necessary he did not, as the Tractarians did, unchurch those who had lost it. The bond of communion might be broken and yet many ties with the Universal Church might still stand. He refused to define the limits of the Church. "I cannot answer the question; I believe only One can

[39] *The Kingdom of Christ* (edition of 1838), I, 287.
[40] *Three Letters to the Rev. W. Palmer*, p. 8.

31

answer it. I am content to leave it with Him." [41] The sixth sign, the Bible, we have already discussed.

▶ The Relevance of Maurice's Thought for Contemporary Ecumenism

Maurice's *The Kingdom of Christ* and many other writings and letters of his set forth a theology of Christian ecumenism that has yet to come into its own. As the Protestant Churches see beyond pan-Protestantism to an ecumenism that is genuinely catholic and as the Roman Catholic Church comes out of its isolationism and loses what one of its own theologians has called its "anti-Protestant face," Maurice's modestly offered "hints" will become increasingly central to ecumenical discussion and action. A surprising number of studies on the nature of the Church by Roman Catholic ecumenists follow a methodology similar to Maurice's. One of these theologians, Father Louis Bouyer, explicitly mentions Maurice's work in these sympathetic and perceptive words:

. . . [Maurice's work], at first misunderstood, is seen now to have been of greater influence in the Church of England than any other of the nineteenth century. A contemporary of the Oxford Movement, Maurice never joined it, revolted as he was by the deliberate scorn and ignorance shown by most of the Tractarians for all that was best in Protestantism. Having come to Anglicanism from Quaker surroundings, he never ceased to uphold the validity of the fundamental principles of the Reformation. At the same time, he constantly maintained that the logic of these principles, far from requiring the overthrow of the Church of tradition, with its sacramental and doctrinal structure, ought to lead to a completely fresh understanding of them, and could not be followed out fully outside that framework or, rather, outside the living organism willed by God. His principal work, *The Kingdom of Christ*, dedicated to this thesis, is certainly of capital importance in the evolution of Protestant thought. That is not to say that it is exempt from prejudices or misunderstandings in detail, both in regard to the ultra-Protestantism it starts from and to the Roman Catholicism it stops short of; in fact, it abounds with them. This only makes the depth and sureness of his thought all the more remarkable. If there is anyone within Protestantism who saw with clarity and depth into the

[41] *Epistle to the Hebrews*, p. cxxxiv.

32

principle needed to resolve the crisis endemic within Protestantism, it is certainly Maurice.[42]

With this awareness of the universal applicability of Maurice's ecumenical principles it may be well to illustrate just how he saw the vocation of his own communion as a reconciler. Anglicanism, he maintained, had never defined itself in sectarian terms. The word sect represents one of Maurice's basic distinctions in ecclesiological analysis. The real opposite of Catholicism, in his mind, was not Protestantism, but sectarianism. The sect-principle was opposed to the principle of Catholicism in that a sect built itself upon some human formulation of truth. To paraphrase his own words, the Church Catholic is a community united in the acknowledgment of a living Person, Christ. Every sect is a body united in the acknowledgment of some notion or system of divinity. The sect invariably considered Christianity as an ecclesiastical organization to which men must adhere to be saved.

True Catholicism, however, looked upon Christianity as the bestowal of a relationship with God. The relationship was given by God himself to all mankind, and the Church existed to bear witness to it in the world. It was, one might say, the means by which God proclaimed to men that they are his sons and invited them to receive their heritage. Thus the Church could never be conceived as a man-made organization pitted against the other organizations of the world. It was part of the "constitution of the race." The sect, on the other hand, always saw itself pitted against the world. It could make no peace with those outside its confines. Its only approach to unity was to demand agreement with or submission to itself.

All of this is common enough today. For a variety of reasons modern Christians are much aware of the sect type of Christianity. Maurice's concern, however, was the manner in which the sect-principle had infected all of Christendom, whether originally sectarian or not. The tendency of church bodies to identify themselves with "the True Church" meant that the sect-principle triumphed almost everywhere in Western Christianity. The ecumenical move-

[42] L. Bouyer, *The Spirit and Forms of Protestantism* (Westminster, Md.: Newman Press, 1956), pp. 189-90.

33

ment is a sign that responsible Christian leadership has now become aware of these evils and is seeking a way out of the impasse. Though he came long before the movement, Maurice too felt the impasse and thought Anglicanism had something to contribute toward its solution.

Anglicanism, he contended, was an important expression of Christianity precisely because it did not have a "system of divinity" or a confessional formulation. It was not a Church that insisted upon an official point of view, but embraced warring factions within itself dedicated to Catholic, Protestant, or Liberal principles. This might be the despair of the strict Roman Catholic or of the pure Protestant, but it did emphasize the fact that the Church was founded not upon a humanly contrived system, but directly upon God. "That peculiar character God has given us," he wrote in *The Kingdom of Christ*, "enables us, if we do not slight the mercy, to understand the difference between a Church and System, better, perhaps, than any of our neighbors can, and, therefore, our position rightly used, gives us a power of assisting them in realizing the blessings of their own." [43]

Maurice did not attribute the advantages of the Anglican position to human wisdom and foresight. Rather he contended that the events of the English Reformation had prevented the Church of England from formulating its understanding of itself in sectarian terms. The result was a church body in which the Catholic constitution of the Church was united to a Protestant protest against the Papacy. In her insistence upon national freedom, in her emphasis upon justification by faith, in her refusal of a human, visible head for the Church, the Church of England was thoroughly a church of the Reformation. Yet none of the classic marks or "signs" of the Church were abrogated. The apostolic ministry, the Catholic creeds, Scripture as the word of God, the two dominical sacraments, and liturgical worship all remain. It is interesting to note that these very items, which Maurice treats at great length in *The Kingdom of Christ*, were later also affirmed by the Lambeth Quadrilateral as essentials of church life.

The Kingdom of Christ gives us an indication of Maurice's views on the unity of the Church. As indicated above, he tries to show

[43] *The Kingdom of Christ*, II, 343.

that in the positive witness of each sect some basic, living, Christian principle is recognized, but not the whole of Christian truth. In constructing a system to embody and defend its partial truth, each sect denied other truths and excluded other Christian bodies from its fellowship. In the process it betrayed the truth it set out to enshrine. The trouble lay in the sectarian conviction that it must construct the Church anew to purify it from error. There was no remedy for this trouble, Maurice contended, unless the Church already existed, built upon the foundation of the living Christ, reconciling all the fragments of truth which the various sects had championed, liberating them from the distorted shapes into which their defenders had forced them. Maurice joined the Church of England because in it he saw the fulfillment of this vision.

Far from claiming anything for itself, Anglicanism simply witnessed to the living foundation underlying all sects. Far from excluding all those who disagreed with it, Anglicanism claimed for itself and others membership in Christ's one, holy, catholic, and apostolic Church. Its role was to affirm and defend major Catholic truths denied by Rome or by Protestant sects. Thus, Maurice saw the ideal of Anglicanism to be just as concerned to defend justification as the Lutheran, just as occupied in proclaiming election as the Presbyterian, just as zealous for the inner light as the Quaker, just as insistent upon the preservation of Catholicism as the Roman. Precisely because it had no system of its own it was in a better position to champion the truths others had perceived. Thus he urged:

Let us make the members of sects to understand that we are setting up no opinions of ours against theirs, no leaders of ours against their leaders; that we desire to justify all that they and their fathers have clung to in their darkest and bravest hours, all that their leaders have taught them when they were inspired with most indignation against our indifferences to Christ and His Gospel; that what we preach is Christ the One Head of a body which time and space cannot bound, Christ the source and object of their faith and ours. Christ is the destroyer of all sects, inasmuch as He joins man to God. Let us make Spaniards, Frenchmen, Italians understand that we do not ask them to leave their churches for ours, to accept any single English tradition

35

which is not also theirs, or to travel through the path by which God led the Teutonic nations in the sixteenth century.[44]

Seen in the perspective of ecumenical vocation, the parties of Anglicanism could be of considerable value. The Tractarians preserved the Catholic witness to a constitution and order for the whole race and to the reality of the Church Catholic in the world. Evangelicals witnessed to the fact that there was a real bond for all men in Christ's sacrifice. The Liberals or Broad Churchmen insisted that the Church must be comprehensive and throw off all partial truths. Each party, unfortunately, became as narrow and as divisive as any sect in the defense of its principles. But between them they outlined the things to which any branch of the Church must witness. The fact that they stayed together in one communion testified to the divine union which the Church was meant to proclaim to the world. Men have often remarked that Anglicanism itself is a sort of ecumenical movement. This is precisely Maurice's point.

How was Anglicanism's ecumenical vocation to be carried out? Not by calling upon other groups to unite with it as one possessing all the essentials of church life. This would be a covert return to sectarianism. Yet neither would it do to propose indiscriminate mergers with other groups. Few of the religious bodies in Maurice's day understood the truth he was driving at. His approach was to invite those of sectarian views to see that they were not really members of a sect at all, but of the Church. On this ground he justified the refusal of the Church of England to permit itself to be called a sect like all the other Protestant sects. Though this seemed pretentious to nonconformist churchmen, its purpose was to preserve a witness against their own view of themselves. "We will not submit to be called an episcopalian sect, because we do not want you to consider yourselves as sects. We want you to feel that you are members of a Church, members of Christ, children of God." [45]

Thus Maurice stumbled across the very principle which has made the ecumenical movement possible—the recognition that

[44] *Lincoln's Inn Sermons*, II, 86.
[45] *Life*, I, 258-59.

somehow all Christians were already united in Christ and members of his Church. He was perfectly willing to associate with other Christians on the grounds of man's "common membership in Christ." But he sharply rejected any sort of union based on the lowest common denominator of belief. Such a union would only be the dead residue of all sectarian systems, perhaps in a more intensive form.

The ecumenical vocation of Anglicanism, on the other hand, was to be carried out by claiming for others the privileges and the position Anglicanism claims for itself. Rather than unchurch those who disagree with it—which is, in effect, the approach of sectarianism—it is to "church" them. It is to insist that what is true of itself is also the truth about them. Even the thorny question of apostolic orders Maurice approached in this way. The doctrine of apostolic ministry, he insisted, was not held in order to cast doubt on the validity of other ministries but to testify to the fact that every minister is more than a denominational official. God himself had brought the pastoral office into being. The nonconformist minister, it was granted, could stand in a deeper, more organic relation to his congregation than he himself recognized or admitted. The intention of Anglican insistence upon apostolic orders was, in part, to enable such a minister to see the real validity of his ministry and the catholicity of his own communion.

Maurice did not feel that the vocation he envisaged for Anglicanism could be undertaken with any sense of self-righteousness. Essentially he was contending that the Church of England was to call others to repent of the sectarian temper which had led them away from Christ and divided them from each other. Such a call could only come out of a like repentance from the Anglican. Maurice was extraordinarily aware of the sins of his chosen church, of the way it had treated its Catholic structure as a pretext for a sectarian temper, of its treatment of both the Bible and Prayer Book as a "series of inspired sentences," and of its neglect of the poor in England. There was no sin in any church that was not also a sin of the Church of England. Only out of repentance could a call for unity come. But come it must, for God was "a destroyer of sects." On the horizon of the nineteenth century Maurice saw a "fearful crushing of sects"; this made him hopeful for the unity of the Church, but not optimistic about the future. "Permitted destroyers of faith" would force the Church back to its oneness in Christ.

Maurice's understanding of the ecumenical vocation of Anglicanism and of the much larger focus, the reconciliation in depth between Catholicism and Protestantism, is clearly the message of the Spirit to the churches in our day. Maurice many times described his whole ministry and authorship as a search for unity. He knew, however, that its deepest ground was there all the time, in the given unity of the Triune God:

The idea of the unity of the Father and the Son in the Holy Spirit, as the basis of all unity amongst men, as the groundwork of all human society and of all thought, as belonging to little children, and as the highest fruition of the saints in glory, has been haunting me for a longer time than I can easily look back to.[46]

[46] *Life*, I, 414.

The Thought of
Frederick Denison Maurice

▶ 1. An autobiographical letter to his son Frederick in 1866

You have often begged me to write down some recollections of the sixty years through which I have passed. A fear of not reporting them faithfully and of being egotistical has kept me from complying with your request. But I hope to be tolerably honest. There will be enough in what I say to mortify my vanity if I am. And what I say will possibly be of use in warning you of tendencies which you may have inherited, and in leading you to seek a more effectual way of counteracting them than mine has commonly been. Above all it must show you, if I can but state the facts as they rise before my mind, what an education God is giving every one of us.

I say *every one*; for you will see nothing strange or exceptional in my biography. It is thoroughly commonplace, without startling incidents or peculiar conflicts, or any results which set me above the level of any of my countrymen. I have longed (how often!) in my silly vanity that I could give myself credit for something rare or great. But there has been a continual disappointment of this ambition, till at last I have learned in some small measure to praise God for teaching me that I am one of a race, that He has been guiding me wonderfully, striving mercifully with my stupidity and obstinacy, setting an object before me when I was most turning away from it, because this is His method with all of us; because each may be brought to know that it is His method far more perfectly than I have been brought to know it, through my experience.

My letter to you last week . . . will have prepared you for the prominence which I give to the fact that I am the son of a Unitarian minister. I have been ashamed of that origin, sometimes from mere vulgar, brutal flunkeyism, sometimes from religious or ecclesiastical feelings. These I perceive now to have been only one degree less discreditable than the others; they almost cause me more shame as a greater rebellion against a divine mercy. For I now deliberately regard it as one of the greatest mercies of my life that I had this birth and the education which belonged to it.

As I told you the other day, it has determined the course of my thoughts and purposes to a degree that I never dreamed of till lately. My ends have been shaped for me, rough hew them how I would, and shape has been given to them by my father's function and this name "Unitarian" more than by any other influences, though I have been exposed to many of the most different kind which have strangely affected and may appear to some to have entirely disturbed that primary one.

My father's Unitarianism was not of a fiercely dogmatic kind. But it made him intolerant of what he considered intolerance in Churchmen or Dissenters; pleased when either would work with him, sensitive to slights from them. I have inherited from him some haste of temper, and impatience of opposition to what he thought reasonable. I wish I had anything like his benevolence, generosity, and freedom from self-indulgence. As I grew up I became far too sensible of what seemed to me his narrowness, and of a certain incoherency in his mind; far too little sensible of his very noble qualities of heart. I have since come to the deep practical conviction that this insensibility was a sin against God, a refusal to recognize the operations of His Spirit. I held that thought while I was with my father, but it was not a firm belief in my mind which could withstand a certain pharisaical conceit that I knew more than he did, and that I was therefore in some sense better. Now I am very sure that if I had this knowledge it made my moral inferiority to him an additional reason for shame and repentance.

My mother had a far clearer intellect than my father, a much more lively imagination, a capacity for interests in a number of subjects, and an intense individual sympathy. In spite of her fancy, which made her very miserable by filling her with the most unnecessary fears about all who were dear to her, she was in all her own trials, even in sudden emergencies, brave and collected, and she had an inward truthfulness and love of accuracy which I have seldom seen stronger in anyone; it gave a sort of curious definiteness to her apprehensions when they were the least reasonable.

For many years after my birth she was entirely agreed with my father in his religious opinions. Great differences arose between them afterward, which had a serious effect upon my life; as you will find if I should be able to continue my narrative. I had three sisters older than myself. Two years before I was born my parents lost a little boy in croup. My mother could never utter his name; in all our intercourse I do not think she ever alluded to him; though I always perceived a shudder when any of us or any child for whom she cared was said to have the complaint which carried him off. In her papers there are many references to the boy. I think I must owe part of the peculiar tenderness which she always showed me to my having come in a certain degree to supply his place, though she was such a mother to us all that the word peculiar is somewhat out of place. . . .

From fictions of all kinds, modern or romantic, I was carefully guarded. Miss Edgeworth's *Parents' Assistant* was the only story-book, I think, which ever came into my hands as a child; afterward I was allowed her *Moral and Popular Tales.* I have never approved or imitated this discipline. I have sometimes murmured against its effects upon myself, but I do not now regret it. I had the same temptations to speak falsely and act falsely as other children. I daresay I yielded to them as often. But I do think there was in me a love of truth for its own sake which has kept alive in me ever since. I do not know that the abstinence from fairy tales contributed to it. I am sure my mother's own sincerity cultivated it much more; and if my father had any hope of making me business-like and scientific, he certainly failed. But I cannot be sure that, along with some dryness and poverty of fancy, I did not gain in this way a certain craving for realities which has been exceedingly necessary to me since I have begun to deal with abstractions of the intellect.

In 1812 we left Suffolk. My mother suffered from asthma. My sister Emma seemed to be in an atrophy. An aunt of mine, to whom my mother was much attached, was suffering from a spinal complaint at Clifton. She urged our coming there for the sake of the climate, and that Emma might be under the care of a medical man in whom she had great confidence. Emma's illness increased. She was attacked with water on the brain. But, to the wonder of all, she recovered and lasted till twenty-three, to be a blessing to every member of her family and to many beyond it.

In the year 1814 we removed to Frenchay, about four miles from Bristol, where I spent the next nine years of my life till I went to Cambridge.

▶ 2. A second autobiographical letter to his son in 1866

When we left Suffolk a very excellent person, Miss Parker, was residing with us as governess to me and to my sisters Emma and Priscilla; the latter was three years old. Being very much attached to my mother she consented to go with us into Gloucestershire. She was, so far as I can judge from my early recollections, a very good teacher. That she was a wise and admirable woman I can have no doubt. My mother had taught me to read. Esther Parker, at her request and my father's, gave me very useful books to read, which I ought to have profited by much more than I did. I remember them now with a mixture of shame and amusement. Gatton's *Birds* and the *Book of Trades* were conspicuous among them. The first I believe was as good a book as any on the subject till Bishop Stanley's appeared. But I never knew the note of a single bird, nor watched the habits of any one. My book information, therefore, if such it was, speedily faded away.

With so little care for natural history, I ought to have sympathized with the Trades. But the records of their wonders also fell quite dead upon my mind. It was not the fault of the books or of my teachers, nor even of the selection of subjects. There are many to whom either or both of these would have been interesting, in whom they would have awakened thoughts and activities which the common teaching of schools do not awaken. I am sure it was no superiority in my case, but a defect both of attention and sympathy, which has caused me much sorrow since, that made me irresponsive to such instruction. I do not recollect that I rebelled particularly against it. My passions, which were violent enough at times, were not excited by a dislike of particular studies or a preference for others. I had no great taste for reading of any kind; that which I delighted in most was anything dramatic. . . . At a somewhat later time I began to care about history, but it was always such history as I could connect with the events which I heard of as passing in our time, or with some party feeling that had been awakened in me. My father being a Dissenter, I took great interest in a heavy and undoubtedly a somewhat narrow book, Neal's *History of the Puritans*. I owe much to the direction which this book gave to my thoughts; much even of the forms which my belief took when I became an Episcopalian.

My mind had thus received an early theological complexion, and my father greatly desired that I should be a minister among the Unitarians like himself. I took it for granted that I was to be so; he was not, of course, unwise enough to put a child upon the study of controversies. I was only recommended to read the Bible regularly, and many discussions about it went on in my presence. My Bible reading was a task which I performed every morning; I did not consider it on the whole an unpleasant task, but was rather proud when I had completed the proper number of chapters. There was something of formality about the old Unitarian conceptions of the Bible. My father believed in it more strongly and passionately than most of his sect, and was an enthusiastic champion of the Bible Society. But he encouraged a kind of criticism on it, which, though far short of that which has prevailed since, would shock many religious people now more than it did then. For the timidity about the contents and authority of the Bible has increased as it has become more exalted into an object of worship. To this exaltation the Bible Society on the one hand, and the Unitarian desire to separate it from the creeds on the other, have perhaps equally contributed.

44

But there came a great change over the spirit of our household. My cousin Anne Hurry had been particularly strong in Unitarian opinions; she had pursued them, I should suppose, more logically and consistently than my father, and had arrived at bolder conclusions. She became intimate with a very superior woman, who had been born a Quaker, and who now was a Moravian. By this lady she was aroused to feel the need of a personal deliverer, such as her old system did not tell her of. The long illness and death of her brother Edmund, which took place in our house, deepened all her impressions. She had broken off the engagement with Mr. Hardcastle because they differed in their religious opinions. It was renewed, and they were married.

My eldest sister went to visit her, and afterward a clergyman in Sussex, whose wife was a relation of ours. She returned utterly dissatisfied with my father's opinions. My third sister, Anne, a very earnest, solitary thinker, who had long been studying such books as Law's *Serious Call*, sympathized with her, though their habits of mind were very unlike. My second sister, who was staying with her cousin when she died in her first confinement, arrived more slowly at the same impatience of Unitarianism. At first they were strongly influenced by Wesley's teaching. Gradually they all, for a while, became strong Calvinists; the form of belief which was most offensive to Unitarians and to my father. It was still more grievous to him that they seemed to cut themselves off entirely from their childhood by undergoing a second baptism, and being connected with a Society of Baptist Dissenters. Very gradually my mother entered into their views. When her youngest child was born, many years after the others, she would not consent that there should be any baptism till it should be of age to determine for itself.

These events in my family influenced me powerfully; but not in the way which either of my parents or my sisters would have desired, nor in a way to which I can look back, so far as my then temper of mind was concerned, with the least complacency.

These years were to me years of moral confusion and contradiction. . . .

▶ 3. From an undated fragment on his desire for unity

The desire for *Unity* has haunted me all my life through; I have never been able to substitute any desire for that, or to accept any of the different schemes for satisfying it which men have devised. . . . I not only believe in the Trinity in Unity, but I find in it the center of all my beliefs; the rest of my spirit, when I contemplate myself or mankind. But, strange as it may seem, I owe the depth of this belief in a great measure to my training in my home. The very name that was used to describe the denial of this doctrine is the one which most expresses to me the end that I have been compelled, even in spite of myself, to seek.

▶ 4. To his mother, on October 23, 1823, about his Cambridge lecturer Julius Hare

Our other lecturer, Hare,* is a very different man from his coadjutor. He is a lively lecturer and an admirable classic, and you have no reason to complain in his rooms that you are employed an hour in hearing difficulties demolished in a most triumphant style which you really did not fancy had ever occurred to anyone. I am particularly pleased with his manner, especially that of recommending books bearing upon the subject in question, but out of the regular college routine. For instance, Schlegel's celebrated work on Dramatic Literature he advised us to study attentively as illustrative of the play we are reading, though it is evidently for the purpose of imparting philosophical views of literature in general that it can possibly be useful, and as such will bear upon the

---

* Julius Hare (1795-1855), who was later to become a close friend of Maurice's, had left law study in London in 1822 for a classical lectureship at Trinity College. Hare later married Maurice's sister Esther. More than has been recognized, Hare was responsible for introducing German ideas into English theology. Rector of Hurstmonceux, he became in 1840 Archdeacon of Lewes. See studies of Hare by Maurice and A. P. Stanley reprinted in the 1874 edition of Hare's *The Victory of Faith*. Soon after Maurice attended Hare's lectures, Hare wrote of him as "a pupil whose metaphysical powers were among the greatest I had come in contact with, but [that] the man was so shy that it was almost impossible to know him."

general examination in May. Nothing at Cambridge is so earnestly recommended as the perusal of general literature, except it be, which is absolutely necessary, the study of the evidences of Christianity—Paley, Butler, etc. So false is the general opinion that the English universities have a regular coachroad system, out of which their members are not for an instant allowed to deviate under penalty of life and limb.

▶ 5. From a sketch of Hare's teaching, written much later by Maurice

I *do* recollect Hare's classroom exceedingly well. I am often surprised how clearly all the particulars of what passed in it come back to me, when so much else that I should like to preserve has faded away.

You will suppose, perhaps, that this was owing to some novelty in his method of teaching. You will inquire whether he assumed more of a professional air than is common in a college, and gave disquisitions instead of calling on his pupils to construe a book? Not the least. We construed just as they did elsewhere. I do not remember his indulging in a single *excursus*. The subject in our first term was the *Antigone* of Sophocles. . . . We hammered at the words and at the sense. The lecturer seemed most anxious to impress us with the feeling that there was no road to the sense which did not go through the words. He took infinite pains to make us understand the force of nouns, verbs, particles, and the grammar of the sentences. We often spent an hour on the strophe or antistrophe of a chorus. If he did not see his way into it himself, he was never afraid to show us that he did not; he would try one after another of the different solutions that were suggested, till we at least felt which were not available.

You will think that so much philological carefulness could not have been obtained without the sacrifice of higher objects. How could we discover the divine intuitions of the poet while we were tormenting ourselves about his tenses? I cannot tell; but it seems to me that I never learned so much about this particular poem, about

47

Greek dramatic poetry generally, about all poetry, as in that term. If there had been disquisitions about the Greek love of beauty, about the classical and romantic schools, and so forth, I should have been greatly delighted. I should have rushed forth to retail to my friends what I had heard, or have discussed it, and refuted it as long as they would listen to my nonsense. What we did and heard in the lecture room could not be turned to this account. One could not get the handy phrase one wished about Greek ideals and poetical unity; but, by some means or other, one rose to the apprehension that the poem *had* a unity in it, and that the poet *was* pursuing an ideal, and that the unity was not created by him, but perceived by him, and that the ideal was not a phantom, but something which must have had a most real effect upon himself, his age, and his country.

I cannot the least tell you how Hare imparted this conviction to me; I only know that I acquired it, and could trace it very directly to his method of teaching. I do not suppose that he had deliberately invented a method; in form, as I have said, he was adapting himself exactly to the practice of English colleges; in spirit, he was following the course which a cultivated man, thoroughly in earnest to give his pupils the advantage of his cultivation, and not ambitious of displaying himself, would fall into. . . .

I believe that Hare gave some lectures on the Greek Testament to the students of the second year, but I never heard any of them, nor had I ever any conversation with him on theological subjects. In fact, I had very few opportunities of conversing with him on any subject. I had no introduction to him. I had never heard his name when I entered the college, and I availed myself of the kindness which he was disposed to show me, in common with others, less than I should have done if I had been older and wiser. When we met again many years after, my theological convictions had already been formed by a discipline very different, I should imagine, from any to which he was subjected; they were not altered in substance, nor, so far as I know, even in color, by any intercourse I had with him. But to his lectures on Sophocles and Plato I can trace the most permanent effect on my character, and on all my modes of contemplating subjects, natural, human, and divine.

48

▶ *6. To his father, about February 10, 1829, in answer to his father's complaint that he was not being consulted about his son's faith and vocational problems*

One reason why I have not enjoyed as much happiness as I might is that I have felt a painful inability to converse even with those who loved me best upon the workings of my mind. I am conscious of the vice, but those only who are unfortunately sharers in it can tell how deeply ingrained it is, and how hard to eradicate. Each person I have been acquainted with who has thought me worth knowing has complained of this defect, and imputed it [to] some particular want of confidence in them, and I have only been obliged to assure them, without much hope of being believed, that if they asked others, who had also a right to expect frankness from me, [they would hear from these] that my lips had been hermetically sealed to them also. I am conscious of having estranged some from me who, from having made me a depositary of their secrets, had a claim upon mine by this unfortunate disposition. All I have ever been able to say in palliation is that the crime involves its own punishment, that I am much more a sufferer by it than they can be. . . .

On ultimate plans I am just as much undecided, though I hope I shall be regulated in them much more by conscience and much less by accident than I have been in those that are past. And there seems to me this difference—that there are several ways of getting a livelihood open to me which will not hinder me from adopting a regular profession at last, or put me out of the way of it, and yet will furnish me abundant occupation for thought and diligence if I should continue in them.

The notion you allude to of my becoming a clergyman has often occurred to me as a subject of consideration within the last three months; before that very seldom indeed, and never with any seriousness. As far as I can tell at present, I should have no conscientious objection to the undertaking except my own inability for it, which at present I feel would be as strong a motive to restrain me from the Church as the most decided dislike of its doctrine or its discipline. All, therefore, that I have ever given those who asked me to understand . . . is that I might possibly adopt that course

49

at last, if I discovered no new reason in an interval of six or seven years (during which time I might be holding a fellowship, taking pupils, etc.) to disapprove of the profession, and did discover many new reasons to think that I might be a worthy member of it. If I look at it in my private moments as a point which I may reach ultimately, it is merely because then [I] think it may be a motive to increased seriousness and more earnest study of the best things. But I have no wish that my friends generally should mistake so loose a speculation for a confirmed intention.

With respect to my views on this and on all other subjects, my dear father, the strongest wish I have is that my self-deceptions may be laid bare, and that I may not fancy that I am acting from one motive when I am really acting from another. I think purity of intention so necessary—quite as necessary as purity of action—that I should be most grateful to anyone who, with the sincerity of a friend, will detect me in any dishonesty which, from want of sufficient self-examination, I have not detected in myself. That there is such evil lurking at the root even of the conduct which seems most outwardly fair I have learned even from the little self-knowledge I possess. And this conviction, I believe, occasions the principal difference between my opinions and yours. I believe with you that if we are sincerely devoted to God, He will not be strict to mark occasional deviations, or rather that He will give us repentance for them; but then it is exactly here that I found I was deceiving myself. My heart was not sincerely devoted to God. I fancied so till I had searched it, but then I saw very clearly that self and the world had far the greatest part of it.

If I could have conceived of God as anything less than perfect love, I might have found less difficulty in satisfying myself that I was conformed to the standard which He requires me to attain. But believing Him to be Love in the most absolute, unqualified sense, I felt the difficulty of approaching Him, or even of comprehending His nature, almost infinite, because love divided my heart with a thousand evil passions, and was itself tainted with evil and corruption like them. The perfect spirituality of God's character I found I had no idea of, though from habit I might bend my knees to Him and use all the phrases which expressed it. Hence the necessity of that perfect spirituality being embodied to me in a human form; hence the necessity of being able to contemplate Him, in whom and through whom only I could contemplate God, as the pardoner and remover of that evil in my heart which prevented any spiritual idea of God from being entertained by it; and hence the necessity, when that obstacle, that disease, was removed, of the Spirit of God dwelling in my heart to enable it to think rightly of and pray rightly to Him.

When I speak of making these discoveries with reference to myself, I speak literally. I cannot tell you how little, how, I fear, sinfully little I have thought of them with reference to other men. I mention this that you may not suspect me of violating the Scripture rule of "Judge not," which I think I hold in greater reverence than any other in the whole Bible. I do not believe that we can any of us know the least of the inward thoughts of another man with reference to God. Therefore, all I would ever wish to do to anyone is to say, These assistances I have found necessary in order to accomplish that purpose of believing and worshiping God which we both wish to keep in view as the end of our existence. These assistances the Bible promises, as I think, to every man. I do not think it would have promised them if our nature had not wanted them.

But to say whether any one individual is availing himself of these assistances or no, this is beyond the province of all other men; we cannot determine whether he is or is not using them, by any words which he uses, for they may bear a different meaning to him and to us. All therefore I think we should do is to exhort each other (and it is on this point that I said I was most anxious for exhortations and warnings) to examine ourselves whether we are seeking them and whatever subsidiary helps God vouchsafes to afford us or no.

I hope there is no uncharitableness in this statement. I am sure there is much less than in the one we hear so much of nowadays, that each person ought to let his neighbor take care of himself, which if pushed to its legitimate length would put an end to all preaching, since if a man is not to care for the interests of his friends, it seems great presumption to trouble himself about those of whom he knows nothing. To stir up self-examination in myself and others, to which I know that I have a disinclination, and to which I believe that all are naturally disinclined, is the only wish I have on this subject, and if they would only adopt the same opinion and endeavor to stir up self-examination in me I should be deeply grateful.

▶ 7. To the Reverend Julius Hare written from Oxford on December 3, 1829, on Maurice's decision to enter Oxford

My dear Sir,

I should not have so long suffered you to imagine that I was insensible of your great kindness, but that I hoped Sterling* would have been the bearer of this letter, and would at the same time have told you how grateful I felt for your valuable advice, your unexpectedly flattering testimonial, and the interest you express in my future proceedings.

I find, however, that he has given up his intention of going, at present, to Cambridge, and I cannot longer defer saying what I wished to say a fortnight ago.

I was almost ashamed to present the letter in which you speak so favorably of my scholarship, lest I should disgrace your good opinion, and, in some degree, the university, by an ignorance which three years of vague and ill-directed thought have done much to increase. I accompanied the delivery of it with the observation that it is nearly five years since I had the advantage of your instructions and that during all that time I have been in circumstances not at all favorable to the growth of the powers which you fancied you had observed in me; but I added that I still hoped by steady application to prove that those instructions had not been lost, and might still bear fruit.

The truth of your remarks upon the superiority of a bachelor's

* John Sterling, Maurice's friend at Cambridge, had worked in London with him on a number of literary journals. Both had agreed to write novels. Maurice was currently at work on *Eustace Conway*. Sterling was trying to decide whether to take orders himself. This he did later, but his ministry was shadowed by doubts about his own faith and by ill health. Tuberculosis caused his early death. For two contrasting evaluations of Sterling see the *Memoir* by Julius Hare attached to an 1848 edition of Sterling's *Essays and Tales* and Thomas Carlyle's *Life of Sterling* (1851).

life struck me very forcibly, and if I had not cut myself off from the chance of a fellowship by removing my name from the books (a measure which I adopted in consequence of some scruples, since entirely removed, respecting the profession of faith required of graduates), I should certainly have acted upon them. I am not certain, however, whether, in my particular case, the subjection of an undergraduate's life and the humiliation of returning to it after three years of fancied independence may not be a useful discipline. I can trace a great deal of mawkishness and unhappiness to a premature wish to shape out my own course, and I hope it is not a superstitious feeling which leads me to think that some penance for this self-sufficiency is needful before I can eradicate it with all its evil fruits out of my character.

The same feeling makes me dread less than I should otherwise do the mere barren orthodoxy which, from all I can hear, is characteristic of Oxford. As all my tendency has been hitherto to be too loose and incoherent in my speculations, I think this habit of the place may operate rather as a useful check than a dangerous temptation to me. If I could hope to combine in myself something of that freedom and courage for which the young men whom I knew at Cambridge were remarkable, with something more of solidity and reverence for what is established, I should begin to fancy that I had some useful qualities for a member of the English Church. At present the difficulties which surround a clergyman seem to me so overwhelming that, even with a strong impression of the grandeur of the office, and of the possibility of entering it with right views, I almost shrink from the thought of encountering them.

I took the liberty of sending your letter to Sterling, well knowing that your advice would have more weight with him than anyone else's. I trust it will induce him to adopt a course which will be as much for his own happiness as for the good of society, to which I am sure his talents might be very useful.

▶ 8. To his sister Priscilla from Oxford, about February, 1830

Believe, my dear Pris, what I am just beginning to learn, and you knew long ago, that the death of Christ is far, very far, more than a mere peacemaking, though that view of it is the root of every other. But it is actually and literally the death of you and me, and the whole human race; the absolute death and extinction of all our selfishness and individuality. So St. Paul describes it in the sixth of the Romans, and in every one of his Epistles. To believe that we have any self is the devil's lie; and when he has tempted us to believe it, and to act as if we had a life out of Christ, he then mocks us and shows us that this life was a very death. Have we not all felt it so?—the death, the absolute death of self. Let us believe, then, what is the truth and no lie—that we *are* dead, actually, absolutely dead; and let us believe further that we *are* risen, and that we have each a life, our only life—a life not of you nor me, but a universal life—in Him. He will live in us, and quicken us with all life and all love; will make us understand the possibility, and, as I am well convinced, experience the reality, of loving God and loving our brethren.

▶ 9. To his father, about February 6, 1832

. . . Your love for every member of your family is felt and acknowledged, I am sure, by every one of them. I can answer for myself that, if I have thought of it with less pleasure than I ought, that is chiefly because it has awakened painful self-reflections on my own poor requitals of it. The more I think of it, the more your happiness is near to my heart, and the more I would labor to promote it. With respect to what you call doctrinal or speculative views, my feeling is just this: I see that every good and wise man who is held up to my admiration and imitation in the Bible, desired nothing less, and could be satisfied by nothing less, than communion with God.

Every word in the Book of Psalms, in the Gospels, in the Epistles, and in the Prophecies tells me this. They wished to know God, not in a vague, loose sense, but actually to know Him as a friend. Starting with no preparatory notions of God, but ready to receive everything He told them, they welcomed each new dispensation only because it told them something more of God; because it enabled them more intelligently, more practically, more literally to converse with Him. I observe that all their sorrow arose from the loss of God's presence, all their joy from the possession of it, all their pleasure in expecting heaven from anticipation of it.

I observe that they shrank from the contemplation of no side or phase of God's character, that His holiness and His mercy were equally dear to them, and that, so far from viewing them as separate, they could not admire one without the other. They could not delight in His love unless they believed that He would admit no sin into His presence, for sin and love are essentially hostile. They could not adore His holiness unless they believed that He had some way of removing their sinfulness and imparting His own character to them. The plain, obvious study of the Bible tells me this.

Now, just as any system of divinity helps me to realize these feelings, just so far do I believe it true. If I can honestly say of any doctrines, these teach me how I may converse with the holy and invisible God as a real living person, for as such the Bible holds Him forth to me in every line; how I may overcome the difficulties to this intercourse which arise from His being unseen, from the evident impossibility of my forming a notion of Him by my own understanding, and from the unlikeness and dissimilarity of our characters; if they show me how my character may be conformed to His, not how His may be brought down to mine; if they inspire me with a desire for this intercourse, a delight in it, and a conviction of its reality, just so far as I can, after strict examination, say this of any doctrines, just so far have I a test that they are the doctrines of the Bible, the true doctrines, the doctrines according to godliness. Call them orthodox, heterodox, or what you will; if they answer this description, I wish to hold them fast in life and death. But if they be anything less than this, I will reject them, and, by God's grace, will tear them out of my heart, though they should have the finest and the best name in the world's books, as something essentially different from that faith which enabled the prophets and patriarchs, the martyrs and apostles, the saints of every age, to endure as "seeing Him who is invisible." I wish and pray, my dearest father, that we may each have grace given to us to try our faiths by this real test—mere speculations you cannot hold cheaper than I do. . . .

I have now three pupils, and hope of another, for which I desire to be very thankful. The tutor recommended me to these two, and very kindly arranged with one that he should pay me at the end of every term.

▶ 10. To his father, about February 12, 1832, on the revelation of God

. . . The whole of history shows me that just as far as the true God has made Himself manifest, just so far has there been light, truth, and honesty in the world; and that in those nations to which He is not revealed, there is darkness, falsehood, and fraud. I know that it is out of the heart these proceed—from each separate human heart. I believe, therefore, that all the honesty and truth in the world has come from God being manifested in the hearts of some men, and from thence affecting the general course of society. Hence I feel sure that just so far as I can hold intercourse with Him, I can be true and honest to myself. Outwardly so, I may, in a Christian country, and with the kind, gentle feelings which are produced by the idea of the relations of life prevailing in Christian countries; but thoroughly true and honest to myself I have no hopes of being, without this real personal knowledge of Him who is Truth.

To attain to this truth, this heart truth—not to fancy that I have it, but to have it—is my greatest wish. I know I was formed in the image of God. I believe if I could behold God I should reflect His image. But I cannot behold Him. God, I am told, is a Spirit, and I am of the earth, earthy. I cannot, and would not if I could, abandon my belief that He is a lofty Spiritual Being; I cannot throw aside my own earthliness. Now, this seems to me the most important practical question in the world. I cannot put up with a dream in place of God. He is a Spirit, but He is reality; He is Truth; a True Being in the highest sense. As such I must behold Him or not at all.

To behold Him, therefore, in that way in which they could alone understand, in which they could converse with Him, namely, as a man, was, I see more and more clearly, the longing desire of every patriarch, prophet, and priest from Adam downward. It was the desire of Abraham, of Moses, of Job, of David, of Solomon, of Isaiah. They were practical men, and they wanted a practical revelation, a revelation which they could understand and grapple. God, they knew, must be forever the Unsearchable, the Mysterious. They would not for worlds He should be anything else; for it was the glory of Judaism that their God was not a visible, intelligible idol, but an incomprehensible Spirit. Yet they longed to behold Him, and to behold Him so as they could understand Him.

I would beseech you to observe attentively whether nearly every verse in the Old Testament does not exhibit these two apparently opposite and most contradictory feelings; an acknowledgment of God as incomprehensible and infinite; a desire to see, to understand, to comprehend that same God. Yes, and just so far as the heathen attained any light did they begin to make the same acknowledgment and feel this same want. Is there a difficulty, a mystery here? Most unquestionably: but where? In the heart of man. *There* is a craving that will not be satisfied with anything less than the reconciliation of these two amazing contrarieties— explain the fact as you may: but is it a fact? was there this want? was there this difficulty? If you never observed it, may I ask you affectionately to look again with this particular view. And if it be a fact, and if this be the one great cry of human nature in all ages, just in proportion as it was enlightened, then cannot any explanation be found for it except only that which will satisfy it.

If the infinite, incomprehensible Jehovah is manifested in the person of a Man, a Man conversing with us, living among us, entering into all our infirmities and temptations, and passing into all our conditions, it is satisfied; if not, it remains unsatisfied. Man is still dealing with an incomprehensible Being, without any mode of comprehending Him. He may be revealed to him as his lawgiver, his sovereign, but he has no means of knowing Him as a friend. It was on the promise of this revelation that every one of the Old Testament good men lived; and through these promises only did they contemplate their lawgiver, their sovereign, with satisfaction and delight.

And it is surely the renunciation of any feeling of this kind, the being content to regard God as their lawgiver and sovereign, without believing in the fulfillment of His promises or being able thoroughly and heartily to think that they will yet be fulfilled, which has converted modern Jews into such an unspiritual, profane, worldly race. I do not say that this is all. I feel that it is not. If the appearance of that Being upon earth awakened all the evil passions of man's breast, and showed him—showed even the twelve apostles—that they had no real sympathy with their God, the mere revelation of [God] in an intelligible [being] was not sufficient.

To pass through that state which had been proclaimed by God and always regarded by man as emphatically the punishment of that hatred and opposition to God; to pass through it and reappear again in the world with God's own glad tidings of pardon in his hand attested by that act; was absolutely necessary [on His part] before there could be any peaceful, comfortable feeling in man toward the Maker with whom he had felt himself at such issue. [It was needful for Him] to leave the world as a real, efficient, known, intelligible human Mediator between [men and] that invisible God whom He had manifested forth (and to suppose any being less than God perfectly manifesting forth God is a contradiction; and to suppose any being an efficient Mediator who did not perfectly manifest Him forth, seems to me no less a one— I mean to my reason). Lastly (since, with all the sense of forgiveness in man's mind, with all the knowledge that he had a Mediator, though all outward impediments to intercourse were removed, there was still an inward impediment—the same kind of impediment which exists between two men who, though they see one another and may be outward friends, are not one in heart), to promise the Spirit, who could be no other than the Spirit of Christ (otherwise there could be no intercourse between Christ and His disciples on earth through Him); and, if the Spirit of Christ (supposing what was before said to be true), must be the Spirit of God; and, if the Spirit of God, could not be an inferior part of God's nature, but must be His very Being, because He is a Spirit.

This, my dearest father, is my faith; it is one [about] which I should be most able to write to you or talk with you. There may be a hundred thousand simpler faiths. It is simpler to believe in a Great Spirit with the North American Indians; it is simpler to

58

worship wood and stone; but what is the worth of simplicity if it does not account for facts which we know; if it does not satisfy wants which we feel; if it does not lead us up to the truth which we desire?

I hope you will excuse the length of this letter, as well as anything in it that may have pained you, which you will believe it was far from my thoughts to have written. Praying that the Spirit of Truth may guide us into all truth, I remain, my dearest father,

Your very affectionate son.

▶ *11. To his mother, written from Leamington, December 9, 1833, to comfort her in her depressed feeling that she was not among those to be saved*

My dearest Mother,

Though I have felt grieved each day at reflecting on my delay in writing to you, I do not regret that I did not send my first thoughts, which I put down about a month ago; for as often, too often, is the case with mine, they are expressed in rather a complex manner, and might not have given you comfort. I now long and pray to be able to speak as simply as I ought to speak when I know that what I say is true.

My text is this, "Know ye not that Jesus Christ is in you?" This question is often put in such a way as to distress poor humble persons very much. But nothing was further from the Apostle's thoughts. To give a proud professor a notion that he had attained anything in having the Lord of life near to him, to give the desponding spirit a gloomy sense of his distance from such a privilege, that was no part of Paul's commission or his practice. To prove it, see what he says, not to a faithful Christian or an unfaithful one, not to a church at all, "For in Him we live and move and have our being." This is spoken to the ignorant, idolatrous inhabitants of Athens.

What, then, do I assert? Is there no difference between the believer and the unbeliever? Yes, the greatest difference. But the difference is not about the *fact*, but precisely in the belief of the *fact*. God tells us, "In Him," that is, in Christ, "I have created all things, whether they be in heaven or on earth. Christ is the Head of *every* man." Some men believe this; some men disbelieve it. Those men who disbelieve it walk "after the flesh." They do not believe they are joined to an Almighty Lord of life—One who is mightier than the world, the flesh, the devil—One who is nearer to them than their own flesh. They do not believe this, and therefore they do not act upon this belief. They do not think they are joined to Christ; and therefore they do not *pray*, that is, ask Christ to fill, animate, and inspire and sanctify them. They believe, for this is all they *see*, that they are surrounded by a *flesh* which shuts them in, that they are surrounded by innumerable objects of sense. Their hearts are wedded in the strictest sense of the word to sense, and they do not wish to be divorced.

But though tens of hundreds of thousands of men live after the flesh, yea, though every man in the world were so living, we are forbidden by Christian truth and the Catholic Church to call this the real *state* of any man. On the contrary, the phrases which Christ and His apostles use to describe such a condition are such as these: "They believe a *lie*. They make a *lie*. They will not believe the *truth*."

The truth is that every man is in Christ; the condemnation of every man is that he will not own the truth; he will not *act* as if this were *true*, he will not believe that which is the truth, that, except he were joined to Christ, he could not think, breathe, live a single hour. This is the monstrous lie which the devil palms upon poor sinners. "You are something apart from Christ. You have a separate, independent existence." See how this works. Separate from Christ, I can bear no fruit to God. Separate from Christ, I am separate from every one of my brethren. Then at once follows disobedience to God's two commands, "Thou shalt love the Lord thy God; Thou shalt love thy neighbor as thyself." God commands *every* man to do this; but to command me, in myself, to love Him and love my neighbor is to command me an impossibility, to mock with a precept which experience and reason and Scripture tell me cannot be performed.

Now, my dearest mother, you wish and long to believe yourself in Christ; but you are afraid to do so, because you think there is

60

some experience that you are in Him necessary to warrant that belief. Now, if any man, or an angel from heaven, preach this doctrine to you, I say, let his doctrine be accursed. You have this warrant for believing yourself in Christ, that you cannot do one living act, you cannot obey one of God's commandments, you cannot pray, you cannot hope, you cannot love, if you are not in Him. But God says, Pray, pray, hope, love; God bids me do that. He has constituted me to do, not something else, but just that.

This condition I have made for myself; this state of independence, this fleshly Adam life is no state at all; it is a lie. In that I cannot please God. It is as impossible as that lying should please the God of Truth, as that enmity should please the God of Love. Wherefore we say to every man, "In your flesh you cannot please God." Wherefore we say to every man, "Believe in the Lord Jesus, and you shall be saved." Not, believe in a distant Christ, not, believe in a dead Christ; but, believe in the *Lord* Jesus Christ. Believe in Him as the Lord of your own spirit. Believe that your spirit is as much His servant as you have believed it the servant of the flesh. Believe Him to be mightier than the world around you, than your own flesh, than the evil spirit. Believe and live.

Now, who is the Lord of your spirit? He who agonized in Gethsemane—He who bled on Calvary—the Lord of all love—the Lord who sacrificed Himself for love; this is the Lord of your spirit, ever near to you, ever present with you, with everyone.

Does it grieve you because I say with everyone, as if I put you on a level, as to hope, with the most vile and unbelieving? Oh, do not so pervert the words of comfort. The fact is, you desire earnestly that you could find One near you who loved you intensely, to whom you could tell your sorrows, your griefs, your sins; to whom you could tell everything in the assurance that He would sympathize with you, and that they, at present, do not feel this want. Then the same words spoken to you have as different a sound—as joy from grief—to them and to you. Yet I cannot disguise it, the words are the same. Ye are children of God; ye are members of Christ. Profligates, hardhearted sinners, yea, hypocrites, this is your condemnation, that you are. It will be your misery to find that you were so, unless you will believe.

Now here is the warrant for *prayer*; here is the *possibility*, here is the *might* of prayer. Christ is in you, submit yourself to Him. Say, "Lord, I submit." Not now, but at every moment of your life; tell Him of whatever sins or sorrows are disturbing you; of *sins* no less than *sorrows*, of *sorrows* no less than *sins*. Of other people's sins no less than your own, of other people's sorrows no less than your own. Believe that He loves you and them. Ask that He will do His will in you, which is your blessedness. Ask that He will separate your spirit from the flesh and from surrounding objects by His Spirit, in order that you may behold His love.

Do not think you will ever have any righteousness or glory except His righteousness, for in perceiving this is your life, your happiness, your virtue, your glory. Ask Him to sanctify the whole body of which you are one member, that the whole body may see and delight in Him as its Head, and may not delight in themselves. For to delight in Him is righteousness, to delight in ourselves is sin. Lastly, ask Him more and more to shine through you, that others may see your good works and glorify your Father in heaven. This He says He wishes, therefore, of course, He will do it for you. Tell me what you think of what I have said. May He bless it.

▶ 12. To his father, on January 25, 1834, the day before his ordination

. . . If you ask me, my dear father, what feelings chiefly occupy me at this most important crisis of my life, I answer that they may be summed up in a desire for greater self-abasement and a more perfect and universal charity. I feel that the minister of the Gospel of peace, the minister of a Church which is called Catholic and Universal, is bound to have a much lower opinion of himself than I have practically and habitually of myself, and also to feel a much more perfect and unlimited love toward all and each than has yet ever been shown forth in me. When I speak of universal love, I do not mean anything which is not perfectly consistent with national and family affection. I believe if we give up ourselves to God and renounce ourselves, He is sure to work these feelings in us, else why did He command us to have them? I long to have them far more strongly, in far more practical operation than I ever had. But I feel the duty of cultivating that universal love more incumbent upon me as a minister than upon others, because I think I am more directly shown the true foundation of it than others are.

It is the natural feeling of all of us that charity is founded upon the uncertainty of the Truth. I believe it is founded upon the certainty of Truth. That God is Truth and Love also; that all men may know Him, that is, know Truth, and that He willeth all men to know Him. On this rock I build my charity. All error, all sin, in myself and in others, is their misery; therefore I wish to hate it in myself and in them, and that they should hate it in me and in themselves, and trust with perfect confidence in God to deliver them and me out of it. Now this I feel is my imperfection that I do not love men's persons enough, and hate that which makes them unhappy enough; that I do not more labor to guide them into truth, and use the only means of doing so, kindness and love. This is my desire, this I am bound by my ordination vows to seek after; and, seeking, I trust that I shall find.

▶ *13. Maurice's answer on his canonical examination to the question: "Specify some of those erroneous and strange doctrines which, on your admission to the priesthood, you promise to 'banish and put away.'"*

1. The doctrine that there is any merit in the creature which can entitle it to God's love; or any goodness in the creature at all disunited from God.

2. The doctrine that there is now any bar to the admission of a sinner into God's presence, except that which his own unbelief creates.

3. The doctrine that there is in God "any darkness at all," that there is in Him the least particle of selfishness, that He is merely a superior will, and not absolute righteousness and absolute love.

4. The doctrine that men are more anxious to attain the knowledge of God than He is anxious to bring them to that knowledge.

5. The doctrine that it is possible for the perfect God to behold

anyone except in the perfect Man, Christ Jesus, or that it is possible for man to behold God, except as revealed and manifested in Him.

6. The doctrine of Antinomianism in all its shapes; that the end of God in bringing men to the faith of Christ is not to make them holy as He is holy; that it is a privilege to be allowed to commit iniquity, instead of a privilege to be delivered from iniquity; that there is any reward so great or glorious which God can offer to His creatures as that of making them partakers of His divine character.

7. The doctrine that man can worship God except in the Spirit; and

8. The doctrine that the Father, Son, and Holy Ghost are not "in glory equal, in majesty co-eternal."

▶ **14. To Acland,* on February 13, 1834, less than a year after Keble's sermon on "National Apostasy," the beginning of the Oxford Movement**

. . . Since we parted I have taken orders, but through unavoidable delays only within the last month. I am now settled in a very small parish (of about 250 souls) in Warwickshire. I am the sole manager of it (bating the very great help which I receive from a sister who lives with me), as my rector is one of the tutors at Wadham. I have also the charge of a young pupil, respecting whom I feel much anxiety, as he has considerable talents and is come of a stock which he ought not to disgrace. I do not know whether it will strike you as the greatest oddity and anomaly that I should be minister to a set of farmers and laborers, most of whom have not a notion beyond their teams, or that I should be appointed to form the mind of one who, if he lives, will be Lord Somers.

Whether my theorizing propensities would make me most unsuitable for the first vocation, or my ignorance of the world, and my gawkiness, for the second, may be an amusing question for

* Acland (afterward Sir T. Acland) had been a sponsor when Maurice was baptized on March 29, 1831.

you; but so God hath ordered it. I have not gone out of my way to get into either position, but have been led by unlooked-for providences into both. I feel my utter incompetency; thanks be to Him who has sent me all other mercies for this especially, and I trust that I shall have strength according to my need. If it is His will to transmit blessings to His creatures they will reach their destination, however awkward the hands which have the honor of bearing them. I wish I had more opportunities of communicating with Harrison,* whom I regard with increasing reverence and esteem, as I feel more of the distance between my state of mind and his. Blessed may he be and all who labor with him in the task of stripping the Church of her Babylonian attire, and clothing her once more in her white and bridal robes.

If they err and stumble in their sincere endeavors after the recovery of old and forgotten truths, if they even are tempted to forget that the Church is Catholic while they are in the act of pleading for its Catholicity, if they do anything unwillingly to hurt that unity which they so earnestly contend for, may their oversights be all forgiven, all corrected, and may they daily advance more themselves and lead others further in the knowledge of all truth.

I sometimes feel a longing desire to set them right when I think they are misapprehending or frightening away sincere Dissenters; to say, "You need not weaken one of your assertions, you may make them stronger, and yet by just this or that little alteration give them a Catholic instead of an exclusive form," but I do not know how to make myself understood. Nobody sees what I mean, and I return humbled if not dejected into myself, half convinced that I have no business with any but my own little flock, who may, I hope, by God's grace, be taught to feel what a Catholic Church is, though they may never understand the name.

I don't mean by this that I have ever attempted formal intercourse with the dons of the Oxford band—Keble, Newman, Harrison, etc.—but that all my chance connections with any of their party had this termination. Of our Liberals I suppose we must not venture to hope good any longer, though I think there are

* Probably Archdeacon Harrison about whom Maurice had ambivalent feelings, although mentioned favorably here.

still among them a better seed, a nobler generation, who only want to have that charity, of which Liberality is at once the counterpart and the greatest contradiction, truly presented to them in order to embrace it, and cast away the miserable idol that they have been worshiping.

The most glaring exhibition of the evils of their own party will not, I think, avail to detach them from it, without this, or if it do, it will but bring them into that last state which is worse than the first, wherein the house being empty, swept, and garnished, stripped of its brilliant hopes and fond expectations, becomes a fit residence for seven brother spirits more wicked than the original occupier.

. . . I have heard of a poor creature in St. Luke's in a lucid moment snatching a lady by the arm who was visiting the Asylum with the exclamation, "Have you thanked God for your reason today?" and then relapsing into fury. Surely one of these men in a lucid interval might say to either of us, "Have you thanked God today for having passed through a debating society with any portion of your souls undestroyed?" and at least to one of us, "Have you meddled with periodicals, and have you thanked God that you still think, love, go to church, and find anyone to love you?"

▶ 15. To Richard Trench,* from Bubbenhall, May 8, 1834, enclosing a copy of his novel Eustace Conway

If I should ever write again, it will be, I think, on the subject nearest my heart, and from which I cannot wander for long together without finding myself the worse for it—the principles and conditions of union among men. Everything without and within seems drawing us to meditation upon this mighty question.

* His friend Richard Trench (1807-1886), later a teaching colleague of Maurice's at King's College, London, then Dean of Westminster, and finally Archbishop of Dublin. He wrote on New Testament themes, composed religious poetry, and played a decisive part in the early stages of the *Oxford English Dictionary*. This selection is taken from *Letters and Memorials of Richard Trench*, edited by M. Trench (London: K. Paul, 1888), p. 158.

▶ 16. To Acland, from Bubbenhall, July 12, 1834

I would wish to live and die for the assertion of this truth: that the Universal Church is just as much a reality as any particular nation is; that the latter can only be believed real as one believes in the former; that the Church is the witness for the true constitution of man as man, a child of God, an heir of heaven, and taking up his freedom by baptism: that the world is a miserable, accursed, rebellious order, which denies this foundation, which will create a foundation of self-will, choice, taste, opinion; that in the world there can be no communion; that in the Church there can be universal communion; communion in one body by one Spirit. For this, our Church of England is now, as I think, the only firm, consistent witness. If God will raise up another in Germany or elsewhere, thanks be to Him for it, but for the sake of Germans, Dutchmen, Frenchmen, Spaniards, Italians—for the sake of Baptists, Independents, Quakers, Unitarians, for the sake of Jews, Turks, Infidels, for the sake of Men, I will hold fast by that Church which alone stands forth and upholds universal brotherhood, on the only basis on which brotherhood is possible.

We stand on the voluntary principle, we voluntarily come into God's order. We refuse to stand on the slavish foundation of self-will.

▶ 17. To the Reverend J. A. Stephenson of Lympsham under whom he interned before his own curacy at Bubbenhall, written from Leamington, July 24, 1834

My dear Sir,

I have been withheld by the fear of occupying any of your valuable time from writing to you hitherto, but I have often desired to express to you how much more lively my impressions of your kindness and of the truths which I heard from you are now than when I was in the neighborhood of Lympsham. A great depression of spirits hindered me at that time from expressing, or even from feeling, as I ought, all the pleasure of that intercourse. But since I have been engaged in preaching myself, I have found the advantage of your instructions in a degree that I could scarcely have believed possible; especially as they have led me, almost unawares, into a method of considering many subjects, and of setting them forth, which I should not have naturally fallen into.

I have not hitherto, nor do I intend hereafter for many years at least, to travel much beyond the Lord's Prayer and the Creed, and the Gospel and Epistle of the day, in addressing the people. But I have found myself in all my private meditations, as well as in preaching, drawn to speak of Christ as a King, and His Church as a Kingdom. Whenever I depart from this method, I feel much less clearness and satisfaction, much less harmony between my own feelings and the Word of God.

▶ 18. To Richard Trench on January 3, 1835

If I write* I shall endeavor to bring out the principles of the question, so far as they have been revealed to me; which are, I conceive, twenty times as important as the question is. To help forward the unity of the Church, a witness for the unity of the race in Christ, [grounded?] on the still deeper and more awful Unity of God, the Father dwelling with the Son in one Spirit, is the want we have to desire. For this I hope we shall be enabled to live and die, for it includes within it every subordinate union: peace of nations, peace of families, peace of heart.

▶ 19. An autobiographical letter to his son, written from Cambridge in 1871, to explain the origin of his Subscription No Bondage

My dearest Frederick,

You have asked me to tell you to what crises in our country's history or my own certain tracts and pamphlets refer which I have

* Maurice was thinking of writing about the controversy on subscription to the Thirty-nine Articles at the universities. This selection is from pp. 180-182 of *Letters and Memorials of Richard Trench*.

written during the last thirty-five years. I will try, as well as I can, to recall them. They will be interesting to you if they only enable you to know me a little better, and to connect together different passages in my experience. If they should also, even by means of my mistakes and imperfect apprehensions, make any of the questions which concern us all as "English citizens" more intelligible to you, I shall think the effort to speak of them, which must be often a humiliating and painful one, well repaid.

I was the curate of a small parish in Warwickshire when I wrote the tract called *Subscription No Bondage*. It was published in the year 1835. I may tell you at once that no pamphlet ever made less impression upon the English public generally, or upon the smaller university public, for which it was chiefly intended. Those who accepted it at first with a certain qualified sympathy as an argument on their side, were those who confuted it most successfully by their subsequent acts. The few who took any real interest in it entirely dissented from its conclusions. It has been out of print for twenty-five years. I have myself confessed that Subscription *is* bondage. Nevertheless, no book which I have written expresses more strongly what then were, and what still are, my deepest convictions.

None is a more curious commentary on my own life during the years which preceded the publication of it. None is a better prophecy of the kind of position which I was to hold in reference to all the parties within and without the English Church. And little as it has affected, or as I have affected, the thoughts and the conduct of those parties, it may explain in some slight degree to you of another generation certain of their views and movements at that time.

You may often have wondered that I should have been a member of both our universities. You cannot wonder more than I do. Considering the circumstances of my birth and early education, it is very strange that I went to either of them.

My father was a Unitarian minister. He wished me to be one also. He had a strong feeling against the English Church, and against Cambridge as well as Oxford. My elder sisters, and ultimately my mother, abandoned Unitarianism. But they continued to be Dissenters; they were not less, but some of them at least more, averse from the English Church than he was. I was much confused between the opposite opinions in our household. What would surprise many, I felt a drawing toward the anti-Unitarian side, not from any religious bias, but because Unitarianism seemed to my boyish logic incoherent and feeble. I had an early interest in the Puritans, but that, except so far as it was embodied in a respect for Milton, had disappeared. I had a great dislike to the thought of being a Dissenting minister; from conscientious reasons partly, but also from something of disgust from what I saw of the class, mixed, I doubt not, with a great leaven in my own mind of vanity and flunkeyism. I wished to go to the Bar, and my father, with his usual generosity and liberality, but with a degree of pain, which I ought to have appreciated, consented. Then it was suggested that I had better study at one of the universities, and Dublin was thought of as being free from tests. But as they were not required at Cambridge before taking a degree, some of my friends urged that there was no sufficient reason why I should cross the Channel.

I look back with shame, and yet with much thankfulness, on my undergraduate life here. I became nothing of a mathematician, little of a classic. My waste of time, considering the reasons which I had for exertion in the kindness and the poverty of my parents, now seems to me incredible. I knew none of the Seniors; I did nothing which could give them an interest in me. Your uncle Julius, indeed, who was Classical Lecturer in Trinity, took a kind notice of me; but I saw him very rarely. On the other hand, I cannot find any words to explain how much my whole life has been influenced by intercourse with men of my own age there. They were often men whose tastes were most unlike my own. One with whom I was especially intimate was devoted to music, and abhorred both politics and metaphysics. The majority of my acquaintances, however, were mainly occupied with these subjects. I had no pretensions to be a speaker, but I mixed with those who were busy in the debates of the university.

Among the younger and cleverer undergraduates of the day, especially in Trinity, Benthamism was the prevalent faith. I had read Coleridge before I came up, and had received a considerable influence both from him and from Madame de Staël's *De l'Allemagne*.

I, in a small society of which I was a member, defended Coleridge's metaphysics and Wordsworth's poetry against the Utilitarian teaching. I was a noisy and often angry disputant, though mixing much shyness with my presumption. In most parties I was reckoned a bore. But Sterling, who was a remarkable speaker, and was in those days brilliant in conversation, fancied all fine things of me because I had exactly the qualities which he wanted, and was deficient in those which he had. He talked of me as having the rudiments of a metaphysician; that opinion he retained through most years of his life. When it was shaken, when he suspected that I had passed into a fanatical theologian, and when I was hard and cold to him, he still showed me the rarest friendship. At college I lived much with him and with others, who, with far less gifts, were far more likely to succeed in the world. Even at that time my obligations to him were more than I knew, or than I can calculate now when I am better able to judge of them. With his frankness and nobleness, which always exaggerated his debts to others, he immensely overrated what he owed to me, and suffered the inevitable disappointment which follows when a supposed hero turns out to be what he is.

I seem to be going a long way round to give you the interpretation of a very insignificant book, but I must travel further still if I am to tell you what it means. I ended my career in Cambridge by entering Trinity Hall (the law college), passing through the examinations and the Act required for a student in civil law. That seemed to be a reasonable preparation for a member of the Temple, and it entitled me to leave the university without making any fuss about not professing myself a member of the Church of England. I did not want to make that profession as I had been brought up a Dissenter, though I should have been much more reluctant to profess myself a member of any of the Dissenting bodies. I had no inclination to infidelity. Coleridge had done much to preserve me from that. I had a real, not a conventional, though far enough from a practical or spiritual, reverence for the Scriptures, and a great dislike, which Sterling felt even more strongly than I did, to the tone of the Liberals with whom we consorted on religious subjects generally.

In London I became a law student, but desultory habits had

still possession of me; I thought I should never make way in the study. I had a certain knack of writing; I joined with a number of my friends in the *Athenaeum*. I was constituted editor, and so far fulfilled the office that I always contrived to fill the paper when there was want of matter, and that my friends most generously gathered round me; otherwise I had no particular fitness for the task, though I persuaded myself at the time that it was better for me than any other.

You may remember how hardly I have sometimes spoken to you and Edmund against the sacrifice of life to journal writing. The bitterness of my own experience may account for such remarks. Not that it was not in some degree useful experience. It kept my mind alive, though the life was of a restless kind. I had strong convictions which I desired to enforce; but the sauciness of my language, and my impertinence in judging those who had a right to judge me produced much self-contempt in me afterward. I wrote partly because I mixed little in general society, and had little power of expressing myself when I did. . . .

I was still under the influence of Coleridge's writings—himself I never saw. His book on the *Ideas of the State*, which appeared at this time, impressed me very much. I accepted to a great degree the principle of it, though not all the conclusions. With the Benthamites, therefore, I was still at war. The few whom I chanced to know regarded me as a very harmless and visionary antagonist.

At last I became weary of my sham creed and pretentious toleration. I began to think that I was wasting time, and that if I could ultimately excel, it should be somewhere else than in a newspaper, even if it could have succeeded in my hands. I left London, and spent many months at Southampton in my own family. It was an important time to me. The conversations of my sister Emma, who was dying, deepened any belief which I had, and made me know how shallow my belief was. She was singularly wise as well as devout. It astonishes me now to think how she bore with my incoherencies; still more, what a method she took to cure me of them. I had begun a novel. It embodied queer conceptions of what I thought was passing around me; with some few of my own vicissitudes of feeling. She encouraged me to complete it. I read it to her chapter by chapter. Scarcely anyone but one so good

72

as she was could have discovered any good in it, but she did. She believed that I was trying to say something that it was better for me to say, and that I should see my path more clearly if I did. It was long before I did see it at all clearly.

Sterling suggested that if I gave up the Bar I should not return to Cambridge, but go to Oxford. The present Bishop of Chester, who was then tutor of Exeter, was a great friend of Sterling's. He entered me at his college almost before I was aware of it. My sister and my friends approved the step, and I went there.

Looking back on that step, I cannot fully justify it to myself. Just at the time it seemed to me a profitable humiliation to begin an undergraduate life again, after I had given myself such airs in a literary course. There was much, assuredly, in the position which might have humbled me; also with the discovery that I was still as irregular a student—much as I wished to be otherwise—as I had ever been. I had good friends here also. . . . The circumstance of belonging to a small society at Cambridge brought me into a similar one at Oxford founded by Mr. Gladstone, to which otherwise I should never have been admitted, as it consisted mainly of Christchurch men destined to hold an eminent position in the world. I had only a very distant acquaintance with the greater number of them; but I had just a glimpse of some of those who were to be associated with the political life of the last thirty-five years. . . .

The time I spent at Oxford was, for the most part, before the passing of the Reform Bill. The agitation about the Roman Catholic Emancipation had just subsided. Sir Robert Peel had been ejected from his seat for the university. The old Tories had evidently lost their moorings; many of them were inclined to join, and were actually joining, the Whigs to punish the Duke of Wellington and Peel for their apostasy. The young men were evidently puzzled, like the elders whom they were to follow or avoid; moderate Churchmanship generally prevailed. There was a party which was favorable to a relaxation of subscription. In the Cambridge pulpit Mr. Hugh Rose, afterward a kind friend of mine, denounced German Rationalism, and seemed to treat all German theology as rationalistic.

Dr. Pusey, who had just been studying at Bonn, wrote an apology for some of those whom Rose had condemned or neglected to notice. There was no decided movement, or at least none which a superficial observer could take notice of, in any direction. Yet there was a feeling, I think, in all that some movement was approaching. The three days of June, 1830, were followed by the coming in of Lord Grey's Ministry, and the agitation respecting the Reform Bill. When that bill had been carried through, and the old party had been beaten, there began to be a great effort among Liberals to accomplish other reforms, especially such as affected the Church. Lord Stanley carried through a bill for abolishing ten Irish bishoprics; and a measure for abolishing subscription to the Articles in the universities was much discussed in them and in the country. The first of these measures gave rise to the Tractarian Movement, of which we have all heard so much. The other produced far less seeming effect at the time, but it gave occasion to a number of academical pamphlets on both sides.

This last was a question which came home to me. In Cambridge it was demanded of every person taking a degree that he should declare himself a *bona fide* member of the Church of England. That, when I left Cambridge, I had declined to do. At Oxford every student at matriculation was required to sign the Thirty-nine Articles. This, when I entered the university, I had deliberately done. Whilst some reformers proposed to admit Dissenters to the university without restriction, or upon some general confession of belief, others argued that the Cambridge plan was a great advance on the Oxford, and might be reasonably substituted for it. I thought, country curate though I was, I had some call to speak on this text, as I had been obliged to give it some study.

Reviewing my own experience with the two universities, and, to some extent, with my own past life in connection with the question which was occupying the public attention, I came to this conclusion: that the Cambridge demand was much more distinctly and formally exclusive than the Oxford, inasmuch as it involved a direct renunciation of Nonconformity; that the subscription to Articles on entering Oxford was not intended as a test, but as a declaration of the terms on which the university proposed to teach its pupils, upon which terms they must agree to learn; that it is fairer to express those terms than to conceal them; that they are not terms which are to bind down the student to certain conclusions beyond which he cannot advance, but are helps to him in pursuing his studies, and warnings to him against hindrances and obstructions which past experience shows that he will encounter in pursuing them; that they are not unfit introductions to a general education in humanity and in physics because they are theological, but on that very account are valuable, because the superstitions which interfere with this education are associated with theology, and can only be cleared away by theology; that the Articles if used for the purposes of study and not as terms of communion for Churchmen generally, which they are not and never can be, may contribute to the reconciliation of what was positive in all Christian sects.

I spoke of Methodists, Baptists, and even Unitarians; only that which is negative in each and incapable of reconciliation being cast out.

Such was the substance of my pamphlet, and you will see, I think, that what I have written since has been intended in various ways to illustrate these maxims. I had a moderately clear instinct when I wrote it that I never could be acceptable to any schools in the Church; that if I maintained what seemed to me the true position of a Churchman, I must be in hostility, more or less marked, with each of them.

The newest form of parties was only then beginning to develop itself. I did not personally know either Mr. Newman or Dr. Pusey. The first I regarded as an eminent Aristotelian divine and popular tutor, who had been in great sympathy with Dr. Whately, and who was then following Mr. Keble in his reverence for Charles I, and in devotion to Anglican Episcopacy. The latter I only knew of as a Hebrew and German scholar, who had answered a book of Mr. Hugh Rose's on the subject of German Rationalism. Both were at this time strongly opposed to any relaxation of subscription; both appeared to take the Thirty-nine Articles, even more than I did, as representing the belief of the English Church. To both my pamphlet was shown—not at my request—in proof; both I was told accepted it as one contribution to the cause which they were advocating; both, I have no doubt, disliked the tone of it.

In a short time Mr. Newman was the declared antagonist of

Luther, the defender of the English Church only as it presented itself in writers like Bishop Bull, who had resisted the reformers' doctrine—that simple belief in Christ is the deliverance from evil and the root of good. That doctrine was still more undermined, as I thought, by Dr. Pusey's tract on Baptism, published a short time after; a tract which drove me more vehemently back on what I took to be the teaching of our Catechism—that by Baptism we claim the position which Christ has claimed for all mankind.

At the same time this conviction put me in direct opposition to the Evangelicals. They were at this time passing into a new phase. They had been the great antagonists of the High-and-Dry school which had made the Establishment everything, the witness of the Spirit with the individual conscience nothing; they had become the most vigorous supporters of an Establishment as such —whether Presbyterian or Episcopalian signified little. They had adopted the maxim of Dr. Chalmers'—that as men are fallen creatures, religion must be distasteful to them; that there will be no natural demand for it, therefore that it must be recommended by all external aids and influences. No doctrine could be so at variance with the notion that it is a Gospel which men have need of, and in their inmost hearts are craving for. Men who had the reverence which I felt for the old Evangelical Movement were obliged to choose between these two conflicting ideas, which were now practically presenting themselves to every young divine.

More and more I was led to ask myself what a Gospel to mankind must be; whether it must not have some other ground than the fall of Adam and the sinful nature of man. I had [been] helped much in finding an answer to this question by your dear old friend Mr. Erskine's books—I did not then know him personally —and by the sermons of Mr. Campbell. The English Church I thought was the witness for that universal redemption which the Scotch Presbyterians had declared to be incompatible with their Confessions. But this position was strictly a theological one. Every hope I had for human culture, for the reconciliation of opposing schools, for blessings to mankind, was based on theology. What sympathy, then, could I have with the Liberal party which was emphatically antitheological, which was ready to tolerate all opinions in theology, only because people could know nothing

76

about it and because other studies were much better pursued without reference to it?

The Liberals were clearly right in saying that the Articles did not mean to those who signed them at the universities or on taking orders what I supposed them to mean, and I was wrong. They were right in saying that subscription did mean to most the renunciation of a right to think, and, since none could renounce that right, it involved dishonesty. All this I have been compelled by the evidence of facts sorrowfully to confess. I accept the humiliation. I give the Liberals the triumph which they deserve. But they feel and I feel that we are not a step nearer to each other in 1870 than we were in 1835. They have acquired a new name. They are called Broad Churchmen now, and delight to be called so. But their breadth seems to me to be narrowness. They include all kinds of opinions. But what message have they for the people who do not live upon opinions or care for opinions?

Are they children of God, or must they now and forever be children of the devil? The Broad Churchman gives no answer. To me life is a burden unless I can find one. All these parties, I knew when I wrote *Subscription No Bondage*, and I know much more fully now, contain men at whose feet I am not worthy to sit. I have longed for sympathy with them all. But God has ordered it otherwise.

▶ **20. From Guy's Hospital, on January 20, 1836, to an unidentified friend**

. . . I do not wonder at your being tormented with the great question respecting the comparative extent of the Fall and the Redemption. It is just the question by which we of this age are, I suppose, to be most tempted. But the language of the Catechism is to me, in general, satisfactory. The human state which the baptized man *claims* is a state of salvation, and the world, the flesh, and the devil are striving to hinder each man from knowing and believing that it is so. I know they harass others, and have harassed me with the suggestion, "It is all a vain subtlety to distinguish between the fact of redemption and the knowledge of it when" (as the redemption has reference to a knowing subject) "the fact without the knowledge is as though it were not." But the answer to the sophism is, "Yes, but the distinction is a most vital and practical one; for it makes all the difference to the possibility of my knowing and believing whether there is something to be known and believed, or nothing."

Why there should be an age in which the whole order of things is settled, but in which men are not yet brought to understand it and acquiesce in it, intervening between that age of the yet uncompleted kingdom which we read of and that one of perfect peace and submission which we hope for, I think the very restlessness of our own minds and our willingness to put our own apprehensions in place of the things apprehended may teach us. Without such a witness for truth as truth, though unbelieved, I think we should not believe that all love and all wisdom are of God, and without this belief there could be no happiness or peace. Still there is another answer to the temptation which I have found very useful: "I know that in me, that is, in my flesh, dwelleth no good thing." This has been proved to me by many experiments; and it has been proved to the world, too, at such crises as the siege of Jerusalem, when men, God-deserted, have shown that all the so-called natural affections dwelt in them no longer. Then where they do dwell, this is grace not nature, Christ not Adam. All family life, maternal instincts, the whole order must perish unless He were bearing up the pillars of it.

▶ **21. To his pupil Edward Strachey, in February, 1837, with advice on a course of study**

. . . I believe, after much thinking, I am more than ever strengthened in my opinion that in this age, at least, we are *not* to lay down plans of study and life which have been contrived with a view simply or principally to the apparent wants of our own minds, the peculiarities of our character, tastes, etc. All the instances I know, or have heard, of persons taking this course convince me that it is a wrong one. . . . I can myself see no course so clear and safe as that which is determined by the answer to the question, What are the most prominent evil tendencies in the age in which I live as I see them manifested in myself and those with whom I am brought into contact? What direction do the cravings after good in myself and in them most habitually and decidedly take? What course of thought and reading will best assist me in understanding these tendencies, and the method by which God would counteract the one, foster the other?

I doubt not that your own experience will accord with mine as to the reply. You will not have much hesitation in deciding that all our minds have more or less a political bias, that we cannot thwart it altogether, try as hard as we will; and that every attempt to thwart it generally does us great mischief. I have come to these conclusions gradually and reluctantly, for I do not think I was born a politician, and there are times in my life in which I have resolved that it was better to be anything than this. But I never could succeed in overcoming the mighty impulse which seemed unceasingly to urge me forward in this direction, and I never was happier than when I discovered that God did not design me to overcome it, and that on the contrary my personal and spiritual life was deeply interested in my yielding to it.

I am quite convinced that if you propose to yourself the science of politics (in its highest sense) as your business that you will compass three great ends: (1) Your social life, the ordinary conversational, after-dinner life, I mean, will acquire something of the lofty tone of the study and the oratory, without it being needful that you should deviate from common topics or that you should seem to force your companions out of their customary materialism. (2) You will acquire a feeling of the reality of the Bible, and will feel how its application to the universe and to everyday events consists with and is sustained by its transcendental meaning. In fact the one will reveal itself in the other. (3) You will be delivered from the fetters of party and the care about confederacies, and will find that we must sanctify the Lord God in our hearts and make Him our fear and these our dreads. I regret deeply that I have not more sedulously pursued this study and cultivated the habits which I am sure if rightly pursued it will engender. For you I have no question of the expediency of making it your prominent pursuit. If you should spend your life as a country gentleman, it will be the fitting course even in the judgment of the world; if you become a clergyman you will find that it is that which makes you the most faithful and useful servant of the Church.

The course of reading I should be inclined to recommend with a view to this object (which I am sure you will find it your interest to keep before you all the time at your College, and to a degree throughout life) is firstly and principally the Jewish law, history, and prophets. Any hints that I can supply respecting the mode of reading them will be contained in the Hebrew part of my *History of Moral Philosophy*, which is short and which you shall see as soon as it is fully made out. In Greek, Thucydides to be read and weighed as a history of the working of the two great principles which governed Greek society. Every part of it is important. Second, the *Politics* of Plato and of Aristotle. Third, as much of Homer as you have time for. It may be read at intervals to explain the order of society in the heroic ages. Fourth, the *Birds* and *Frogs*, *Knights*, and *Acharnians* of Aristophanes, all bearing upon the Athenian democracy, and illustrating Thucydides. Fifth, some of Xenophon's smaller treatises; but of these I know little.

In Latin read Cicero's *Letters*, his *Political Orations*, and the parts of his philosophical writings which bear upon politics. Read Livy, and the *Annals* of Tacitus: in illustration of these, Machiavelli's *Discourses on Livy*, and Niebuhr [the German historian]. In all your modern reading, I should recommend you to put ecclesiastical history foremost. There may be no good ones; but if you read Mosheim, Milner, and Neander, and remember that not one of the three had more than a faint dream what a Church means, you may make out something. Read Augustine, *De Civitate*, for yourself. Study the history of great crises, especially these: the Age of Constantine (with the Arian controversy); the Age of Justinian; the Age of Charlemagne; the Age of Hildebrand; the Age of the Reformation; the English period from 1603 to 1688; the French Revolution. Read a little of Sir Thomas More and Erasmus; what you can get of Luther; read Hooker.

Burke belongs to another era; he is the index to all modern

thoughts and speculations on political subjects. But never read him or any of the moderns without keeping your mind steady and hopeful by the study of St. Paul's and St. John's Epistles and the Apocalypse. There we learn the sure triumph of order, unity, and love over confusion, divisions, and hatred; learn to expect that we shall pass through all these in their most dreadful manifestations; learn to understand the grounds of our safety and of the Church's safety when all is in wreck and ruin. I have thus hastily given you my notions, on which I will enlarge more in a future letter if these are intelligible to you and seem to promise you any assistance. In the meantime, as I am rather fagged, I will wish you good night, and all blessings spiritual and temporal. Among the former, that you may be able to work out the hints in this letter into practical life till you quite forget where you first heard them, and yet have reason to give thanks for them to Him who can by the most unworthy hands transmit most precious gifts to us. . . .

▶ 22. To Edward Strachey, in the spring of 1837, on the Oxford Tracts

I do not fancy that you will get much satisfaction from the Oxford Tracts, but I cannot tell. To me they are, for the most part, more unpleasant than I quite like to acknowledge to myself or others. Their error, I think, consists in opposing to "the spirit of the present age" the spirit of a former age, instead of the ever-living and acting Spirit of God, of which the spirit of each age (as it presents itself to those living in it) is at once the adversary and the parody. The childlike spirit of the fathers, say they, must be brought in to counteract the intellectual spirit of these times—the spirit of submission to Church authority against the spirit of voluntary association. Nay, I contend, but the spirit of earnest and deep reflection is that which God would cultivate in us to oppose the superficial intelligence of the day, the spirit of Christian or Church liberty (the service which is freedom) to counteract the lust for independence, the spirit of unity to overthrow the spirit of combination. Thus I am entirely opposed to them, while yet our lines of thought will often coincide, and while I can yet recognize them as doing part of that work (though I think doing it ill) which must be done for us.

If you bring out the spirit of earnest meditation, that will be a childlike spirit, and is a spirit which loves the parent and loves the fathers; yet it will be the spirit of the man, not of the child. If you bring out the idea of the Church freedom and unity, you will lead him to submit to the Church, but it will be a submission of the reason for the reason's sake, not because it is to be crushed. It is useless to talk these things to them, they must have their own way, and so I said three years ago to the friend who has been most active in persuading them to think me a very decent, genteel sort of person, and me to believe that they did think me so. Unfortunately, I took off the mask when he was not looking, and they were quite frightened at my ugliness.

▶ 23. To his fiancée, Anna Barton, on July 23, 1837

I am rejoiced that you at least have understood exactly, most exactly, what was the object of my letters to the Quakers.* That truth, of Christ being in us the hope of glory, is the one which I have found most necessary to sustain my own spirit when it has been sinking with the sense of its own utter unworthiness; for it shows that we can have no goodness apart from Him, that all our goodness must be by union with Him who is perfectly good. Baptism seems to me to declare this truth to everyone, and to be moreover that act in which the Holy Spirit takes charge of us and promises to guide us into the knowledge and love of Christ if we will submit to His guidings; the Lord's Supper to be that in which, as you express it, we may have life and have it more abundantly by ever fresh communication from the source of it. I know in myself that if I had not had the faith that I was a member of Christ and child of God confirmed to me by the simple assurance of this ordinance, and if I had not felt that it was a sin not

* Maurice's letters to the Quakers became his *The Kingdom of Christ*, 1838. This was expanded and completely rewritten in the edition of 1842.

to believe God's words, I should have sunk into utter indifference or wretchedness.

I know that you, my dearest, can never have the same miserable self-reproach that I have had; but yet it is so comfortable a truth that we are bound to trust in God and to believe ourselves one with Christ, on His own assurance given in His own way, that I would wish you to receive it, though you may have a multitude of pleasant and holy feelings which seem to give a better warrant for the same confidence. If you have such—oh! let me share them with you, but take in exchange for them the trust which I am obliged continually to maintain, when my soul seems in utter drought and dreariness.

▶ *24. An autobiographical letter to his son, written December 10, 1870, as an "Explanatory Letter" mainly about his book,* The Kingdom of Christ, *and headed by the title of his pamphlet,* Reasons for Not Joining a Party in the Church

My dearest Frederick,

The next pamphlet, if I remember right, in the collection which you saw bears this title. . . .

I had become the Chaplain of Guy's Hospital. That change in my circumstances did not bring me much into contact with London life. I was in an obscure corner, and my duties were such as would not have brought me acquaintance with any who lived away from it. . . .

I had been much impressed in my Bubbenhall curacy among laborers and farmers; I was still more impressed in the midst of this London population of sick men and women, with the language of our Catechism—that language which caused most offense to the Evangelical school. It seemed to me that except I could address all kinds of people as members of Christ and children of God, I could not address them at all. Their sin, it seemed to me, must mean a departure from that state; it must be their true state, that which Christ had claimed for them.

I thought I had no Gospel for the sufferers in Guy's Hospital, if it was not that. I was ignorant enough of their sufferings and sins, I knew that I was; my ignorance was unfathomable. If I might not say, God your Father knows it all, He is able and willing to raise you out of any depth into which you have fallen, I must despair. I could not think that they had ever resisted God's goodness as much as I had. I could not scold them, I could only speak to them of trust in One who could raise them. That became the principle of my preaching. I understood very little the way of making it intelligible to individuals, rich or poor, sick or well. But when preaching in the chapel or the ward, I found this language the only possible one.

I felt therefore much sympathy with those who spoke of baptism as bearing witness of the state into which men are redeemed. I felt the worth of that direct appeal to the hearts and consciences of men which had distinguished the Evangelical preachers of the last century from the dry moralists, but I thought they had become weak, because they assumed sin, and not redemption, as the starting point.

The new form of Churchmanship which was set forth in the Oxford Tracts had so far an attraction for me that it appeared to treat of a regeneration as dependent on the will of God and the death of Christ, not the individual faith of men. I did not care much for the other peculiarities of it, which were chiefly negative. It asserted that Presbyterians were not Churchmen, that Protestants and Romanists were equally departing from the standard of Anglican moderation. Such opinions had a certain influence, not a healthy one, on my mind, but they took no real hold of it. With that part which concerned baptism I dreamed for a while that I should have a real point of union. This dream was entirely scattered by Dr. Pusey's tract on Baptism. Instead of affording me the least warrant for the kind of teaching which appeared to me alone scriptural and practical, it made such teaching utterly impossible. The baptized child was holy for a moment after its baptism; in committing sin it lost its purity. That could only be recovered by acts of repentance and a system of ascetical discipline. I remember to this day the misery which this tract caused me as I read it in a walk to one of the London suburbs. I saw that I must be hopelessly and forever estranged from this doctrine and from those who taught it unless I abandoned all my hopes for myself and for the world.

Just about this time my eldest sister drew my attention to a movement in the Quaker body. The old Quakers had spoken of the divine Word as the light which lightens every man that cometh into the world. A younger body of them, who were in strong sympathy with the Evangelicals, declared that this doctrine interfered with reverence for the written word and with the doctrine of human depravity. Evidently the new party had much life in it and was conscious of a dryness and formality in the elder school. Reflecting much on this controversy and connecting it with what was passing in the English Church, it seemed to me that the old Quakers were affirming a most grand and fundamental truth; but that it had become narrow and contradictory because they had no ordinance which embodied it and made it universal; that we, on the other hand, forgetting their Quaker principles, or rather the words of St. John, necessarily made baptism a mere ceremony or a charm. The two being united expressed to me the reconciliation of the High Church baptismal regeneration with the Evangelical demands for personal faith.

Starting from this text, I wrote a series of tracts addressed to Quakers, but really concerning ourselves more than them. They formed the book called *The Kingdom of Christ*, of which a second edition, much altered, appeared in 1842. In the second of these tracts I commented on Dr. Pusey's theory of baptism. Nothing I have written had so important an effect on my life. It set me in direct antagonism with his school, to which I had many attractions, and by some members of which my *Subscription No Bondage* had been partially approved.

Soon the most advanced members of that school began to be exceedingly impatient of the Articles for which they and I had pleaded. The younger men perceived that Dr. Pusey's baptismal doctrine was in spirit even more than in terms opposed to the maxims of the Reformation which had impressed themselves so deeply on our formulas. In his 90th Tract Dr. Newman undertook to show that there was a possible construction of the Articles which they might with a safe conscience recognize. His intention was, I am satisfied, honest, but to ordinary readers his interpretation appeared highly sophistical.

Four Oxford tutors, one of them the present Archbishop of Canterbury, denounced it as fatal to all sincere subscription. This pamphlet called forth Dr. Hook, the present Dean of Chichester. He had sympathized much with the earlier tracts; he disliked the 90th; but he could not consent to abandon friends from whom he had learned much. He said that the Oxford tutors compelled him to choose his party in the Church, and that he did choose that of their opponents. His book was the occasion of my *Reasons for Not Joining a Party in the Church*.

Since my coming to Guy's Hospital I had become acquainted with Archdeacon Wilberforce, now the Bishop of Winchester. He was seeking, I believe, for a common ground between the two parties in the Church. He had a natural desire to see if anyone else had found one. It was very unlikely that a man with his wide sympathies and knowledge of the world would do more than take a glimpse at the opinions of a solitary thinker and pass on. Everyone who has been in temporary communication with him must be aware how great a power he has of receiving and reflecting impressions even from the least important persons.

Dr. Hook, who never sympathized with any of my opinions and knew little of me personally, yet wrote to me afterward with characteristic generosity that in this instance I had been right, and he had been wrong. The confession was far more honorable to him than to me, but no praise bestowed on me personally could have pleased me so much.

Thus you see that the principle with which I started became, almost in spite of me, the growing one of my life, that which every new circumstance made me more aware that I must live and die for, more aware also that it would separate me from those with whom I should most wish to act, and would give me not only the appearance of isolation and self-conceit, but often the reality of both.

I knew also that I was in danger of attaching myself to a party which should inscribe "No Party" on its flag. Many had fallen into that snare. I was as little likely as anyone to escape it. . . . Our common dread of the Liberals, the Evangelicals, and the

High Church school might have bound me slavishly to their modes of thinking if God had not given me a nearer friend who understood me better than they understood me or than I understood myself. Your mother knew the secrets of true Churchmanship better than any of my male acquaintances, and oh, how much better than I did!

"If you only act on your conviction," she once said to me, "that Christ is in everyone, what a much higher life you might live, how much better work you might do!" There was in that sentence the clearest divination of what I feel and know to be God's purpose in all His teachings and discipline which I have received, and of my failures.

I was sent into the world that I might persuade men to recognize Christ as the center of their fellowship with each other, that so they might be united in their families, their countries, and as men, not in schools and factions; and through forgetfulness of this truth myself I have been continually separating myself from relations, letting go friendships, and sinking into an unprofitable solitude.

Your mother sought to save me from this vanity, making home more delightful than any other society could be, and yet giving me an interest in that, yet teaching me that the poorest man is Christ's brother and should be dear to us for His sake. She mourned over my want of sympathy with nature, and many deeper wants than that; yet she entered into all my thoughts and pursuits. She and your second mother have shown me how much a married man may be, if he will, educated by marriage in the kingdom of God, how much the true union of hearts may make party ties unnecessary to him. God's love has been at the root of their wedded lives; if it had been equally of mine there would not be so much shame mixed with joy and thankfulness in the recollection of what I have written and what I have been.

But joy and thankfulness should and shall triumph over the shame. God blots out sins and keeps alive all that is pure and good. I can bless Him that He has not suffered me to join a party in the Church in my youth, or manhood, or old age. I can believe on this tenth day of December, 1870, your mother's birthday, that she is helping you, and your brother, and me, and teaching us more than if she were visible to us of our union with each other and with all in Christ.

▶ 25. To Mr. Woollcombe, on February 14, 1838, answering problems arising from Woollcombe's earlier letter to him

. . . To know that God does not depend upon our feelings, but our feelings upon God, to know that we must claim a certain spiritual position as our right before we can realize it in our apprehensions, to be assured that we have the Spirit of God within us, and that He is distinct from all the emotions, energies, affections, sympathies in our minds, the only source and inspirer of them all, this is most necessary for us, the peculiar necessity, if I am not mistaken, of this age. To learn that what they could grasp by faith was theirs, was the task of our forefathers; it is a precious truth which they have left to us, and we must not let it go.

To learn that there is a substance for faith to lay hold of, and that faith does not create this substance; that there is a deep ground and source of faith—deeper of course than all the acts which proceed from it, this is our task. The consciousness of positive, tangible evil drove them to their truth: the consciousness of an unutterable hollowness of heart, a consciousness that seems like strangest unconsciousness, and yet at the furthest remove from it, because it is not simple and innocent, this seems the appointed path to ours.

Through it, I suppose, not perhaps every Christian, but almost every Christian minister in this day, must at some time or other pass, and, what is more, I do not fancy that till our life's end we shall find where it terminates. But of this I am well assured, that the truth which we learn by walking in it is strength to support us through it. The confidence of a power always at work within us, manifesting itself in our powerlessness, a love filling up our lovelessness, a wisdom surmounting our folly, the knowledge of our right to glory in this love, power, and wisdom, the certainty that we can do all righteous acts by submitting to this Righteous Being, and that we do them best when we walk in a line chosen for us, and not of our choosing, this is the strength surely, and nothing else, which carries us through earth and lifts us to heaven.

And here is the answer to your second series of difficulties—those which arise out of your tendency to look at all questions as merely puzzles for the intellect. This tendency is, I suppose, in most of us. But we cannot gratify it, we may try as hard as we will, but that discipline of which I have spoken does, in spite of us, bring all, who desire not to resist it, into another state of mind altogether.

There are some who would give us only the husks of truths in systems; there are [others] who would give us only the juice of truths in feelings and sympathies.

The Spirit of Truth will not suffer us to be content with either gift, nor yet to be alternately choosing one and the other. He compels us to feel that the whole truth, in all its substance, in all its juiciness, lies at the roots of our own being, and sustains it.

I have given you an instance in the demonstration by which the truth of the distinct Personality of the Holy Ghost is brought home to us; and when this truth is once cheerfully received, every other is appreciated by degrees in the like manner. And assuredly this is, after all, but that of which our baptism has been all along testifying, and which God, by the other sacrament, will settle and ground us in, let our intellects struggle against it as much as they will. Meantime, it is the wisdom of a cultivated layman, it is the solemn duty of a Christian priest, to give that intellect its proper employment in examining the history of opinions and heresies; of all studies, I fancy the most profitable and the most helpful to a mind which starts with great moral and spiritual wants, and does not expect that anyone but God can satisfy them. It signifies little what are your textbooks; those in which the Bishop examines—Pearson or Hooker—will be quite as good for authors as any which we could invent for ourselves.

As to episcopacy, I certainly should encourage everyone to ask for "the wherefore" as well as "the what," but he must start with "the what," he must believe that he has a position, and not begin with abandoning it. I should say the same to a Presbyterian. Start from your own ground, do not give up anything you hold now; get as much more to strengthen it with as you can. Having adopted this precaution, I have no fear of his not finding that episcopacy is necessary to the idea of a Church. I have no doubt of his perceiving that without the third order, the grand truth of Christ's own episcopacy is lost sight of and becomes a mere dream; that comprehension and universality cease to be constituents of the Church; and that, as a consequence, Christianity becomes a notion or doctrine, instead of a kingdom. With these internal reasons for episcopacy, the external facts and authority in support of it will assume quite a new weight and character, and this faith too will become that of his being as well as of his creed. I shall be truly happy if these few hints are of any use to you.

I shall be very glad whenever you have the kindness to write, and will answer as well as I can.

▶ *26. To Edward Strachey, on November 9, 1838, about the subjects of the New Testament books*

. . . Could you contrive to come and spend a little time with us? We are expecting Carlyle and his wife to dinner some day soon, and we shall try and get Scott to meet them; if you could come and stay a week with us, you would be sure of seeing them, and the fatigue of coming would have time to go off.

I drew up a collection of heads for ecclesiastical history for Mrs. Maurice, and in the course of them introduced some remarks on the different books of the New Testament. I do not know whether they are what you want, but such as I have give I thee.

. . . From the birth of Christ to the destruction of the Jewish polity. This period connects the old with the new world. It contains the history of the growth of the Christian kingdom out of the Jewish. First, we have the four Gospels exhibiting the person of Him to whom the law and the prophecies had been pointing— Jesus Christ, the son of David, the son of Abraham. In this character He is especially presented to us in St. Matthew's Gospel. Mark announces that his is the Gospel of Jesus Christ, the *Son of God*. He exhibits to us the living, acting Man, the Image of God in human flesh, rather than the Jewish King. Luke's primary object is to present Him as the Light to lighten the Gentiles, the

90

Head of the new dispensation. John's is emphatically the Christian Gospel, exhibiting the relation of Christ as the Head of humanity to Christ as the Son of God.

The Acts of the Apostles describe the establishment of the kingdom in the name of the Father, the Son, and the Holy Ghost; its assumption of the character of a universal kingdom by the preaching to the Gentiles, the different forms of opposition it meets with, which are so classified that it serves for a prophecy of the future condition of the Church as well as a history of the past.

The next documents relating to this period are the thirteen Epistles of St. Paul, developing different leading ideas of Christianity in reference to the condition of different Churches. In that to the Romans is developed the idea of God's personal righteousness exhibited in Christ as a ground of faith, in contrast to the righteousness of mere law, which is a ground of fear and condemnation. In the First Epistle to the Corinthians is developed the idea of Church unity as resting in the person of Christ, and not in any theories or philosophy concerning Him. In the Epistle to the Galatians is developed the idea of the Christian covenant as the covenant of sonship in opposition to the Jewish covenant, the covenant of servitude. In the Epistle to the Ephesians is developed the idea of the Church as a constitution in Christ before all worlds. In the Epistle to the Philippians is developed the idea of Christian perfection, and of the Christian life as a continual progress toward the apprehension of it as already existing in Christ. In the Epistle to the Colossians is developed the idea of the headship of Christ and of the direct connection of men with Him in His risen glory. In the Epistle to the Thessalonians is developed the idea of the second coming of Christ. In the Epistles to Timothy and Titus is developed the idea of the ministerial and episcopal character. In the Epistle to the Hebrews is developed the idea of the priesthood of Christ.

The next set of documents are the Catholic Epistles of St. James, St. Peter, St. John, and St. Jude. St. James's Epistle develops the idea of the law of liberty, of the Christian admitted into the privilege and power of keeping God's commandments. It presents us with the other side of the idea of law from that which St. Paul takes—of what St. Paul himself calls the law of the Spirit of

Life, in opposition to the law of the flesh. St. Peter's Epistles develop the idea of the Christian life in the opposite form to that which is taken in the Epistle to the Philippians, not as the pursuit of a righteousness above ourselves, but as in the submission to a power working upon us and in us. Of course, both ideas are assumed in both Epistles; but in one the first is made prominent, in the other the second.

The Epistle of St. John is the reconciliation and completion of the ideas which St. Paul, St. James, and St. Peter have been bringing to light in the revelation of God's character, and of men as enabled by Christ to enter into communion with Him. It is emphatically the sacramental Epistle. Finally we have the Book of Revelation developing the complete idea of the Church, and of its relation to the kingdoms of the earth, and exhibiting the history of its triumphs over them. . . .

In my last letter, correct "Established Church." I never used the words in my life—at least in the last ten years—in my senses; it should be "English."

▶ 27. To the Reverend A. J. Scott, afterward Principal of Owens College, on February 20, (probably) 1839

. . . I have endeavored in my tracts to prove that if Christ be really the Head of every man, and if He really have taken human flesh, there is ground for a universal fellowship among men (a fellowship that is itself the foundation of those particular fellowships of the nation and the family, which I also consider sacred). I have maintained that it is the business of a Church to assert this ground of universal fellowship; that it ought to make men understand and feel how possible it is for men as men to fraternize in Christ; how impossible it is to fraternize except in Him. Now the denial of a universal head is practically the denial of all communion in society.

This universal fellowship in Christ, I believe that the Church of England asserts by its ordinances; and believing this (rightly or wrongly), I feel that *I am bound* as a good member of that

92

Church not to narrow my terms of intercourse or fellowship. I meet men as men because I feel that I have a ground on which I can meet them, and that this is the deepest, safest ground of all. If they do not acknowledge it distinctly, or even if by their works they deny it, I may still hope in some way or other, by God's blessing, to make them conscious of it. If they do acknowledge it, and exhibit the practical results of the acknowledgment, I have as strong and full a sympathy with them as my own miserably imperfect and feeble apprehension of the truth on which we stand permits. If the person whom I thus meet fraternizes elsewhere, on another principle, that is nothing to me. Still less does it signify to me that he may support in conversation certain theological theses to which I cannot assent, or may deny doctrines which I hold very earnestly. I should make no compromise, I should hope to be enabled to tell him honestly what I think, but my friendship with him would not be interrupted: or, if it were, I should attribute the breach to my infirmity of temper, and not boast of it as a sacrifice to duty. This would be my way of acting in society.

But if the same person said to me, "Let us meet tomorrow at some meeting of the Bible Society; I am an Independent, or a Baptist, or a Quaker; you, I know, are an Episcopalian; but let us forget our differences and meet on the ground of our common Christianity," I should say, instantly, "I will do no such thing; I consider that your whole scheme is a flat contradiction and lie. You come forward with the avowal that you fraternize on some other ground than that of our union in Christ, and then you ask me to fraternize with you on that ground. I consider your sects—one and all of them—as an outrage on the Christian principle, as a denial of it.

"And what is the common Christianity which you speak of? The mere dead residue of all systems! You do not really mean us to unite in Christ as being members of His body; you mean us to unite in holding certain notions *about* Christ; just as you hold certain peculiar notions about baptism, the independence of congregations, etc. But you say I am an Episcopalian. It is true; I acknowledge the authority of bishops. But I do not fraternize in the belief of the authority of bishops. I would refuse the right hand of fellowship to anyone who asked me to stand with him on that ground, as I now refuse it to you. If you do not understand this; if you cannot see that just as I meet Englishmen, not on the ground that I agree with them in thinking a limited monarchy the best form of government (though I may think that), but on the ground of our being Englishmen, of our having the same Queen, the same laws, the same ancestors, recollections, associations, language, so I meet Churchmen on the ground of our being Churchmen, of our having one head, of our having the same relation to an innumerable company of spirits that are on the earth and that have left the earth. If you cannot perceive this, I see more clearly than ever what your sect system has done for you; I see more need than ever of protesting against it by word and deed, in season and out of season."

I trust that this statement will enable you to see what I meant by meeting "sects as sects," and why I accused Mr. Noel of a contradiction in inviting us to acknowledge ourselves members of a sect that we might associate with the good men who belong to the sects. I think, also, you will see how I might allow "sects as sects," the very existence of separation, to have done good as "volcanoes and tornadoes have done good," while yet I could confess far more cheerfully that *every* good man in every sect has done good of quite another kind, especially by being a constant witness against sectarianism. . . .

▶ 28. To Edward Strachey, April 17, 1839, after the birth of a stillborn child to Mrs. Maurice

Our little still infant had a very delicate and beautiful countenance, and its form was, I believe and hope, the shrine of a spirit which has its dwelling somewhere else, though not here. It is a mystery—so all our life is; but I do not know that it is harder to believe this than the wonders which we must believe respecting ourselves.

▶ 29. To Edward Strachey on May 25, 1839

. . . Sterling, I take it, will be at Clifton the week after next. I hope you may see something of each other. His residence abroad has done him good in many ways, and if you are not mutually determined to get on uneven ground—which is not wise, as I know—you will find enough to sympathize in. My own nature is very prickly and disputatious, but it has caused me so very much trouble, such bitter present pain, from the conflicts into which it has brought me with others, and such remorse in the retrospection, that I hope I am now become more watchful and determined, so far as in me lies, to live peaceably with all. One can find enough that is not good and pleasant in all; the art is to detect in them the good thing which God has put into each, and means each to show forth.

You must practice this art with your Bristol clergy. The Church is in a sad state; we all know that—little light, little life. So much the more careful should we be not to quench any that there is. Our great misery has been our resolute worship of our own notions, our hatred of every notion that clashed with them. If we have begun to see this, and to feel the real importance of fellowship in a person instead of a notion, it will not do to make that discovery into a notion too, and to break our neighbors' heads with it. I know I am preaching what I practice very miserably, nay, scarcely at all. But in my inmost heart I wish to practice it, and to stir up all persons to do the like. I think a great responsibility is laid upon those who have any vital perceptions as to the nature and conditions of Church unity, to see that they *keep* the unity of the Spirit in the bond of peace, using their intellects to help forward spiritual fellowship, as intellects have been used to disturb it. We know that the Word of Wisdom does dwell in all; in those who kick against that very doctrine as in those who receive it; the reception of the doctrine being, indeed, in *their* account everything, not in ours. To make them aware of its presence, to bring them to submit to it, and for this end to sympathize with whatever of light there is in them, however hidden under dark notions of life, however stifled by unkind and uncharitable surmises, must be our aim.

I cannot tell you how hard I find this to be: nothing, I believe, but the daily, hourly discovery that there is a depth of darkness and death in myself, which at least I do not know of in any other, and that there are the sparks of light and the announcements of life in others, to which there is little corresponding within, would save me from most intolerable conceit and dogmatism. These frightful disclosures God in His mercy appoints for me; and so they be compensated, as I am bound to hope against hope that they will be, by such disclosures of His own excellence and beauty as shall fully raise me out of self and transfigure me into His likeness, I have abundant reason for thankfulness.

But I must believe that all want this as well as myself; and if none deserve it less, I should have some of the same confidence in asking that all may receive it. I have got into this train of talking I know not how, instead of answering your particular request about a book on the importance of a learned ministry, which I believe I am so far competent to write that, being a minister, I feel the want of learning most grievously. I fancy I must get love first, and then, possibly, in this or in some other sphere, I may have learning added. At present I lack both.

▶ *30. From a letter to his wife, on May 9, 1840, about Carlyle as a lecturer*

. . . I felt throughout how much *more* kind and tolerant toward the truth in all forms of faith and opinion he can be and should be who does in his heart believe Jesus Christ to be the Son of God, and that all systems are feeling after Him as the common center of the world, than Carlyle can ever be while he regards the world as without a center, and the doctrine of Christ's Incarnation, Passion, and Resurrection, as only one of the mythical vestures in which certain actions—which, without such a vesture, he secretly knows and confesses to be good-for-nothing abstractions—have wrapped themselves up.

At the same time the miserable vagueness into which he sometimes fell, his silly rant about the great bosom of Nature, which was repeated in this lecture several times, which, as you observed, he would laugh to scorn in any other man, together with the most monstrous confusions both intellectual and moral, even while he evidently wished to assert the distinction between right and wrong, convinced me whither his tolerance would lead in any mind in which it was not corrected, as it is in his, by a real abhorrence of what is base and false, and by a recklessness of logical consistency, if so be he can bring out his different half-conceptions in some strong expressive language. . . .

▶ 31. From a letter to Mr. Thomas Erskine* of Linlathen on August 8, 1841

. . . There is one passage in Mr. ———'s letter which showed me clearly how much I must have injured the principle which I wished to set forth by my way of stating it. He speaks of the English Church as being in his judgment more faithful than most of the sects which despise her: but not as fulfilling his idea of the Catholic Church. Now, certainly this is as much my faith as it can be his. The English *Church* I look upon as merely one branch of the true Church; and every *system*, whether called Evangelical, Liberal, Catholic, or purely Anglican, which has been invented by the members of that Church in former times and in our own day to express their notion of the Church, I look upon as "of the earth earthy," and as much carrying in it the seeds of destruction as the systems of the different sects which have revolted from her.

The Church—it seems to me—is a part, the highest part, of that spiritual constitution of which the nation and the family are lower and subordinate parts; implied in the acts we do and the words we speak, established before all worlds, manifested as the

* The Scottish Erskine of Linlathen (1788-1870) was both a lawyer and a theologian. He early influenced Maurice by his *Brazen Serpent* (1831) and responded to Maurice's thought with friendship. Both agreed on the universal nature of Christ's atonement. See the interesting collection edited by W. Hanna of *The Letters of Thomas Erskine of Linlathen* (1877).

true and everlasting kingdom when the Son of God died, rose, and ascended on high, testified as the common property and inheritance of men by certain forms and ordinances which convert it from an idea for the mind into an actual reality for all who will enter into it and enjoy it, and which prove God to be true though all men be liars.

The Catholic Church, I think, has established itself in the East and the West, and is acknowledged by God as His kingdom upon earth. It has been preyed upon by diseases of all kinds in the shape of human systems: by the Romish system, which is the most successful parody and counterfeit of its Catholic character, and practically contradicts and outrages that, as well as its spiritual character; by Protestant systems which parody its distinct and personal character, and really outrage that as well as its principle —universal human fellowship. Yet in spite of these, and other different systems which have attempted to make a middle way between them, and so, I think, to combine the mischiefs of both, the Church, I think, is coming forth, and will manifest itself as something entirely distinct from them all—distinct, too, from the faith which exists in the minds of those who spiritually dwell in it, though requiring it and supposing it.

This last conviction—that it is necessary most carefully to distinguish the objects of faith from its exercises, and that the permanence and eternity of the one are manifested to us as much by the weakness and poverty of the other as by the warrant which they give, if we will receive it, that they shall be stronger—has been brought home to me by such painful experience, that it has become, I think, the deepest and strongest in my mind. How liable it is to be perverted into an excuse for shameful indolence and recklessness, I know too sadly; but I know also, by proofs sufficient to myself though not I fear to anyone who converses with me, that it is the best deliverance I have from such sins. I could indeed wish to ask you for your help in this fight. I cannot easily tell you how much comfort I received from your kindness when you were in London in November.

It would delight me at any time to hear from you or see you.

▶ 32. To Strachey, whose health was always precarious, November 24, 1841

I am grieved at your report of yourself both in this and in the former letter, for though I think you bear up against pain and suffering more manfully than most men, I am not willing that you should have so much and such constant call for the exercise. However, I am quite sure that sufferers have a wonderful appointment and ordination. No men give me the notion of the privilege of being priests unto God so much as they; and kings, too, they are in a sense, though a less obvious one. You do not know the pains and temptations of doing, the self-accusations of strong health, the sense of weakness of the spirit when the flesh is strong. These are struggles within me, and they seem to touch the will more nearly than the others, though I feel assured at the same time that, were I called to your task, I should perform it most miserably; at least, I should need a degree of grace which has not yet been vouchsafed to me.

As for your thought that the sufferer lives less for others than the doer, I think it is a mistake, though a very natural one. We shall know more about it hereafter, but I suspect the cross will be found to have been the great *power* of the world, both in the members and the Head. You approved of my paradox about form being more spiritual than spirit; you, therefore, embolden me to another, that suffering does more than doing. . . .

▶ 33. To Mr. de Vere, in the summer of 1842, concerning the Jerusalem Bishopric

I was very glad to receive your kind letter, though I have delayed so long to tell you that I was. . . . I had for two or three weeks interrupted the progress of my second edition [*The Kingdom of Christ*]—which has dragged its slow length along till this time—for the purpose of writing a pamphlet on passing occurrences. The text of it is the New Bishopric at Jerusalem, and the occasion the very violent brochures by a Mr. Palmer of Magdalen College, Oxford (not Lord Adair's friend)—one on that subject, and one containing a general anathema upon Protestants and Protestantism. I have addressed three letters to him; the first on the name Protestant, the second on the position of the English Church, the third expressly on the Bishopric.

The object of them is to show that the turning point of modern controversies is the question respecting the center of unity, and whether there is one for the whole Church; whether, if there be, it is a visible center. As I maintain, of course, the necessity of a real center, and affirm the doctrine of a visible center to be a monstrous practical heresy, the evil effects of which upon the order and unity of the Church all ecclesiastical history is manifesting, I find Protestantism to contain a great positive witness needful for the support of Catholicism, and never more necessary than in our day.

I then proceed to consider the position of the English Church as enabling us, if we will, to unite ourselves with any part of the Eastern or Western Church which will meet us on the ground of our Catholic institutions, provided it recognizes the true Center of Unity; as enabling us, on the other hand, to unite with any Protestants on the ground of our recognition of that true center, provided they do not refuse to adopt the Catholic institutions which connect us with that center, and with each other.

Then upon this ground I defend the course which the rulers of the Church have taken in reference to the Jerusalem Bishopric; maintaining that no principle has been sacrificed in it, and a great principle asserted.

▶ *34. To his wife, on July 20, 1842, with reference to the publication of his* Three Letters to the Rev. W. Palmer on the Jerusalem Bishopric

The Archbishop wrote last month to the King of Prussia, stating the terms of the relation between the Bishop of Jerusalem and the German Protestants. He gives up the Thirty-nine Articles, and the Augsburg Confession, and merely requires the three creeds. This was the plan I always maintained to be the right one. The King has adopted the proposal and published an Ordinance about it. As these documents have not yet found their way into any English paper (the *Berlin Gazette* which contains them being that of the 12th of July), Bunsen is very anxious that I should insert them in my pamphlet, and though it is published, Parker (the most accommodating of publishers) has consented to add some flyleaves. I am, therefore, translating, and should be very glad of your help, though I can manage pretty well.

▶ 35. To Daniel Macmillan* on May 22, 1843

I thank you very much for sending me Dr. Brown's letter. The kind expressions in it, coming from a person of so much thought and earnestness, were, of course, very gratifying; it was still more so that he gave me credit for wishing rather to know the actual effect which my book [*The Kingdom of Christ*] had produced on minds educated in different schools than to receive any expressions, even of sincere sympathy with it, from those who might happen to find it confirming their previous opinions.

For this reason I was not least pleased (perhaps I might say, more pleased) with the part of his letter which expressed dissent from my views than with that which seemed to be panegyrical. I can conceive that the reading of the first volume may have been gratifying to him; because, though not in all its details perhaps, yet in substance, he had admitted the truth of it beforehand. In this day no one who has not forcibly, like the writers in the Oxford Tracts, determined his mind in the opposite direction, is unprepared for a recognition of truth under various sides and aspects in different sects. It is the common faith of our age. My wish has been to show how heartily I embrace it, not the least to put it forward as a novelty of my own; and then to consider under what conditions it is reasonable. It seemed to me poor work to say, "There is something of good or true in all sects," unless one found some

---

* From 1840 to 1854 corresponded and worked with Archdeacon Hare and Maurice in an attempt to give workingmen and poor of London decent reading matter. In 1843, with his brother, began bookselling business which, after his death, became the famous book publisher Macmillan & Co.

method of ascertaining whereabouts the truth lay, and how it became mixed with the other ingredients.

In this attempt I have certainly arrived at a conclusion somewhat different from that which our Carlyles and Emersons are, at least in words, inclined to adopt. The *personal* element in those sect-opinions, that which requires the acknowledgment of a living Being; the *social* element, that which requires that this Being should be the Head of a body, of a fellowship—these, in all cases, and under their various one-sided forms seem to me the essential indestructible portion of them, with which the negative elements are always at war, and which they are always attempting to swallow up in themselves. I have said that this is not what in words Carlyle and others are disposed to acknowledge, but rather to contradict; but, nevertheless, I do think, and have partly stated in my book why I think, that they too are in their hearts crying after a Commonwealth with a personal center, and why all their apparent contentment with particular heroes or with a vague naturalism is not genuine, not really in accordance with their own deeper and more unconscious utterances.

I can understand also, I think, why Dr. Brown should have felt the part of my book with which he was most inclined to sympathize "emasculating." Nothing is so emasculating—I know it well—as the vague feeling of potential right in all things when there seems to be actual right in nothing. To lie down and sleep till the fates accomplish their own purposes, which it seems impossible that we can promote and very likely that we may hinder, is the inference from such appearances which the devil has whispered to everyone a thousand times, and which most of us have obeyed till a louder whisper has awakened us. Oh, there is nothing so emasculating as the atmosphere of eclecticism! Who that has dwelt in it has not longed for the keen mountain misty air of Calvinism, for anything, however biting, that would stir him to action? And if we could get back into that air it might be worth trying; others before me have said that it is impossible.

I agree with Dr. Brown that we must move onward, that we must find somewhere a reconciliation between the comprehension or Universal which the reason of this day sighs after and the heart-stirring faith of other days. The point is, where are we to seek for

102

it? He says, in a progress beyond Protestantism, as Protestantism was a progress beyond Romanism. And this progress must somehow lead us beyond "isms." Just so; these are the conditions which must determine whether that which is offered to us is that which we seek after. But if we are to invent our own faith, and our own symbols, we must, it seems to me, by an everlasting law, be still shut up in "isms"; we cannot get beyond them.

Carlyle partially admits this. He says that each age must have its own formulas, the next must discard them. The reality lies beneath them; to see *that* is the privilege of a few gifted seers who then create a vesture through which realities shall be apprehensible, in some measure, to the multitude of their day. And so there is to be an endless repetition of half truths and half falsehoods; the time when there shall be no symbols, when there shall be a mere naked recognition of an undefinable something, being one which they themselves tremble to contemplate.

Let a man but steadily look these difficulties in the face, not as they are stated by me but by those who seem most contentedly to adopt this theory of the universe, and *then* I would ask him to consider what I have said about divine symbols, about media of communication with the Absolute and Eternal, not devised by men but appointed by God, not meant for sages but for all creation. But till the difficulties have been fairly grappled with by a mind fully convinced that there must be a solution of them somewhere, I dare not the least expect that what I have said on this point will be regarded as anything but an attempt to methodize shams, to idealize shovel-hattery, to build up not earth only, but heaven also upon a ground plan of the Thirty-nine Articles.

"We want a Church," it will be said, " a Church of living men; we will go any way to look for it, to England, Italy, Australia! But you show us no such thing, only some mysterious pictures of water and bread and wine, an obsolete creed, an office which enables men to put 'Cant.' and 'Ebor.' after their names, a book worn to shreds with commentaries." All this, and more contemptuous words than these, I am quite prepared to hear, and it shows the exceeding kindliness of Dr. Brown's nature that he has abstained from the utterance of them.

Of this point I am well assured, that *the* difficulty in our day is to believe in a revelation as our fathers did. I find it so myself. I see it in others. Second, that this difficulty arises in great measure from the intense necessity of that belief to us. Our minds bear a stronger witness than the minds of our forefathers did to the idea of a revelation; so strong a witness that we think it must have originated in them. We cannot think it possible that God has actually manifested himself to us *because* the sense of a manifestation is so near to us that we think it is only our sense and has no reality corresponding to it. I wish this remark to be tested by the experience of any thoughtful man. I think it will explain many strange phenomena to him, which are passing around him. And it may be at least some help toward a reconciliation with those who are telling him, often I am sure in most perplexing and conscience-insulting language, that he ought to believe a revelation in spite of the natural disinclination of his heart to do so. On the other hand it may serve to remove a great many perplexities about the nature of faith.

. . . But whatever there is in it [*The Kingdom of Christ*] of truth is certain to live, though some of it should for a time fall into the ground and die. That I believe will be the fate of the doctrine of Ordinances, perhaps Ordinances themselves. But a butterfly will come forth out of the chrysalis; a perfect Church, united in Him who is one with God and with Man, will be seen hereafter to have been contained in these which seem but husks and shells. Let us wait and long for its full manifestation.

▶ 36. To Daniel Macmillan, from Bonchurch, August 31, 1843, on The Kingdom of Christ

. . . I tremble to think what a crushing of all systems, religious and political, there must be, before we do really feel our gathering together in Christ to be the hope of the Universe; before we acknowledge that the manifestation of the actual center of society, not the creation of some circle for ourselves or the indefinite enlargement of the circumference of our thoughts and notions, is what we should be looking for. Such men as Strauss and Feuerbach do not seem to me exactly in the light in which they once did;

but rather as appointed or permitted destroyers of philosophical and religious systems, that in the utter atheism of men's hearts they may be driven to tears and prayers for a Prince and Deliverer who will be the very same they had fancied they had rid the world of.

That every wish and panting of the heart and reason is fulfilled or on the way to be fulfilled, when we acknowledge the crucified man to be indeed Lord of all, when our thoughts and desires are brought to revolve round Him, and not around our own selves, I feel more deeply and assuredly every day. But neither in our modern Church notions which leave us so generally to the dream of a new scheme or system into which we are artificially put for the purpose of being fitted and ripened for what is called our salvation; nor in the Protestantism which sets up individual salvation as the end, only not admitting the Church as the necessary means to it; nor in Rationalism which equally glorifies self, only deifying it under the name of Intellect or Insight instead of soul, do I find that which we and all men have need of. The inference would *seem* most reasonable. Have nothing to do with either of them; stand aloof from them all; take up an independent position.

But the counsel defeats itself. If the disease of all those be their independency, their selfishness, I am only becoming more deeply tainted with that disease when I try to draw a *cordon sanitaire* around myself and dwell in my own exclusiveness. And how can I do so? Do I not carry about High Churchism, Evangelicalism, Rationalism, Atheism in myself? Is not everything I see in them working within? Is it not to be acknowledged and tested there first? Therefore I believe that the true position for escaping the evils of each is the position which God has given us and our countrymen, not one which we choose for ourselves.

I feel that I ought to be High Churchman, Evangelical, and Rationalist; that, being all, I might escape the curse of each; that I only fail in realizing this idea because I fail in acting out the position which has been bestowed upon me. All the discomforts of this view I know and am experiencing every day of my life. Alienation from those whom I love, an impossibility of making them understand what I mean, a continual suspicion of cowardice and dishonesty from one side, of disaffection to the truths which I profess from another; what is far worse than all these, the inward self-accusations of dishonoring God and setting up a way of my own, even when I most disclaim one; the feelings of pride, of self-exaltation, of division, which are so adverse to all that, after the inner man, I love and aim at; finally, the often recurring hopelessness of ever being able to exert any beneficial influence on any class of my countrymen. In my case there are ten thousand blessings to compensate for these evils; yet we ought all to count the cost before we enter upon any line of conduct, and I would most strongly warn anyone against the self-deception of fancying that he who wishes to be an ambassador of peace can do otherwise than weep bitterly.

▶ 37. To Daniel Macmillan, from Guy's Hospital, June 28, 1844

. . . The one thought which possesses me most at this time and, I may say, has always possessed me, is that we have been dosing our people with religion when what they want is not this but the Living God. We are threatened now not with the loss of religious feeling, so-called, or of religious notions, or of religious observances, but with Atheism. Everywhere I seem to perceive this peril. The battle within, the battle without is against this; the heart and the flesh of our countrymen are crying out for God. We give them a stone for bread, systems for realities; they despair of ever attaining what they need. The upper classes become, as may happen, sleekly devout for the sake of good order, avowedly believing that one must make the best of the world without God; the middle classes try what may be done by keeping themselves warm in dissent and agitation to kill the sense of hollowness; the poor, who must have realities of some kind, and understanding from their betters that all but houses and lands are abstractions, must make a grasp at them or else destroy them. And the specific for all this evil is some Evangelical discourse upon the Bible being the rule of faith, some High Church cry for tradition, some liberal theory of education.

Surely we want to preach it in the ears of all men: It is not any of these things or all these things together you want, or that those want who speak of them. All are pointing toward a Living Being, to know whom is life, and all, so far as they are set up for any purpose but leading us into that knowledge, and so to fellowship with each other, are dead things which cannot profit. There are some things which I sometimes feel, like Dr. Arnold, I must utter or burst. But then, again, the despondency and weariness and shame which come over me, the numberless discomfitures and wrong-doings, the dread of hurting the good which still remains, the fear of dishonoring what is right or of proving at last an undoer —these are terrible hindrances.

My *Church History*, over which I toiled, idled, and lamented for a year, till the burden of it became too much, and I was obliged to tell Parker that, for the sake of all other duties and of the quiet of my conscience, I must be quit of it, has been a great lesson to me, not, indeed, to abstain from work, but to enter upon work which does not lead to hopeless laziness. This blunder has, perhaps, been at the bottom of my discovery that I ought to labor for the objects more directly set before me—as in writing tracts for a hospital and helps to the students of King's College in reading history or some such book. . . .

▶ *38. To the Reverend Charles Kingsley,* on July 19, 1844, from the Chelsea vicarage of Kingsley's father in which Maurice was then staying*

My dear Sir,

I am sorry that I was prevented from writing to you by yesterday's post to express my gratitude for your kind expressions toward me; how much pleasure I should have in making your acquaintance, and how it grieves me to think of the disappointment you will experience when you find in what degree I deserve the opin-

* The Rev. Charles Kingsley (1819-75) was a social reformer and novelist. With Maurice he worked in the Christian Socialist Movement, contributing articles as "Parson Lot." Some of his better-known novels include *Alton Locke, Hypatia,* and *Westward Ho!* See G. Kendall, *Charles Kingsley and His Ideas* (1946).

ion you have formed of me. I have now taken a long sheet that I may say a little about the interesting subjects to which you refer; not that I expect to throw much light upon them, or that I do not agree with you in believing that conversation is, on the whole, better than paper and ink, but that I should be sorry not to give you the benefit of any blunders I may have committed in past time, with such experience as has been the fruit of them, and that it is sometimes easier to recover the different fragments of this experience and to piece them together in writing than in speaking.

With respect to the study of the Scriptures, my own great error has been that I have formed and abandoned so many plans, any one of which, honestly pursued, might have led to good results. I fancy this is a prevalent temptation, though I have yielded to it and suffered from it more than any of my acquaintance. As I would turn diseases to commodity, or, at least, as God is sometimes mercifully pleased to do this for us, I think I may say that all the deplorable waste of time which these changes have occasioned has brought with it this compensation, that I had been solemnly and inwardly impressed with the truth that the Bible, as a means of attaining to the knowledge of the living God, is precious beyond all expression or conception; but, when made a substitute for that knowledge, may become a greater deadener to the human spirit than all other books.

The method of the Bible itself and the reasons of its being over-looked, I think, become more and more clear to us as we keep this consideration before us. If it be a human history containing a gradual discovery of God, which discovery awakens the very faculties and apprehensions which are to receive it, the treatment of it as a collection of notions either about the invisible world or our own duty must entirely mislead us in all our studies; and, whether we rate it high or low, whether we accept it as the one rule of faith, maintain its authority to be concurrent with that of Church traditions, or look upon it merely as a set of fragments containing the speculations of a certain nation about religious questions, the result will be much the same. In each case the end of the book will be lost, and therefore all the steps to that end will be confused and incomprehensible.

But if once the teachers in our theological schools would have

108

courage to proclaim theology to be the knowledge of God and not the teaching of a religion, I am satisfied that the scientific character of the Bible would be brought out as conspicuously as its practical character, one being seen to be involved in the other. Then it would not be necessary to assert for theology its place as the *scientia scientiarum*, or to bid others fall into their places in connection with it and subordination to it; far less would it be necessary to be perpetually proclaiming Church authority in favor of such and such doctrines. . . . But since our universities afford us no teaching of this kind at present, we must try to profit by the helps which we have.

Our actual work is, I think, the best of these helps. It forces us, whether we will or no, out of the routine of sects and systems, and leads us to seek for something in Scripture which is altogether unlike them. And though I would strongly urge anyone not to lose the idea of that method of which I have spoken, I would by no means recommend anyone who was not working as a professed theologian in the schools to spend his time in contriving how he may adjust his own reading to it. The use of it to him will be far greater if he recollects that it exists when he is reading a single book or chapter or text, than if he determined doggedly to make out the traces of it from Genesis to Revelation.

The subject of his studies, I should think, must be always best determined by the wants of his parish. In preaching, I have always found it best to follow the order of the services, taking my subject from the Epistle, Gospel, Collect, or First Lesson; and, I think, if we read on a plan we can hardly find a much better one. The study of words also, I think, is of immense profit, especially of families of words, e.g., "just, justify, justification" through an Epistle or through many. . . .

I think, too, that it is desirable cautiously and deliberately to question ourselves about the leading idea of any Epistle; I say cautiously and deliberately, because the mere taking up with customary formulas on the subject, such as that the Epistles to the Romans and Galatians are about justification, will, I am satisfied, lead us astray. These Epistles are, I am convinced, strikingly different in their object and character. With respect to the Romans, the great mischief is that commentators generally start from the third chapter, looking upon the first and second as merely an introduction or prologue, whereas any simple reader must perceive that St. Paul enters at once on his subject, and that it is really the "manifestation of God's righteousness," and not an abstract theory of justification. . . .

The great misery of the Calvinist is his constant substitution of the idea of sovereignty for that of righteousness, which is the one always brought before us in Scripture. I would seek to deliver him from that evil, but as far as possible keeping entire and unhurt that which he has already. But I must not enlarge any further. Any day you can come to us next week, if I may hear from you the day before, we shall be happy to see you and will take care that you shall not be without a bed in your own house.

▶ **39. To friends on the death of John Sterling whom Mrs. Maurice nursed to the last, written from Ventnor, Friday evening, September 20, 1844**

You will understand from what I have said that the struggle is over, and that we have parted with our brother. There are many things in this dispensation which seem strange and dark, but I believe it is better for us far that there should be such things—that "Even so, Father, for so it seemed good in Thy sight" may be our rest, and not any dreams or desires of our own.

You do not need to be told what deep and tender affection there was in him, and this became more marked toward all his friends latterly, though he said he was losing his interest in what he had once cared for. His honesty and desire never to pass for other than he was also became even more remarkable than ever, and a disposition to charge himself with faults toward those whom he had treated with unbounded kindness, and who had the deepest sins to reproach themselves with, toward him, was very touching and humbling. I cannot easily tell you how many instances of this and of the most thoughtful, untiring kindness, in the midst of great suffering and weakness, we were allowed to witness. And I am sure that for all these qualities he took no credit to himself whatever; nor can I conceive that they had their source anywhere but in divine grace and love.

You know it was his temptation to magnify the intellect, and on that, as it seems to me, the greatest cloud rested; but I think those who know their exceeding sinfulness and yet can believe in the love of God in Christ will be the least inclined to doubt that this love may be imparting its warmth to the spirit through all these clouds. And what one feels for oneself, I believe we must feel for others, that the love which has manifested itself in redeeming mankind is a safer rock and resting place for our hopes than all signs and tokens which we may crave for. Simple and awful submission, not to a dead fate but to a perfectly loving will, seems to me the best state for us always.

Almost the last time I saw him he was speaking of your father with the strongest affection and reverence as one of the most striking examples of Christian benevolence he had ever known. He often alluded to the poor people he had known, and the patience he had witnessed in them under suffering, which he said had none of the outward alleviations he was blessed with. Quite lately he had been taking the liveliest interest in hearing that two of his friends for whom he had cared much, Julius Hare and my sister Esther, were likely to be united to each other. They hoped to have received his blessing, and they have come down with me to see at least the case in which his spirit once dwelt. But I must not go on, as it is very late. I could write much to those on whose sympathy we can reckon as we can on yours. Pray remember us most affectionately to your dear sister.

40. To his mother, toward the end of 1844, when she asked him about the problems of a boy whom she had befriended and who now had written despairingly to her from India

. . . In reference to his questions about good and evil and hell punishments, I should say that he was perfectly right in believing God to be the Good, the perfect Good, and in rejecting any doctrine which interferes with that belief. I would add that he was evidently not believing this, though he seemed to himself to believe it; for he thinks that his own affairs had been arranged by some evil spirit. I should tell him that hell, according to the idea of Christians, is simply separation from God, who is the perfect Good; that this separation must exist in everyone whose own heart is not in correspondence and tune with that of the true and perfect Being; that his conscience would tell him that in his late disputes with his father, he had indulged feelings and tempers which were not right and good, and that if he considered he would see that these tempers in him and in others, these tempers which are contrary to God's will, had been the cause of all their misery. Thus his own heart would testify to the truth that God is love and that all unlovingness is war with Him, and that the more this war increased the nearer any man's heart and the whole man would come to the condition of hell.

In reference to his comparison of the Christian and Hindu theology I should say that his young friend was quite right in supposing there was a connection between them. You cannot go north or south, east or west, without finding men full of restless desires after a knowledge of God and of union with Him. All the Hindu mythology expresses this in the wildest, most incoherent way, but still does express it. We do not wish to strip the natives of these longings, but to satisfy them. We do not say they are wrong in thinking that God must have become incarnate if He was to reveal Himself to men and make them know Him. We only say that all their conceptions about incarnation are crude, strange, and confused; that the incarnation of our Lord is that to which all these are pointing and by which they are explained; that He exhibited God as the perfectly holy, pure, loving Being; that the extreme simplicity and greatness of the thought that the Most High should not come down among men in some great royal form but as a peasant to claim fellowship with the whole race, is that which scandalizes men, though it is really the truth which binds all men together and establishes a fellowship between them and good.

I would say, with reference to the *Age of Reason*, that I supposed those who had warned him against the book were afraid of its taking unfair hold of a mind not sufficiently educated to be

112

aware of the weakness of the arguments; that, in fact, no cultivated infidel in Europe of this day would ever think of quoting Paine, knowing how very shallow he is; that a young man is, however, more likely to be taken in by a shallow book than by a deep one. You might tell him that all the greater and wiser thinkers in Europe, even if they be not Christians, believe that the reason in man, instead of rejecting all that is deep and mysterious, cannot be satisfied without mysteries; that the reason requires truths which are above itself, just as the eye delights in looking upon an immense expanse of sea and sky. . . .

▶ 41. To Edward Strachey who had recently suffered the loss of a friend, written from Guy's Hospital, December 24, 1844

I do not myself think that the previous expectation of a bereavement makes much abatement of it when it actually occurs. That is one of the topics of consolation which I have always found fails me most, and which I am the least disposed to use in the case of anyone else. I scarcely think that in general there is any but simple reliance on the love of God in Christ; all others give way sadly; at least, that is my experience.

Thank you for your kind inquiries about Mrs. Maurice. I have need of some sympathy from my friends, and they always most gladly give it me, for though I have some hope that the disease [tuberculosis] is not necessarily a fatal one, for one lung is certainly sound, and of the other there is good hope, yet the difficulty of reducing the complaint—water in the side—without reducing the patient too much, and she is already very thin, is so great that I have sometimes the darkest fears. Annie lives now in two upper rooms communicating with each other, which we try to keep at one even temperature night and day.

In the midst of our troubles comes this blessed Christmas, and comes with as bright a face, as goodly pledges and promises as ever. May we be able to keep it with glad hearts, singing and making melody in our hearts to God. God bless it to you and all yours.

My dear, dear Mother,

I am much grieved to find from Harriet's note to Esther that you are so very poorly. Do not let me think that your deep sympathy with me is hurting yourself. I know you loved Annie very dearly for her own sake, and her love to you was exceedingly great, and was constantly expressed throughout her illness. But do not let thoughts of me or my little children add to the pain which it must give you to see a dear daughter taken away. It is good for me to bear the yoke, most necessary; and so far from wishing to lose any of the sorrow which is appointed for me now, I have no greater or more earnest wish than that I may never seek to exchange it for anything that is called ease and comfort.

I do not mean that I would nurse any unnatural and violent grief. The deepest anguish I suffer now is the sense of having neglected high duties and abused precious privileges, and I shall not, I trust, be permitted to indulge any one feeling which will keep me from entering heartily and cheerfully upon all tasks which God ordains for me. But I would seek to be sustained in these by the Spirit of Love, and not by any effort after enjoyment, which may come to me if it will, but which, I think, I can quite bear to leave in her grave.

I am grievously ignorant of what a father ought to be, and I feel I must begin to learn that and many things anew. And so far as God enables me to remember her, her words and her whole life as it unfolded itself to me for eight years, I shall have a help in working, which nothing else but divine grace itself can give me. For she was certainly the most unselfish person I ever conversed with, and the one who most mourned over our failure in referring every thought and act to Christ as its source and end. If I did not feel that I had held her from the higher life and standard she would have aimed at, I should have no thoughts of her but the most calm and peaceful. That reflection is often quite crushing, and no human sympathy—even dearest Esther's which is most soothing and delightful—can reach it. You, dearest mother, know not that burden. May the Holy Spirit deliver you from every other, and comfort you with His own comfort.

▶ 43. To his sister Priscilla on Whitsunday, 1845, about the Spirit

I thank you for your kind Whitsuntide letter, which would have been as cheering as it was kind if it had not brought so bad a report of you. "The Spirit helpeth our infirmities" is perhaps the most comforting text of all just now, though there may be other aspects of this season which are more wonderful and exalting. If I may say that any Church festival has been one of help and instruction to me—and I have profited by them so little that I hardly dare venture to say so—I should fix upon this, partly, I suppose, because a clergyman needs the sustaining, life-giving power and the faculty of utterance, more than others, and partly because I have always been conscious of an especial need of it, and have more realized the sense of utter incapacity of thought, feeling, and speech, than any other. I am sure that many times I should have sunk utterly under the feeling of utter hopeless vanity of mind, of dreariness in the affections, feebleness in the will, if the words "I believe in the Holy Ghost" had not been given me as an expression of the best thing I could believe in, and that out of which all other belief might come. To recognize the Spirit of Life, the Spirit of Truth, as a power acting upon me and in me, has seemed to me possible when any act of power, any exercise of faith would have been like the efforts of a man under a nightmare.

And I have sometimes seen very strongly how much in a dead divided Church this was the one thing needful to speak of; the prophecy of a breath which could come into it and make the dry bones unite and live. However, this is not all; the whole mystery of the Father, Son, and Spirit is necessary to restore animation to the dead limbs or a dead body, and we have no right to speak of the Spirit except as proceeding from the Father and the Son, as testifying of them, as uniting us to them, as uniting them in one bond of Eternal Love. But Whitsunday, as connected with Trinity Sunday, and leading to it, seems to me to contain the most marvelous and blessed witness of the whole year, and that without which all the rest would be in vain. . . .

▶ 44. Again to his sister Priscilla, on May 17, 1845, about Trinity Sunday

I have great comfort in connecting your birthday with Trinity Sunday. It is to me the most sacred day of the year, the one which seems to me most significant of universal blessings, and also which blends most by strange and numberless links with my own individual experience and inward history. The idea of the unity of the Father and the Son in the Holy Spirit, as the basis of all unity amongst men, as the groundwork of all human society and of all thought, as belonging to little children, and as the highest fruition of the saints in glory, has been haunting me for a longer time than I can easily look back to.

It seems to blend with every book I read and to interpret it, to connect itself with all the sick and dying people about me; to direct all my thoughts about my children, and more than all others together, to bring my vanished saint to me or me to her; which indeed is not strange, as the ascription "Glory be to the Father," and the last verse of the ordination hymn, "Come, Holy Ghost," seemed always to kindle her whole spirit, soul, and body, far above the utterance of what is sometimes called personal religion, though anything more truly personal than hers I never saw. . . .

I am sure you will be glad to hear that I have a letter from Wilberforce today, expressing entire concurrence in the views I had expressed to him about the Borough, and holding out the hope that they will not begin with raising wretchedly cold-looking churches, into which no poor person will go, but will open schoolrooms in the worst courts and lanes, first for the children, then for worship. On this plan I do trust a blessing will come; the twenty churches made me shudder, for it seems to me a pompous way of doing almost nothing.

I had a very kind note last night from Bunsen. I am afraid he is very anxious to get me preferment. I was obliged to tell him very earnestly and strongly how little I desired it for myself, and what a distress it would be to me if it came. The freer one is from the Church system in this country, the better one is able to serve the Church; at least so I think: and what do I or the children want in the way of social position or means of self-indulgence?

▶ 45. To Miss Georgiana Hare, afterward to become his second wife, written from Guy's, January 14, 1846

I think it is probable now that we shall leave Guy's. They are establishing a theological department at King's College, which is likely to exercise an important influence. Dr. Jelf has asked me to be one of the professors; and I have agreed to give up this place.

In many ways the trial of parting, when it comes (much as I have wished for a change on the children's account), will be a severe one; my whole married life is bound up with Guy's and there is nothing about it which is not in some way associated with her. Still I shall be glad, for I could not have well desired to see you, or anyone who very greatly cared for her, and had seen her here, again at Guy's. . . .

I am surprised at X's wishing you to read Newman's book [*The Development of Christian Doctrine*], for it is not one that appeals to any of the devout sympathies whereby ladies are generally tempted toward Romanism. It is a very clever book, and one which is likely to produce an effect upon young men, for it addresses itself to the state of mind in which so many of them are, which Newman understands, and which very few English Churchmen do understand. But of all books I ever read it seems to me the most skeptical; much more calculated to make skeptics than Romanists, though probably it will make some of each class. I should not be afraid of your reading it, for I think you would feel its exceeding hollowness, and would tremble at the state of mind into which a person would get who yielded to its influence.

You do not tell me what Z had said that so much perplexed and distressed you. If it was that none of our parties, Evangelical or Anglican, is able to satisfy the wants for which so many men and women are flying to Rome, he is perfectly right; every day convinces me of it more. And I do not speak from theory; those who have left say how utterly false and hollow the English attempts to supply a kind of Romanism have long seemed to them; how utterly untenable the position which they had taken up was. At the same time, it is equally certain that the violence of the Evangelicals, and their hard, artificial, yet feeble, theology is alienating numbers, and that the younger members of their families are specially feeling the Romish temptation.

Deepest humiliation for the low tone of feeling and conduct which all of us, and especially the clergymen of all kinds, have kept up ourselves and encouraged in others, should, I am sure, be earnestly sought after. But, though I see everything to deplore in our own condition—nothing to boast of—I feel more deeply convinced than ever that the remedy these people are trying must aggravate the evil a thousandfold, and introduce a number of new evils. Our misery is, that we have not been setting God before us; that we have been seeking ourselves in our religion and in everything else. And this system, though it may be qualified in its operation by a multitude of blessed spiritual influences upon those who have been brought up in it; though to them it may be identified with all that is most holy and godly, will to us—I see it clearly— be a refuge from God, a more entire hopeless pursuit of selfish objects.

They want the living God, and they fly to the fiction of ecclesiastical authority; they want to be delivered from the burden of self, and they run to the confessor, who will keep them in an eternal round of contrivances to extinguish self by feeding it and thinking of it. It is nothing to me that they are in raptures at their first experience of the rest from doubt; at the sense of being united with the whole of Christendom. That was to be expected; it is no more than Blanco White felt and expressed when he first worshiped in a Unitarian meeting. No doubt they have been in a most uneasy, miserable position for a long time; no doubt it is delightful to have made a decision, exceedingly delightful to be welcomed heartily by their new friends when they had found much want of heart among their old ones. But all that is nothing, nothing to us even if their first-love feelings should abide, which I know they will not.

To go anywhere for the sake of getting comfortable feelings is a deep delusion; to go anywhere for the sake of truth is the greatest of all duties; but truth they do not really believe in: it means, with them, "probable security as to the notions we have upon certain subjects." The words "I am the Truth," words which take us out of the world of notions, and opinions, and theories altogether; and those other blessed words, "You shall know the truth and the truth shall make you free," have lost their significance in the Roman Catholic system, not, thank God, in the hearts of Roman Catholics, though they are in continual peril of this infinite loss; and they, it seems to me, are in still greater hazard of incurring it who adopt the system only because they despair of finding truth, and are willing to put up with a plausible substitute for it.

For my own sake I could wish you to adopt X's advice about Newman's book, as I am writing upon it—not a formal answer—but in a preface to some lectures on the Epistle to the Hebrews which I hope to publish in the course of next month (they are the first section of my Warburton Lectures), and I would rather, of course, you should read it, and know to what it alludes. But I could not, for so selfish a reason, advise you to a task which I think and hope would be a painful one.

And from the feeling of sadness and oppression, as if I were in the midst of a country under a visitation of locusts, with which I rose up from the volume, I will counsel you not to take it up, except when you are in tolerable spirits, and, at the same time, have a deep sense of dependence and of the necessity and possibility of prayer. I do not fear its converting you; but the weariness and discomfort which I think it would produce in you are in general so little salutary that I question if anyone not professionally obliged to the duty should be encouraged to perform it.

▶ *46. To Edward Strachey, on becoming Chaplain of Lincoln's Inn, from 21 Queen's Square, Bloomsbury, June 14, 1846*

I wish I could get as far as you are in my summer vacation, and spend a little time with you, but such dreams I must not indulge. Indeed, I scarcely know whether Italy could have any charm for me now; the exertion of speaking another language, nay the exertion of pleasure-hunting and beauty-hunting, seems to me rather more oppressive and fatiguing than any other. If my dear boys are permitted to grow up, and I can show sights to them, the case will be different, but what people call relaxation and bid me seek, I do not feel equal to; work one can generally get through without much struggle.

You will see by my direction that I have left the place in which you knew me, where I have spent the ten best years of my life. For the reason of my leaving I have much to be thankful. The Council of King's College have established a theological department, and the bishops have consented to ordain those who receive certificates of fitness from its professors after two years' instruction. I have been chosen, without my seeking, to one of the professorships; Dr. McCaul and Trench have the two others. This position I felt would be incompatible with my Guy's duties, which therefore, I at once determined to resign. But the treasurer, thinking rightly that I should suffer a good deal in income, kindly advised me to take a curate, which I had agreed to do, when the chaplaincy of Lincoln's Inn fell vacant. . . . This office was exactly the one I should have wished, and it harmonized perfectly with my duties at King's College. I therefore became a candidate for it, and after two or three months was elected by a majority of two among the benchers. . . . I have held the office about six weeks, and within three days have moved into a house in this very quiet and antiquated square.

Guy's, as you may believe, was crowded with associations and recollections, but I felt very glad to leave it; not because I do not think the duty a most honorable and delightful one, but because I never did it justice. In respect of that and every part of my past life I would ask for a broken and contrite heart, for repentance unto life instead of remorse. I am surrounded with causes of gratitude, and I hope I feel a little more every day that God is indeed a home and a refuge. I should not find this house one—even with my children, and my kind sister, whose health is as bad as ever— if it were not so. I have written one book lately. It consists of my three first Warburton lectures, on the Epistle to the Hebrews, and a preface on Newman's book of *Development*. This, with seven lectures a week, professor's lectures, Lincoln's Inn, and moving, has been as much as I have been equal to, though not more if I had done it better.

▶ 47. To Charles Kingsley, December 23, 1847, with a Christmas greeting

. . . Oh! bring up your children to fly from [religious] periodicals more than from any plague. Why is there not a prayer in the Litany for deliverance from them? These are not Christmas thoughts, I fear, but they may help us to rejoice in Christmas. Peace on earth and good will to men, must have come from above, for verily they do not grow in this soil; apart from Glory to God in the highest, they must wither. It is when the Church looks to us most leafless, most frosty, that we can most enter into the mystery of the divine spring, the second birth, the Lord from heaven appearing in swaddling clothes, and growing as we die. May all Christmas gifts and blessings be with you and yours.

▶ 48. To Miss Georgiana Hare, December 29, 1847

. . . I have just been reading a long and elaborate review of my *The Kingdom of Christ* in a German periodical. It is written by Sack, who is very courteous and complimentary, though he differs from me in nearly every point, and takes great pains to show how wrong I am. He has taught me to see more clearly than I ever did what the ground of my difference with the Evangelicals, both of England and Germany, is. The latter, though so much wiser and more cultivated, still seem to make sin the ground of all theology, whereas it seems to me that the living and holy God is the ground of it, and sin the departure from the state of union with Him, into which He has brought us. I cannot believe the devil is in any sense king of this universe. I believe Christ is its king in all senses, and that the devil is tempting us every day and hour to deny Him, and think of himself as the king. It is with me a question of life and death which of these doctrines is true; I would that I might live and die to maintain that which has been revealed to me.

I think that one who understood what I meant better than all the doctors, and only lamented that I acted so little up to my conviction, is now sharing my faith with me, strengthening me in it, and in the darkest hours giving me increased tokens and assurances of its truth. I think that is no dream, nor yet that she is with you, teaching you and cheering you.

▶ 49. To John M. Ludlow,* following his reports on Socialism in France, March 24, 1848

This letter is decisive, I think, as to the question of your going to France at present. . . . I have put your letter in circulation where I think it is doing, and is likely to do, good. It will set many thinking, will inspire some to hope and prayer. Meantime, the necessity of an English theological reformation, as the means of averting an English political revolution and of bringing what is good in foreign revolutions to know itself, has been more and more pressing upon my mind. We have no right to talk of atheistic France, atheistic Germany, true as the charge may be even now, fearfully as it may be proved hereafter.

Are not we atheistic? Is not our Christianity semi-atheistic? We have theories of sin, of justification, of apostolical succession, schemes of divinity Protestant, Romish, semi-Romish, Anglican, Dissenting. But where is God in them all? Not first at least, not a Father; but merely the provider of a certain scheme for our deliverance, the setter-up of a Church system which is to go on without Him by help of popes, kings, doctors; the great assertion is that everyone is to think what he likes. None of these systems is broad enough that a man may stretch himself in it; all are beginning to feel that. But it is more hopeless as systems to incorporate them;

* John M. Ludlow, a lawyer, with Kingsley and Maurice formed a triumvirate in the Christian Socialist Movement. Ludlow edited their journal, helped to organize workingmen's co-operatives, and worked with Maurice at Queen's College and the Working Men's College.

thank God! Alliances having that ground, or any such ground, must come to nought. He must unite us; if we all return to the root and ground of all things, we shall find the fruit. Of course, our attempts to make one and find one in our systems will more and more prove abortive. When we have confessed our own Atheism and repented of it, we can call upon all nations to abandon theirs. But do not let us preach a Protestantism, Catholicism, Christianity without God.

▶ 50. To his student Barry, afterward Principal of King's College and Bishop of Australia, written early in 1848

I can assure you that I had not forgotten my promise of writing something to you about a course of metaphysical reading, when I received the present of your essay . . . which I have read with great satisfaction. It indicates, I think, a power of taking clear, sober, manly views of great historical crises and periods—a capacity which I especially desire to see developed in young Englishmen, and which if my lectures have, as you say, at all awakened in you, I should feel very thankful. I confess I should be sorry if you were tempted to turn your thoughts out of this direction into one which seems to me far less intended for us, or even if you learned to look upon historical and political studies as one part of knowledge, and metaphysical as another. That way of labeling our pursuits may do in an encyclopedia, but it will not do for a man who must be content to be something less than an encyclopedia if he would be something more.

I do not mean, however, by these remarks to excuse myself from the task which you kindly assigned me. I only wish to explain the course which I would recommend. I don't think metaphysics has been separated by any real and consistent thinker from politics, or that he has applied one method to the one, and a different method to the other. In the men who, for good or evil, have exercised most influence upon England of a psychological or metaphysical kind— Hobbes and Locke—the connection between their (so-called) abstract theories, and their theories of government and political society, is most direct and obvious. The Leviathan is the explanation and embodiment of the treatises on Liberty and Necessity. The essay on Government is the proper key to the essay on the Human Understanding.

Among Hegel's works you will find as many bearing upon history and politics as upon any question which, we should say, was within his province; his doctrine of a state seems to be one of the most characteristic features of his philosophy. Cicero's philosophical treatises, proud as he was of the Greek wisdom displayed in them, derive their chief worth from his manly Roman sense and political experience; though the charm of his language must make anything that he writes delightful. I think most are glad to escape from the *De Officiis* to the *Laws*. Aristotle avowedly makes everything subordinate to his polity; his ethics and metaphysics are only the porch to that temple. It is not less evident that Plato regarded the *Republic* as that which was to explain and harmonize all the other dialogues. I should be strongly inclined then to recommend you to study the works on "politics" which have been written by the most eminent metaphysicians in different periods, and to view their more abstract speculations chiefly as illustrating these.

The two great treatises of Plato and Aristotle will be master-keys to the minds of these men; you will see them both in remarkable contrast. Both, Aristotle especially, will cast light upon and receive light from all contemporary and preceding Greek history. The *Republic* of Plato is, in its highest aspect, the dream of a universal Church, in its lowest it touches closely upon French Communism. It is very wonderful in both respects, and will not at all disengage you from present interests, but rather will help you to contemplate them from a higher point of view. Aristotle's, with no ecclesiastical or generally human characteristic, is as beautiful an account of the conditions and forms of national life and its relations to family life as I can conceive. Its true complement is in the Old, as that of Plato is in the New Testament. I should be content with these great works—for Greece.

Cicero's is admirable for Rome, as much by his philosophical defects as his merits. His *Laws*, the fragment on the *Republic*, and the *Offices*, contain what he really understood. He can talk splendidly about everything. I think I should not meddle with Seneca, but should rather take the *Meditations* of Marcus Aurelius, being

124

an emperor and a man of business, for the link between Stoicism and the later Roman age.

The *Paedagogus* of Clement or his *Stromateis* will give you the best view of the Christian philosophy in the Alexandrian school. If you want to see the violent protest against it in the Carthaginian, you must read the treatise of Tertullian on *Praescription*. The *De Civitate* of Augustine is very important as illustrating his feeling of the connection between the Christian and all previous polities, as well as for its direct metaphysics.

I should advise you to look over the *Monologicon* of Anselm, the *Sentences* of Peter Lombard, and part of the "Prima Secundae" in the *Summa Theologica* of Aquinas, that you may understand the scholastic method. Perhaps it might be well also to read a little of Abelard in Cousin's new edition as a help to the nominalist controversy of the twelfth century.

That controversy had taken a new form in the fifteenth under William of Occam. His life and writings are closely connected with the history of the new relations between the papacy and the kings of Europe at that time, so that they are illustrative of the remark I made at the beginning of this letter.

I have no doubt that a person better acquainted with the sixteenth century than I am might point out some book which distinctly embodies its philosophical as well as its political tendencies. I can hardly think that you can collect either except from the books of the Humanists at its commencement, then the Reformers, and at the close of the period the Jesuits—in the first of whom literature, and in the two last theology, is of course predominant. For England, Hooker is the metaphysician as well as the politician of that age. Cousin will tell you that Descartes in the seventeenth century is the real beginner of Western philosophy, and that he is the most important of all the writers of that period. According to the view I am taking, Hobbes (with whom of course I am more at variance than with the Frenchman) is a more significant name, because he more explains the relation between speculation and action, and shows what theory of government is the inevitable and logical consequence of what scheme of human nature.

Locke represents the whole meaning and character of the Revolution of 1688 in his books on Toleration, Government, Education, the Scripture, as much as in his chief work. The parallel work to his on the first French Revolution is the *Contrat Social* of Rousseau, with this great difference, that Locke's was a cold ratification of that which had taken place; Rousseau's, the torch which set the combustibles alight. I have adhered to my maxim of connecting, as far as possible, politics with metaphysics. I should not have deviated from it very much if I had suggested a comparison of the low notions of humanity in the *De L'Homme* of Helvetius with the three sermons of Butler, and I should, perhaps, have seemed ultra-political if I had spoken of Montesquieu and Burke as falling within a course of reading such as you propose.

About the later Germans I will not venture to give you advice. I should suppose that some of the treatises of Fichte would interest you much; Hegel's *On the Philosophy of History* I have found valuable, and I think I could get glimpses into his philosophy generally from it. Schelling's later lectures are not published except in a discreditable and mangled report by an enemy, Paulus.

My feeling about the relation between English thought and German is generally this: that we must always be, to a considerable extent, unintelligible to each other, because we start from exactly opposite points; we, naturally, from that which is above us and speaks to us; they, naturally, from that which is within them and which *seeks* for some object above itself. Supposing these two vocations faithfully fulfilled, then there must at last be a meeting point. But, in the meantime, neither nature quite understanding itself assumes to be more and to do more than it can. They are, I think, of right, philosophers, seekers after wisdom. But they will bring all things under philosophy; they will explain politics and history, which demand to be looked at from both sides, as well as theology, which is emphatically the opposite of it—not the contrary—upon its conditions.

We, on the other hand, deny any scope to the search after wisdom, insisting that it is precluded by theological decrees, or else make theology and philosophy altogether separate as to their subject matter, so depriving both of their reality. I am most eager to assert the worth of our English position, to prove that the truth must look down upon us if we would look up to it, that Truth must be a person seeking us, if we are to seek Him. But so far from feeling that this belief interferes with the free exercise of our

126

powers or the most earnest search, I cannot find any other equally strong proof of its necessity or warrant of its success.

I have thrown out this last hint partly to explain what I said before about our English tendencies and the preference I would give to historical and political over merely abstract studies. You will feel, I hope, that I did not mean to say anything against philosophy properly so called. I only wished to find out the way in which we might best hope to profit by it, and to pursue it with real, earnest interest. Politics and history are a middle ground between theology and philosophy. In them each has a share; by them, I believe, far better than by any eclectical theory, they are reconciled.

P.S. Whether you adopt these hints, or find some that are much better, let me advise you to read only significant books, books of really remarkable men, and that have had a great moral influence. I do not limit you to one class of views, as you will see by what I have written. But mere books (digests and reductions, etc.) which have no human feeling and human interest, if they are ever so clever, and set forth a system ever so well, I should avoid.

▶ **51. To his friend Archdeacon Hare who had protested against one of Kingsley's articles in Politics for the People, May 28, 1848**

My dear Julius,

I could not have suppressed the article if I had wished to do so, for the number was published on Thursday before I knew of your objections. But I should not have suppressed it if I could; for I do not look upon it as mischievous. I feel quite assured that there are quarters in which it will be especially useful.

Every paper which has any circulation among the Chartists regards the clergy as preachers of mere slavery out of the Bible. The question is whether we shall acknowledge that we have far too much read our own slavish notions into the Bible or whether we shall leave it to bear our disgrace. You say, "Confess you are wrong in asides to each other"; I say that will do no good to us or to anyone else. We have sinned openly and we ought to confess, especially to those against whom we have sinned. . . .

And it is not fair of *you* to say of one who takes the like course that he looks upon everybody as having been wrong till Parson Lot.* Such a charge is, of course, brought against all persons who have courage to speak the truth; it has been brought against you a hundred times. I always accounted it the vulgarest of all formulas, and would have given a good deal that you had not sanctioned the use of it.

Kingsley spoke from his heart, I am sure, without the least of that conceit which you impute to him. He felt he was confessing his own sin, not taking honor to himself for discovering it in others. And there are hundreds of young men at Oxford and Cambridge, and I believe a great many Chartists and workingmen, who will have a faith in him and in the clergy which they never had before, when they find he does care to take the beam out of his own eye before he begins to take the mote out of theirs. Parker tells me that the expressions about that letter have been especially warm. There has been one fine cordial letter about it from a young man preparing for orders, to whom it seems to have given quite a new hope.

You say that Kingsley and Ludlow are very conceited and that young men are so generally. I am sorry to hear you using that language; for I am sure either of those two would be glad to sit at your feet and receive your instructions and admonitions. I never met with men of a more reverent spirit.

And as to young men of this age generally, though I find them very unhappy, very discontented, almost hopeless, I do not find in them nearly as much of what I should call insolence and arrogance as in their seniors. . . . Kingsley and Ludlow are, it seems to me, the very best mediators possible between the one and the other, between young England of the middle and upper classes, and the working people. To be so they must speak out their own thoughts, which I am sure are pure and free, and not trouble themselves with the question how they may please or offend the bishops. I believe we must offend them and a great many more; but if we bring the poor people to have more respect for the rich people who hate us, it will be a good revenge, and one worth the death of the paper or our own.

* Kingsley's pseudonym.

The King's College authorities have deliberately rejected Kingsley, not preferring another to him but simply saying they will not have him. This is of course a new bond between us. Their refusal of him is intended as an admonition to me to set my house in order, and as such I shall take it.

▶ 52. Maurice's description of the weekly Bible class at his house during this period *

I was known to a few friends who frequented a Bible class at my house. Our intercourse was of the frankest kind, but this was the foundation of it. They found that I was far less accomplished in general science and literature than numbers of my order, than most of themselves, but that I regarded the knowledge of God as the key to all other knowledge, as that which connected knowledge with life. They found that I accepted the Bible as the interpretation of the history of mankind. They found, as they might have expected, that I did not demand that they should bring that conviction with them. They might if they pleased bring just the opposite conviction. They might think that the Bible was no better than any other book, or that it was a worn-out book. The truth, it seemed to me, would establish itself. I at least was not afraid to subject that belief which had possession of me to any test. I thought that it would only be proved and spread if it was brought to the severest test.

If the Bible shrank from difficulties, if it needed some preliminary evidence to show that such difficulties ought not to be fairly met, if it had not a stronger evidence in itself than all the ingenuity of apologists could supply, it was not the book which I took it to be, it had not the power for which I had given it credit. I desired, therefore, that all who read it with me should express their thoughts of what they read with entire freedom. I had no confidence that any wit or reasonings of mine would be able to change their thoughts; I had the greatest confidence that a Wisdom higher than theirs or mine could impart itself to them.

* From *Working Men's College Magazine*, III, 14.

▶ *53. To his fiancée Miss Hare on February 6, 1849*

You are mistaken that I am overworked. The sense of time lost and seemingly wasted certainly oppresses me more than any duties, which really fill up a very short portion of my day. I could do ten times as much as far as mere physical strength goes. But I am naturally most indolent, and neglect every work to which I am not obliged; and therefore I am glad to be obliged. I dream sometimes of times when one might have more inward and less outward business; but after forty years' experience I find that the inward is not better in my case but worse, for want of the outward, and that I really seek God most when I need His help to enable me to do what He has set me to do.

I think I have learned by many proofs that the words "It is not you which speak but the spirit of your Father which is in you" are always true, and that we ought always to remember them and to depend upon them. And when I am forced to speak and have not leisure for all the preparation I should think desirable, my faith is more called out than at almost any other time.

▶ *54. Again to Miss Hare, written February 7, 1849, concerning the helpfulness of Maurice's sermons to Coleridge's son Hartley, recently deceased*

I heard something just now which seems too good to be true, and which I don't quite believe, as so many things of the kind are said to please writers. It is that my sermons on the Lord's Prayer were of some use to poor Hartley Coleridge, who died at the Lakes about a month ago. He was a beautiful fallen spirit, overcome by one accursed habit, with his father's [Samuel Taylor Coleridge's] weakness of will, but with a freshness and geniality and nobleness which are very rare and which made him the delight of all the people among whom he dwelt, especially the poor. He seems to have died most sincerely penitent for the prostration of his great powers and for all that was wrong in him, and I doubt not has more knowledge of God's forgiving love than most of us who have been outwardly more respectable. I have often mourned,

130

though not as I ought, for him, and it would indeed be a cause of thanksgiving if God had permitted me in anywise to repay the debt which I feel I owe to his father, a man whom I can never cease to reverence for what he taught me, though I think I am as sensible of his errors as anyone can be.

▶ 55. Also to Miss Hare, February 10, 1849, on his daily schedule

I am going to give a lecture this evening to governesses, and generally on Saturday evenings. They are part of a gratuitous course which we are beginning at Queen's College for those who cannot come out in the day, being already engaged in situations. My subjects are the Scriptures one week and Moral Philosophy the next. I will tell you my business for the week that you may know where I am at different times. 8 A.M. every morning, except Sunday, at Lincoln's Inn, Prayers. 9:45 A.M., Monday, Queen's College, Moral Philosophy; 1:45 P.M., Queen's College, Scriptures. Tuesday, at 9:00 A.M., Ecclesiastical History, first three centuries, King's College; 2:30 P.M., General History. Wednesday, at 9:00 A.M., Ecclesiastical History, first three centuries; 10:30 A.M., Ecclesiastical History, eighteenth century. Thursday, 11:30 A.M., Pearson on the Creed; 1:30 P.M., English Composition. Friday, 1:30 P.M., English History. Saturday, 11:00 A.M., Ecclesiastical History, thirteenth century. Saturday evening as aforesaid. Sunday, at 11:00 A.M., and 3:00 P.M., at Lincoln's Inn Chapel. There you have my week, which you see is very poorly filled up, so you must not complain on that ground. . . .

▶ 56. To Miss Hare on February 14, 1849, with premonitions of trouble

If I could see my way clearly, I would, for both your sake and the boys', seek for some employment in the country, but at present I hardly feel as if I ought to change my calling for any other, but we can never tell what new duties may open upon us, and how

131

soon we may be turned out of our old positions. Mine at King's College, I suspect, may not be very secure; indeed, in this age of distrust and fear, no clergyman who thinks and speaks strongly, and not exactly in the prescribed mode of thinking and speaking, can reckon upon the tolerance of his superiors and equals for a long time. He must be ready for kicks and cuffs. And public bodies and episcopal personages cannot afford to stand by a man if there is any strong run against him. They must not, as they say, compromise themselves.

I always, therefore, regard myself as a tenant at will, who may be ejected at a very short notice. More than once I have asked myself whether I ought not to relieve my employers of any uncomfortable suspicions that may rest upon them, on my account, by resigning; but I believe the time for that is not come, and that they would at present be, on the whole, rather sorry than glad to part with me. It may be otherwise in a very short time.

▶ 57. To Strachey, on criticism and the Prayer Book, March 2, 1849

I intended long ago to have thanked you for the [critical edition of] *Hamlet*, which I read with much attention and with persons whose judgment in questions of the kind I reckon much above my own—Charles Kingsley and his wife. He differed with you, I think, in a good many points, and I confess you seem to me to overrate the worth of Coleridge's criticism and to make it too much your standard. Nevertheless we read it with great interest, and I hope learned a great deal from you. What I object to in Coleridge generally as a critic is his tendency to abstraction; his acquired incapacity for looking straight at a man, and his passion for conceiving him under some forms and conditions which, if they belong, as I readily admit they do, to a higher logic than the ordinary one, are for that very reason apt to deceive more and to put themselves forth as adequate substitutes for life and humanity. I think your style, and in some degree your critical faculty, has suffered from too close following of him as your guide. . . .

About the Prayer Book I must answer you another time. I do

not want to force anyone to like it; nor do I care a sixpence for it as a piece of fine composition. I never called it "an excellent liturgy" in my life, and hope I never shall. But it has helped me to see more of the love of God and of the bonds by which men are knit to each other, and to feel more hope as to those whom I should naturally regard as foes, than any other book except the Bible.

It is my protection and the protection of the Church against Anglicanism and Evangelicalism and Liberalism and Romanism and Rationalism, and till these different devils cease to torment us, I will, with God's help, use this shield against them, whether other people prefer their party prayers to it or not. You say I must let people be as narrow as they like. To be sure I must; how can I help it? But if God has provided me with a witness that there is a ground of fellowship and comprehension, can I hold my tongue and not say so, because I may chance to offend some of my dear friends who are asserting their undoubted, inalienable English right to hate and curse one another? . . .

▶ 58. Answers to questions put to him by his Principal Dr. Jelf, who was worried at the effect upon King's College of the attacks by the religious press on Maurice, March 14, 1849

My dear Mr. Principal,

Your first question to me is this: "Am I right in believing that the main object of your letter [to Archdeacon Hare], after disposing of the *English Review*, is to protest against the dictation of religious periodicals, to whatever party they belong?"

Certainly this was one of my objects; but not my "main" object. I had been accused of not believing in the doctrines of the Prayer Book. No evidence had been produced for the charge; the writer had been compelled to confess that he could produce none. Still he continued to propagate the insinuation and to direct it against me especially as a Professor of Divinity. I wished as a Professor of Divinity to explain why I always should be liable to these attacks from him and from all other party writers. They, I said (in the page next to that in which the passage respecting systems occurs), "boast that they represent the genius of the Church as it is set forth in her formularies. I was one of those who turned with especial love, and reverence, and hope, to these formularies as guiding to the eternal foundations which lie beneath their [the party writers'] fragmentary crumbling systems." This was my main object. Your second question I will divide into portions.

(1) "Do I rightly construe your meaning by supposing that when you speak of popular English religious systems as certain not to last, you speak of them as contradistinguished from the Church of England, (2) which you characterize as a foundation deeper than them, (3) and that when you speak of High Churchmen and Low Churchmen, Romanists, Anglican Liberals or Rationalists, you mean either *parties* within the Church or heresies without her pale as distinct from her vital Catholic essence, and (4) that you hold her to be the appointed instrument in this country for getting rid of parties and divisions and heresies in proportion as she is studied and loved, apart from their discordant cries and watchwords?"

I need perhaps hardly reply to (1) after the answer I have made to the first question. I will simply quote one sentence from my letter, because it especially refers to my feelings as a teacher in the College. "It would be a blessing beyond all blessings and worth encountering all the indignation of all the reviews in Europe, if we could send forth a few priests feeling that the word and sacraments are really committed to them, and that the trust is a most real and awful one, and that they have nothing to do with the catchwords of this party or that, and that they may be messengers of truth and peace to high and low, and that the Lord hath founded Zion and that the poor of His people may trust in it."

(2) I should not say the Church *was* the foundation, but that it *stood* upon the foundation which would remain when all systems crumble, even the name into which we are baptized, the name of the Father, the Son, and the Holy Ghost. (3) When I speak of High Churchmen, Low Churchmen, Anglicans, etc., as distinct from the Church of England in which they are found, I merely say what I suppose everyone says about the parties in our Lord's time. No one, I think, could say that the Jewish Church

was identical with the Pharisees, Sadducees, and Essenes who divided it—with any one or all together. That Church was set up by God Himself, theirs were different human theories about its principles and constitution, which might contain fragments of the truth that was embodied in it, and might be professed by some excellent men, but which ultimately were found to have no reality or substance in them, and which were one and all set in opposition to the Son of God.

(4) I could not wish for a more clear and beautiful statement than that which this paragraph embodies of the principles which I have tried to express in my letter to Archdeacon Hare, in every book I have written, in every sermon I have preached, in every lecture I have delivered.

Your third question is: "Am I right in gathering from your words that you accept and embrace as living and (under Christ) life-giving truths and realities (1) the divine constitution of the Church of England as a branch of the Catholic Church, (2) her 39 Articles, (3) her three Creeds, (4) her Liturgy, believing that these are truths upon which you may rest when sects and systems have crumbled into atoms?"

(1) It is to the divine constitution of the Church that I have always turned, especially as a deliverance from systems. The Church, I have said, is represented in Scripture as a kingdom. When we treat it as a theory instead of a kingdom, we dishonor it and destroy its life.

On this ground I have always loved episcopacy as expressing the fatherly and Catholic character of the Church, and have maintained that when it is lost the Church of necessity becomes hard, narrow, formal. On this ground I have always condemned these systems about episcopacy, which seem to me to rob it of its character and make it merely an anti-Presbyterian scheme, which when they are carried out imitate Presbyterianism in its dogmatism and exclusiveness. I do not think those who maintain these systems wish that we should resort to the methods and habits of the Fathers of the Church, they would far rather appeal to public opinion.

(2) I mentioned in my letter that, when the question of subscription was debated at Oxford, I wrote a book to prove the unspeakable value of the Articles to the student of humanity and

divinity as guiding him into a pathway of truth, and pointing out to him the different forms of truth. I had one right to speak on that more than on any other subjects, for I may mention—since one of the newspapers has been at the pains to rake up the fact in my biography—that I left Cambridge without signing the Articles. I had been brought up among the Dissenters. I said at the time: Those whose parents are Churchmen may sign them honestly if they have not been convinced that they are false. Precisely on that ground I cannot sign them honestly if I have not been convinced that they are true.

After two years, when I believe I may say that I had less outward motive to bar my judgment, I had been convinced that they are true, and I did sign them. I have seen many people of all shades who have been attacking them. I have valued them more each year that I have lived and each argument that I have heard against them. I expressed in my pamphlet on *Subscription* my conviction that if students would throw the arguments of the newspapers about them into the fire and would study them, they would come out triumphant. I think so now as I did then.

(3) I have declared that I hold these creeds, and I do hold them: those who hear my lectures or sermons know with what earnest love. I always speak more of the Apostles' and Nicene: the Athanasian I have defended upon grounds which I believe to be perfectly tenable. Otherwise I should not use it. I was called upon by a newspaper a few days ago to say whether I used it in the sense of that newspaper. I gave no answer, first, because I did not choose to recognize such an authority; second, because I do not know what its sense is. I have declared solemnly—I can assure those who say that it is at variance with our Lord's words, "Judge not that ye be not judged"—that I never in my life felt I was judging anyone when I pronounced it, but only myself. I cannot be sure that the newspaper writer does and could say the same, therefore I cannot assert I speak it in his sense.

(4) I have spoken of the Liturgy already, and am about to publish a set of sermons upon it. The object of these sermons is especially to show that it is the most satisfactory witness, guide, and deliverer from the Romish system, and all others which divide the Church and hinder one from drawing nigh to God.

"Do I understand you to say that you desire the Creeds, the

136

Liturgy, the Articles to be taken as the tests of orthodoxy, and that you consider it a part of that orthodoxy to make the Bible a key to all other studies?"

I used this language, simply, solemnly, deliberately. I further challenged the *English Review* or anyone else to take any means for ascertaining whether my teaching in the College or my sermons in the pulpit are or are not in accordance with this profession. I beg now to renew that challenge.

▶ 59. To Miss Hare about Dr. Jelf, March 17, 1849

. . . My foolish business is, so far as I know, at an end for the present. I am afraid it has done my good friend Dr. Jelf more harm than me. He is ill in bed, and I am afraid I have some of his nervous feelings to answer for. One is sorry to be the cause of keeping worthy people in a fever, but that comes of their inviting such dangerous explosive reformers to enter their quiet orthodox schools. He asked me to be a theological tutor when it seemed to my friends a very unwise step that I should become so, for it involved giving up Guy's. I had committed myself to all my "heresies" then, and there were my books to tell the tale if he had been pleased to look at them; so that really I do not feel guilty of any great imposition. I think on the whole he likes me—not perhaps quite as well as you do—but with a fair, reasonable Anglican middle-way sort of liking; and I have no notion that he will ever throw me off rudely or harshly. . . . The rest I must leave in better hands, especially asking not to be allowed to suppress or qualify a single conviction or to state one conviction with unnecessary harshness or point.

▶ 60. To Miss Hare, on biography and love, March 27, 1849

. . . I am so glad you like my sermons. I do not think you are the fairest and the most impartial critic in the world, and yet I gulp down all your commendations just as if you were and I might trust you implicitly. And I am afraid I like your judgment better than that of all sagacious reviewers, and agree with it in my heart, though not without some protest. Well, I can say honestly that I only carry out in my own case a principle which I have always professed. I always tell my pupils not to read cold, impartial biographies, but to study a man's life in the book of someone who loved him. Such a person, I tell them, will alone have found out what he really was. There is no fear of their not making allowances enough for his prepossessions, or not seeing them quickly enough. We are only too sharp-scented in such cases, but if he had any heart in him, any good that could be drawn out, the loving man will have found it and expressed it; if he was nothing, we shall be more aware of that by his failure. Is that true? Tell me if you see any fallacy in it.

. . . Love must be truth to the very heart and must feel the evil it comes near with proportionate acuteness, even as it feels the good. God does so. Christ's life on earth was the continual recognition of good in and imputation of good to those among whom He dwelt—and therefore a continual agony from the wrong and falsehood which grated against His love and would not acknowledge it. Oh! if we could but know what that all-embracing discriminating love of His is, the meaning of the perfect sacrifice there was in it, and of the joy which lay beneath its sorrow! Some day we may be permitted to understand something of it, and we may be spelling at it and helping each other to spell at it now. We shall do it best when we try to carry out the image in ourselves, and make our own love on earth the feeble manifestation of it.

▶ 61. To Miss Hare, on Passion Week, April 3, 1849

I do not think we differ at all about Passion Week. It is the violent effort at *realization,* as it is called, which I think disappointing and mischievous; just the remedy for the temptation to make it is the quiet simple recognition of Christ as entering into our sufferings and the sufferings of all we know. That is *real.* It is not trying to wind ourselves to some conception of what He may have passed through, but apprehending by that which we have experienced what He must have passed through.

This would not be sufficient alone: the divinity of the suffering consists in its love. We must begin from that; and confess that His love was the reflection of His Father's love; so we understand the difference between His grief and any which is soiled with selfishness. It does not differ in intensity—the more love, the more suffering; it is not taken out of the range of our sympathies by the difference—the more love, the more sympathy. And we can only sympathize with anyone in that which is not selfish in him. But these two thoughts together—the divine Love perfected and manifested in submission and sacrifice, the human sympathy with all actual sorrows—seem to me to constitute the mystery of Passion Week. If we strive to think of a certain infinite amount of suffering, it seems to me we lose ourselves and lose the blessing which comes from the more practical consideration of it in reference to ourselves and to humanity. Declamative and extravagant phrases on the subject seem to me irreverent, irreconcilable with the spirit of the Gospel narratives, which are so calm because they are so deep and awful.

► 62. To Miss Hare on the prospect of meeting with some Chartists who were considered dangerous revolutionaries, April 23, 1849

. . . This evening I am to meet a set of Chartists at a coffee house, in the hope of organizing some regular meetings with them at some other place. I have not sought these interviews—the proposal came from one of themselves; but I felt it as a call which I ought not to decline. They seem to think very much of a clergyman being willing to hold conferences with them in a friendly spirit, though they are quite used to meet members of Parliament. This seems to me very sad: that any class of people should feel the clergy to be strangers, and that it is a novelty to be fairly brought into contact with them.

These men have many very interesting points: they have shown remarkable delicacy in wishing to save me from what they suppose I should feel discreditable. A worthy bookseller, one of my Lincoln's Inn congregation, would have allowed the use of his rooms if we agreed to hold no religious discussion. These terms I could not consent to. I think it is very desirable that the poor men should feel the connection of politics with Christianity and that

139

they should be allowed to state all their infidel difficulties frankly. I have not much hope unless they are encouraged to do so. The whole experiment is perhaps a bold one—at least for such a person as I am to enter upon. But I cannot help feeling that if God has taught me to make it He will give me wisdom for it. I do not enter upon it, I hope, lightly.

▶ 63. To Miss Hare on spring and the resurrection, May 2, 1849

All the blessings of the spring be with you! surely they are great and manifold and even divine. The symbolism of spring seems to me very wonderful. I wish I could see more into it. But it speaks to me of that which just now God seems to be forcing most upon my thoughts: Reformation, Revival, Restoration! A very dull dark winter, and heavy frost the Church is surely groaning under. It seems to me sometimes as if all were dead. But I am certain there is a root lying beneath every withered stem which may one day send forth blossoms, and flowers, and fruits.

I do find the resurrection the most cheering and wonderful assurance that together with His dead body the Church shall arise a living body out of the grave into which it has sunk. I do think we are all called in some way or other to work for this great end —I mean, to be fellow workers with God in it. And I earnestly desire to know what He will have me to do. There seem to be a number of persons now, as in our Lord's time, waiting for the kingdom of God: Doctors of the Law like Simeon—counselors like Joseph of Arimathaea—the orthodox Nathanaels and good Samaritans. . . .

▶ 64. To Miss Hare, during his son's birthday party on May 24, 1849

. . . I have just run away for two or three minutes from Freddy's party to write you a line. I have been showing them with Edward's help a magic lantern which was sent me thirty-five years ago by one of the friends of my childhood. It was strange to see them looking at the slides I used to delight in at Edmund's age, and to think of all [who] used to share this pleasure with me. I think I never had much capacity for enjoyment, and this generation has it would seem even less. But Freddy and Edmund do heartily exult in sights and sounds, at least for a time.

They both went to the British Museum this morning, and my mother, who has been reading Layard and longing to see the Nineveh wonders, joined us there. . . .

▶ 65. To Miss Hare, on the new reformation of the Spirit, written on May 26, 1849

. . . I should like to be with you on Whitsunday; but this year we must be content to wish each other the infinite blessings of it at a distance. They seem more wonderful the more I think of them. Sometimes it seems as if they were the very root of all our life. I cannot but think that the reformation in our day, which I expect is to be more deep and searching than that of the sixteenth century, will turn upon the Spirit's presence and life, as that did upon the justification by the Son. But I rather suppose the larger reconciliation of the two truths in the name of the Father, the Son, and the Holy Ghost may be that which one is to keep continually in sight, and which God will teach us if we wait for Him.

▶ 66. To Miss Hare on a picnic, his wedding, and meetings with workingmen, written June 27, 1849

It is only seven o'clock and I have not yet received your letter; but as my friends Ludlow and others have asked me to join them in going out with a set of their ragged boys on a picnic in the country at nine, I am afraid I might miss writing altogether if I did not leave a letter behind me. I am not much used to such expeditions, and am likely to be a wet blanket on this; but the notion is so good of giving a breath of fresh air and one day of simple enjoyment to these smoke-dried boys, that I hope we shall

all have a heart given us to join in it. More feeling I should think of God's kingdom and goodness may be given by such a day than by much teaching, and I repent of nothing more than the unthankful heart with which I have taken part in such things hitherto.

I look upon this as a kind of preparation for our wedding, for it is thankfulness I especially want for the highest blessing as well as the least; and the sight of so many whom God has made as good as oneself with such an apparent want of everything, at once makes one ashamed of one's own treasures, and desirous to claim them and rejoice in whatever one can enter into with them.

You know what the joy of light and air is as I—who have always had health—do not. Oh! teach me to bless God for them. One does not praise Him for the kingdom of heaven when one does not feel the goodness and the richness of the earth. I desire nothing so much as that our married life should begin with thanksgiving as well as with confession; indeed the two always go together.

We had another meeting of the workingmen last night—and I spoke to them for some time. I believe the thing is right and will work good, for I find that though I can only stammer in a speech after dinner among bigwigs, words are put into my mouth when I am addressing these people, who have very little conventional respect for my profession or me, but a great suspicion of both, yet do seem ready to meet any who meet them frankly as men. I think the meetings have been more good for me than for them.

▶ **67. To his mother, from Rockend, July 4, 1849, the day of his marriage to Georgiana Hare**

My dearest Mother,

I know you will like to have a line from us, though it be only a line, to say that we are here and that God has blessed us this day in making us one. Georgiana is better than I had dared to hope I should find her, and has gone through the day wonderfully well. We would fain say to my father and you, and all, something of what is in our hearts, but I know you will believe it is there, and will be glad to hear only that we have begun to bear each other's burdens and share each other's joys. Best love to all. The post leaves this place at four, and we did not arrive till three. May God be with you.

▶ 68. To Mr. F. J. A. Hort,* then unknown to Maurice, and who had asked help from him on the subject of "eternal punishment," written from 21 Queen's Square, Bloomsbury, November 23, 1849

My dear Sir,

Perhaps I shall best show my interest in the subject which is occupying your mind, and my gratitude for your confidence, if I tell you something of the processes of thought through which I have myself passed, while endeavoring to arrive at the truth.

I was brought up in the belief of universal restitution; I was taught that the idea of eternal punishment could not consist with the goodness and mercy of God. When I came to think and feel for myself, I began to suspect these determinations. It did not seem to me that the views I had learned respecting sin accorded with my experience of it, or with the facts which I saw in the world. I had a certain revolting, partly of intellect and partly of conscience, against what struck me as a feeble notion of the divine perfections, one which represented *good nature* as the highest of them. Nor could I acquiesce in the unfair distortions of the text of Scripture by which, as I thought, they justified their conclusions; for I had always learned to reverence the Scriptures, not to set them aside. I did not see how *aionios* ["eternal"] could mean one thing when it was joined with "punishment" and another when it was joined with *zoe* ["life"].

I do not mean that these were very deep, vital *convictions*; they

* F. J. A. Hort (1828-92) became a distinguished New Testament scholar. With Westcott he produced the famous work on the Greek text of the New Testament. Maurice took the time to answer the letter of this unknown student, making Hort his friend for life and providing a clear statement of his understanding of "eternal" long before the King's College episode. Hort shared the social ideals of Maurice and Kingsley. See *The Life and Letters of F. J. A. Hort*, edited by A. F. Hort (1896).

were honest *opinions* as far as they went, though mixed with much intellectual pride. I despised the Universalist and Unitarian as weak; I do not know that I found anything at all better.

When I began in earnest to seek God for myself, the feeling that I needed a deliverer from an overwhelming weight of selfishness was the predominant one in my mind. Then I found it more and more impossible to trust in any Being who did not hate selfishness, and who did not desire to raise His creatures out of it. Such a Being was altogether different from the mere image of good nature I had seen among Universalists. He was also very different from the mere Sovereign whom I heard of amongst Calvinists, and who it seemed to me was worshiped by a great portion of the religious world.

But I thought He was just that Being who was exhibited in the cross of Jesus Christ. If I might believe His words, "He that hath seen me hath seen the Father"; if in His death the whole wisdom and power of God did shine forth, there was One to whom I might fly from the demon of self, there was One who could break his bonds asunder. This was and is the ground of my faith. The more I have thought and felt, the more has the Scripture met my thoughts and feelings, by exhibiting God to me in Christ, reconciling the world to Himself; the more have I been sure that I was meant to trust this Being absolutely, universally—that my sin was *not* trusting Him. The certainty of One absolute in goodness whom I could call Father, has more and more obliged me to believe in a Son, to believe Him, as the Church believes Him, to be consubstantial with the Father; the more have I recognized the impossibility of a perfect all-comprehending unity, or of any living fellowship between me and my fellow men, or of any practical faith in myself unless I confessed a Spirit proceeding from the Father and the Son, distinct from them, perfectly one with them.

I can say, I did not receive this of man, neither was I taught it. Every glimpse I have of it has come to me through great confusions and darkness. With it has come the belief that God has redeemed *mankind*, that He has chosen a family to be witnesses of that redemption, that we who are baptized into that family must claim for ourselves the title of sons of God, must witness to others that they have a claim to it as well as we.

144

You may think I am going a long way round to get at your question; but I really know no other road. The *starting point* of the Gospel, as I read it, is the absolute Love of God; the *reward* of the Gospel is the knowledge of that love. It is brought near to us by the Gospel, so the apostles speak: the kingdom of God is revealed to men; they are declared to be inheritors of it. The condemnation is declared to be choosing darkness rather than light, "hating Christ and the Father." A rebel state of will, at war with God, is the highest, completest misery. So far I think all go, in words at least. All will admit that damnation is in some sense loss of God's presence, that the curse lies in the rejection of love, separation from love, abandonment to self. All admit that God has sent His Son to save us from this perdition; from every other as included in this or the consequent of it.

St. John repeating our Lord's most awful prayer takes me a step farther. "This," he says, "is *eternal life*, that they may know thee the only true God, and Jesus Christ whom thou hast sent." At first we shrink from the strict meaning of these words. We suppose they do not mean that eternal life is the knowledge of God, but only that those who obtain that knowledge or that life will retain it through eternity. But when I ask myself, "Do I then know what *eternity* is? Do I mean by eternity a certain very, very long time?" I am shocked and startled at once by my want of faith and want of reason. Our Lord has been training us by His beautiful, blessed teaching to see eternity as something altogether out of time, to connect it with Him who is, and was, and is to come. He has been teaching me that I have a spirit which cannot rest in time, which must strive after the living, the permanent, the eternal, after God Himself. He has been telling me that He has come to bring me into this state, that He is the way to it. How dare I then depart from His own definition? How dare I impute my own low meaning of "eternal" to Him, and read myself into His words, when He is raising me to another meaning infinitely more accordant with the witness of my conscience, not involving the contradictions which my own does?

Now, believing from my heart that the words in the twenty-fifth of St. Matthew are quite as much our Lord's words as those in the seventeenth of St. John, I am bound by reverence to Him

—and if not by that, even by ordinary philological honesty—to apply to the former the meaning which I have learned from the latter, this being the strictest I can get. I am bound to apply that meaning to both cases in which the word is used, getting rid of the difference which our translators have (not honestly, or with great carelessness) introduced between "everlasting" and "eternal." I am bound to believe that the eternal life into which the righteous go is that knowledge of God which *is* eternal life; I am bound to suppose that the eternal punishment into which those on the left hand go, is the loss of that eternal life—what is elsewhere called "eternal death."

Now, if you ask me on the strength of this passage, or of any similar one, to dogmatize on the *duration* of future punishment, I feel obliged to say, "I cannot do so. I find *here* at least nothing on the subject. I cannot apply the idea of time to the word 'eternal.'" I feel that I cannot; everybody feels it. What do the continual experiments to heap hundreds of thousands of years upon hundreds of thousands of years, and then the confession, "After all we are no nearer to eternity," mean, if not this? Do they not show that we are not even *on the way* to the idea of eternity? Might we not just as well have stopped at the hundredth year or the first? But this trifling becomes very serious and shocking if there is a great and awful idea of eternity which our Lord would teach us, which belongs to our own inmost selves, and which we are flying from by these efforts to get it into another region. For the idea of enjoying God or being without God, we unawares substitute that Mahometan felicity or Mahometan torment which you speak of, and the whole of Christianity becomes depraved in consequence.

And yet do I then dogmatize on the other side? Do I fall back on the theory of Universal Restitution, which in my early days I found so unsatisfactory? No; I find it cold and unsatisfactory still. I cannot speak of God punishing for a number of years, and then ceasing to punish, or of the wicked expiating their crimes by a certain amount of penalties. The idea of a rebel will is, to those who know in themselves what it is, far too awful for such arrangements as these. A man who feels what sin means, who feels it as the contradiction to God's nature, the perfectly holy, and blessed, and loving nature, cannot find any comfort in the thought of God

146

leaving men alone, or hold out such a prospect as a comfort to his fellows. He feels that God is altogether Love, Light with no darkness at all. But then that which is without God, that which loves darkness, that which resists Love, must not it be miserable? And can it not fix itself in misery? Has it not a power of defying that which seeks to subdue it? I know in myself that it has. I know that we may struggle with the Light, that we may choose death. But I know also that Love does overcome this rebellion. I know that I am bound to believe that its power is greater than every other.

I am sure that Christ's death proves that death, hell, hatred, are not so strong as their opposites. How can I reconcile these contradictory discoveries? I cannot reconcile them. I know no theory which can. But I can trust in Him who has reconciled the world to Himself. I can leave all in His hands. I dare not fix any limits to the power of His love. I cannot tell what are the limits to the power of a rebel will. I know that no man can be blessed, except his will is in accordance with God's will. I know it must be by an action on the will that love triumphs. Though I have no faith in man's theory of Universal Restitution, I am taught to expect "a restitution of all things, which God who cannot lie has promised since the world began." I am obliged to believe that we are living in a restored order; I am sure that restored order will be carried out by the full triumph of God's loving will. How that should take place while any rebellious will remains in His universe I cannot tell, though it is not for me to say that it is impossible; I do not want to say it, I wish to trust God absolutely, and not to trust in any conclusion of my own understanding at all.

My duty then I feel is this: (1) To assert that which I know, that which God has revealed, His absolute universal love in all possible ways, and without any limitation. (2) To tell myself and all men, that to know this love and to be molded by it is *the* blessing we are to seek. (3) To say that this is eternal life. (4) To say that the want of it is death. (5) To say that if they believe in the Son of God they have eternal life. (6) To say that if they have not the Son of God they have not life. (7) *Not* to say who has the Son of God, because I do not know. (8) *Not* to say how long anyone may remain in eternal death, because I do not know. (9) *Not* to say that all will necessarily be raised out of eternal

147

death, because I do not know. (10) *Not* to judge any before the time, or to judge other men at all, because Christ has said, "Judge not that ye be not judged." (11) *Not* to play with Scripture by quoting passages which have not the slightest connection with the subject, such as, "Where the tree falleth it shall lie." (12) *Not* to invent a scheme of purgatory and so take upon myself the office of the divine Judge. (13) *Not* to deny God a right of using punishments at any time or anywhere for the reformation of His creatures. (14) *Not* to contradict Christ's words, "These shall be beaten with few, these with many stripes," for the sake of maintaining a theory of the equality of sins. (15) *Not* to think any punishment of God's so great as His saying, "Let them alone."

These rules I have laid down for myself, and have tried to act upon, how imperfectly God knows. One remark I would wish to make further on this point. You speak of the Liturgy and Athanasian Creed as if they laid upon us some new burden. But they merely adopt the language of Scripture respecting eternal punishment. Whatever meaning you give it in the New Testament, that you must of course give it in our services. And I am very sure that in this case, as in others, they are instruments of deliverance from the corruption and materialism of the popular theology. They do lead us to feel practically that the knowledge of God is eternal life, and the loss of God is eternal death. If we use them faithfully, we shall be educated out of the carnal into the Christian idea of eternity. Do you not find that it is so with bed-ridden women and humble peasants? They know inwardly that Christ does not mean millions of billions of years of enjoyment by eternal life. They are not good at numeration. But they worship the Father of an infinite majesty, His honorable, true, and only Son, and the Holy Ghost the Comforter. Thus they find His promise made good to them, and they are not afraid of His ever ceasing to make it good to them.

You think you do not find a distinct recognition of the devil's personality in my books. I am sorry if it is so. I am afraid I have been corrupted by speaking to a polite congregation. I do agree with my dear friend Charles Kingsley, and admire him for boldness with which he has said that the devil is shamming dead, but that he never was busier than now. I do not know what he is by theological arguments, but I know by what I feel. I am sure there is one near me accusing God and my brethren to me. He is not myself; I should go mad if I thought he was. He is near my neighbors; I am sure he is not identical with my neighbors. I must hate them if I believed he was. But oh! most of all, I am horror-struck at the thought that we may confound him with God; the perfect darkness with the perfect light. I dare not deny that it is an evil will that tempts me; else I should begin to think evil is in God's creation, and is not the revolt from God, resistance to Him. If he is an evil will, he must, I think, be a person. The Word upholds his existence, not his evil. That is in himself; that is the mysterious, awful possibility implied in his being a will. I need scarcely say that I do not mean by this acknowledgment of an evil *spirit* that I acknowledge a *material* devil. But does anyone?

When I spoke in the first edition of my *The Kingdom of Christ* of satisfaction offered by Christ to the devil, I was quoting from Bishop Hooper, and I wished to startle the admirers of our Reformers with the thought how vast a difference there must be between a theology which described the devil as demanding a price of blood, and God as demanding it. I did, however, recognize a deep practical meaning in Hooper's statement. It seems to me that in sore conflicts with the tempter one may find great comfort in saying, "Thou hast no claim on me; thou hast been paid full measure, pressed down and running over." And if justice is done to the feeling which is implied in this language, I believe the mind is freer to receive the full idea of that satisfaction which the Son made to the Father, that perfect reflex of His own love which He presented to Him, when He gave up His soul and body to death; when He showed forth the fullness of the divine love in human suffering. I cannot think there is any object so perfectly satisfying to Him who is absolutely and perfectly Love as this sacrifice. Though I see but a very little way into its meaning, I do feel that it is the atonement of God and man; and that to feed upon it must be the communion between God and man, the bond of fellowship between all creatures, the rest of each soul. In that sacrament, and in the acts of trust and charity which belong to it, we shall, I think, enter into the deepest sense of Christ's substitution—by which I mean His entire identification of Himself with our sufferings and sorrows; His intense feeling and endurance of our sins, as only One perfectly pure and loving could feel and endure them; His representation of us as the living, victorious Head of humanity at the right hand of His Father. There may be more, must be infinitely more, in it than I perceive; but this I am sure is there. If He has redeemed men from the devil and atoned them to God, He has done for us that which we need—that *is* eternal life—we may be content. And to return to the first subject, I believe that in prayers, sacraments, sorrows, works for our fellow men, we shall see more than we can ask or think, more than all the theories in the world can enable us to ask or think, of that ransom made for all, to be testified in due time. . . .

▶ 69. To Mr. Ludlow in December, 1849

. . . Oh! the bitter scorn which I have seen Newmanites in-dulging at the schemes of Evangelicals, scorn in which I have been well inclined to join; and now the frost which has come on them-selves, their incapacity of all healthy action. I could get the good will of you all very soon by flattering that habit of mind, and I am often tempted to do it. But God will not let me: and therefore He will not let me ever be the leader or subleader of any school or party in this land. For the only condition of the existence of such a school or party is the denunciation and execration of every other. I find myself becoming more and more solitary. I see that I am wide as the poles from Hare about the baptismal question. He wishes to make everyone comfortable in the Church; and I want no one to be comfortable in it, so cross-grained am I. Yet I seek for unity in my own wild way. He will be here tonight if you can possibly come in to meet him. Tennyson may also perhaps be here.

▶ 70. To Charles Kingsley on January 2, 1850

. . . I like your tract exceedingly.* So far as it is done it is as good as can be. One or two words may perhaps be spared which one would like for one's own sake, but which may damage the cause in some people's eyes, whom we would wish if possible to

* Kingsley's tract was *Cheap Clothes and Nasty.*

150

have with us. I like your method of dealing with the subject, because you do not commit yourself to any specific social plan or any approbation of the partnership scheme for its own sake.

I do not see my way farther than this. Competition is put forth as the law of the universe. That is a lie. The time is come for us to declare that it is a lie by word and deed. I see no way but associating for work instead of for strikes. I do not say or think we feel that the relation of employer and employed is not a true relation. I do not determine that wages may not be a righteous mode of expressing that relation. But at present it is clear that this relation is destroyed, that the payment of wages is nothing but a deception. We may restore the whole state of things: we may bring in a new one. God will decide that. His voice has gone forth clearly bidding us come forward to fight against the present state of things; to call men to repentance first of all, but then also, as it seems to me, to give them an opportunity of showing their repentance and bringing forth fruits worthy of it. This is my notion of a Tailors' Association, which I see must lead to something serious and should not be undertaken except with great seriousness; which may or may not lead to any new arrangement about work and profit. . . .

▶ 71. To Mr. Ludlow, defining "Christian Socialism," dated Hastings, Wednesday Evening, 1850

My dear Friend,

I see it clearly. We must not beat about the bush. What right have we to address the English people? We must have something special to tell them, or we ought not to speak. "Tracts on Christian Socialism" is, it seems to me, the only title which will define our object, and will commit us at once to the conflict we must engage in sooner or later with the unsocial Christians and the unchristian Socialists. It is a great thing not to leave people to poke out our object and proclaim it with infinite triumph. "Why, you are Socialists in disguise." " 'In disguise'; not a bit of it. There it is staring you in the face upon the title page!" "You want to thrust in ever so much priestcraft under a good revolutionary name." "Well, did not we warn you of it? Did we not profess that our intended something was quite different from what your Owenish lecturers meant?" This is the fair play which English people like, and which will save us from a number of long prefaces, paraphrases, apologetical statements which waste time when one wants to be getting to business.

▶ 72. To F. J. A. Hort,* about 1850, regarding Hort's essay "Evidences of Christianity as Exhibited in the Early Apologists down to Augustine"

You must think again of your division of heresies. I do not say that it is wrong, but it requires a good deal of reflection before you put it forth even roughly. I should be disposed a little to expand what you have said about internal and external evidence; it is a point which requires so much clearing to make people aware of your meaning. You are on the right track, I am convinced. The external evidences of the last century substituted Nature . . . for God. The reaction against that mischievous dogma is the substitution of human intuitions, or at best the Reason from which they flow, for God. . . . The idea of revelation in the seventeenth and eighteenth centuries was the announcement of certain decrees, imperative laws enacted by God. In the nineteenth it is the discovery of an endless flux, of which the source is in the creature energy of man. The Gospel of God concerning Himself in His Son is, as you have happily indicated, the reconciliation of two ideas, each of which by itself tends to Atheism and to superstition.

▶ 73. To Hort on March 5, 1850

. . . I never have taken up any dialogue of Plato's without getting more from it than from any book not in the Bible. I do not think it signifies much where you begin. The attempts to systematize his writings seem to me in general unfortunate. His own beautiful and wonderful method is contained in each one,

---

* This letter of Maurice's (not in his son's edition) may be consulted in *The Life and Letters of F. J. A. Hort*, edited by A. F. Hort (1896), I, 176.

and any one, thoroughly studied, is the initiation to the rest. I would advise you to reject no helps. Cousin and Schleiermacher will both be very useful; but Plato is the commentator on Plato, and it is a great mistake, I am sure, to fancy that anyone else can interpret him as well. . . .

I have always contended that Plato is quite as practical as Aristotle; nay, that if he is rightly studied as he would have us study him, in connection with the life and purposes of Socrates, he is more practical. But I am sure Aristotle has excellences of a very high kind which Plato has not, and I am very glad that Dr. Whewell has given him so conspicuous a place in his curriculum. I would advise you to study the *Politics* as well as the *Nicomachean Ethics*; and not to forget the *Rhetoric*, though I should not be disposed to give it as much time as one might be tempted to do by its remarkable acuteness, vivacity, and variety. The *Politics*, though it may be difficult always to trace the course of the thought, seems to me a book of the highest value; I am most thankful for what it taught me. It should be combined with the study of the *Republic* by anyone who is meditating on ecclesiastical or civil polity. I think I learned to feel the preciousness of the Bible as a history and the absolute impossibility of a Church which had not a divine history for its basis—supposing it to have the finest philosophy in the world—very much through these books illustrated by the experience of my own life and of our own times. . . .

Our modern Socialist questions which, as you say, must press more and more upon us will, I conceive, present themselves to you again and again while you are busy with these ancients. And it is a grand thing to read the newspapers by their light, and them by the light of the newspapers. . . .

▶ 74. To the Reverend Charles Kingsley on February 25, 1851

I am sure that you are right; Wordsworth's *Prelude* seems to me the dying utterance of the half century we have just passed through, the expression—the English expression at least—of all that self-building process in which, according to their different schemes and principles, Byron, Goethe, Wordsworth, the Evangelicals (Protestant and Romanist), were all engaged, which their novels, poems, experiences, prayers, were setting forth, in which God, under whatever name or in whatever aspect He presented Himself to them, was still the agent only in fitting them to be world-wise, men of genius, artists, saints. For us there must be something else intended—either the mere science millennium of Comte, from which good Lord deliver us, or the knowledge and life of God as the ground of all human and earthly knowledge and life. You have a right then to wind up the biography of a sporting man with the Trinity better than Berkeley has his tar-water treatise. Let no one rob you of the right.

▶ 75. To Dr. Jelf, the Principal of King's College, written from 21 Queen's Square, November 12, 1851

My dear Mr. Principal,

I write these lines in consequence of some remarks which fell from you in the course of our conversation this morning.

It has been objected to me and to some of my friends that we are countenancing doctrines, and promoting practices, which are connected in a great many minds with a disbelief in Christianity, which are connected in the minds of most with the subversion of order and property. I answer that we have tried to teach the workingmen in our words what we have tried to show them by our acts—that Christianity is the only means of promoting their well-being and counteracting the moral evils which lie at the root of their physical evils. I answer again that we have protested against the spirit of competition and rivalry, precisely because we believe it is leading to anarchy, and must destroy at last the property of the rich as well as the existence of the poor.

It is objected that we do not fully believe in the Bible as an authoritative teacher, and seek for some modern rationalistic way of explaining its origin, or its doctrines, or its facts.

I answer—we have found an unbelief in the authority of the Bible very common among the workingmen; we have found in-

154

fidel notions of all kinds prevailing among them; we have found these notions gaining immense strength from the notion that the Scripture refers to a future world, and not to the present.

Our great object has been to encounter this infidelity, by showing them that the Bible, taken in its most simple literal sense, declares God to be the present ruler of the world, and that if they have faith in Him and in His word, they will find a help and teacher in their daily perplexities, in their common life, which will save them from resorting to demagogues as ignorant as themselves. We are therefore obliged to discredit all fantastical neological notions of the Bible, and to present it as the authentic declaration of God's mind and will to His creatures. . . .

It has been objected to me individually, that as a professor in a college I have no business to occupy myself with associations of workingmen. I answer: both my colleagues in the theological department are occupied most beneficially to themselves and to others, out of college hours, in parochial duties, one in London, the other in the country; both of them in writing books, one of them in special labors for his Hebrew brethren. One of my colleagues in the general department has the care of the soldiers of London; all I believe have some duties or other which bring them in contact with persons of a different rank, besides those whom they teach in the college.

Their classes in the college I believe are infinitely the better for their labors and studies out of it. I think it should be shown, not taken for granted, that mine are the worse for any humble tasks in which I may have been engaged.

If they can be shown to be evil in themselves, I am condemned of course. If not, I venture to submit that they are not made evil by my connection with the college. Should the Council see fit to decree that I should cease to aid the efforts of those friends who are striving to improve the physical and moral condition of the workingmen, or cease to be a professor in the college, I shall, without a moment's hesitation, take the latter alternative.

For there are hundreds of men in the English Church ready and able to fill the honorable offices which I should vacate. There are not at present many (I have no doubt there will be soon a great number) who feel as strongly as I do that, unless we on our side strive heart and soul to show the working classes that the Church is their best friend, and is ready to make every sacrifice for their sake, we shall not only lose all hold over them, but over the upper classes to which we have sacrificed them. Of course this conviction of mine is nothing to the Council or to anyone else, but it is everything to me, and therefore, with God's help, I shall act upon it.

▶ **76. To Archdeacon Hare, concerning the committee appointed by the trustees of King's College to inquire into Maurice's activity, written November 19, 1851**

My dear Julius,

Very hearty thanks for Esther's letters and yours. I entirely agree with you about my own duty in this business. I think also with you that I ought to be very thankful that the secret mutterings have brought forth an open act, and that I have an opportunity of explaining myself. I am perfectly satisfied with the tribunal to which my conduct is submitted; if I had had to choose, I should have made scarcely any alterations. I expect all justice from them, but I do not expect that I shall retain my place in the college. They are appointed to consider what may be done to "allay the just apprehensions of the Council." Now I can do nothing whatever to allay them. If I gave up the working associations, which I believe would be a great sin, I should feel myself obliged to begin some similar undertaking the next day. I cannot promise to be less responsible for the teaching of the society than heretofore. I shall probably be more responsible, as the promoters wish to make their teaching more definitely Christian, and therefore propose to put it under my direction. I shall confess no imprudences, for though I may have been guilty of thousands, the word might mean one thing to the Council and quite another to me. I shall not disclaim any friend or consent to give up the name "Christian Socialism," or pledge myself to avoid any acts in future which have given offense in time past. I should merely patch up a momentary reconciliation if I did any of these things, and be accused continually of violating the compact.

156

Therefore my best hope is that the clerical committee should express general approbation of my behavior as far as the college has been concerned, should speak honorably of the Socialist Movement, and should then recommend me to depart; which recommendation, upon these conditions, I should at once comply with. For I should get a clerical, even Episcopal sanction for the associations; I should cease to be under a government which will never regard me except with suspicion; and the Church would not be committed with the workingmen, and the freedom of my colleagues could not be prejudiced by any unfair treatment of me. This, therefore, is the result which I look forward to as both probable and desirable. At the same time, I hope that I shall do nothing to precipitate a decision of this kind. And I am quite sure that God will manage the matter better than I should. . . .

▶ 77. Dr. Jelf's letter to Maurice, written from King's College, London, December 20, 1851, and enclosing the report of the Committee of Inquiry

My dear Professor Maurice,

I am requested by the Council to forward to you the report of the Committee appointed to inquire into the tendency of certain of your own writings, and also of certain others which appear to have been sanctioned by you; the copy which I enclose having been furnished to me by order of the Council for that purpose:

"The Committee appointed the 14th of November, 1851, for the purpose of considering, in conjunction with the Principal, the tendency of certain works alleged to have been published by the Rev. F. D. Maurice, resolve to make the following report:

"1. The Committee desire in the first place to record their grateful sense of the value of Professor Maurice's services, of the earnest zeal with which he discharges the duties of his office, and especially of the beneficial influence which he exercises over the students of the college generally, and of the theological department in particular; and they see no ground for an abatement of confidence in the soundness of his theological teachings as a professor in this college.

"2. With respect to the particular subject which the Committee were appointed to consider, they are well assured that, whatever may be the merits or demerits of what is called 'Christian Socialism' considered as an economic theory, the scheme which has been set forth under that designation—a designation in their opinion not happily chosen—is believed by those who have devised it to be the most effectual antidote to 'Socialism' commonly so called; and the Committee cannot doubt that Professor Maurice has lent his aid to the carrying out of that scheme, under a deep sense of his responsibility to the Church, and in a spirit of genuine Christian philanthropy directed to the removal of great social evils, the existence of which is acknowledged and deplored.

"The Committee entertain a high sense of the feelings and motives which have prompted him to such efforts; and, allowance being made for occasional obscurity or want of caution in certain modes of expression, there appears to them to be nothing in his own writings on this subject, which does not admit of a favorable construction or which is inconsistent with his office as professor of divinity in this college.

"3. At the same time the Committee cannot refrain from expressing their regret at finding that Professor Maurice's name has been mixed up with publications on the same subject which they consider to be of very questionable tendency, so as to give rise to a general impression in regard to him which the Committee are persuaded is not warranted by the character of his teaching in the college."

▶ 78. To Charles Kingsley, on February 11, 1852, suggesting the inclusion of a representative of Latin civilization in his Hypatia, then appearing serially in a magazine

You will not arrive at the differentia of the Latin merely from the *Confessions*, important as they are. If you have time to take a glance at the *City of God*, especially the metaphysical parts of it (that on "Man according to God" and "Man according to Man" taught me more than all the metaphysical books I ever came in contact with, and threw back a wonderful light on Plato), you will, I think, discover, far better than I can tell you, wherein the Latin excelled the Greek, and was the witness and prophet of a regenerate social order for the universe, not merely, which is the best that can be said of Cyril or of Chrysostom, a brave antagonist, as a regenerate individual man, of a detestable social system.

The real strength of Augustine was acquired, I conceive, through his early baptism in the Styx of Manichaeanism, and his discovery that God must be the deliverer from it. I do not say that he ever shook off the distemper; it came back again frequently in his battle with Pelagius, and I think also with the Donatists, to whose real conviction I should suppose he never did justice, but was content to produce an unsatisfactory exposition of the parable of the good and bad fish against them. Nevertheless, he did learn and believe inwardly, however he might waver, that the world which God has made must be good. And therefore he had to believe also that there is an order at the bottom of it, and that this may and must vindicate itself some day. This inward persuasion belonged, as I hold, to Augustine *qua* Latin, though it was rooted in him by peculiar experiences, and was affected, on the whole not expanded or improved, by his African birth and education. . . .

The love of order and concentration in the Latin may have given birth to popedoms, empires, military despotisms without end; the savage old Goth may have had his independence, private judgment, Germanic conceits, and all the rest of it; but the two together make something better than has yet been, though, I trust, to be hammered into Greek and Jew in the days which are to be. Now what strikes me is that as you have different Greek and Jew specimens of the expiring world, you ought not *only* to have a Gothic specimen of the new world. Merely as a lively contrast to Alexandrian civilization and corruption he may be sufficient, not as a complete picture of the elements out of which God would make a Christendom. But though I speak decisively, I have a very strong secret opinion that you know infinitely more about the laws of dramatic art, and the demands of your own subject, than I do, and I should be sorry if I tempted you to put any figure upon the canvas, which would disturb the grouping of those which are there already.

▶ 79. To a friend, on March 21, 1852, concerning the subjects for discussion with workingmen at conferences over which Maurice was to preside

My dear Friend,

I thank you very heartily for your letter. I do not think I can at present make my feelings respecting Christian Socialism intelligible to you. . . . So long as it is a question between capital and labor, I am satisfied there will be endless controversies. . . . You will all feel that you are supporting a principle; you will be very apt to give that principle an exaggerated, exclusive, distorted character. For you will not be clear whether you are supporting a new and juster arrangement of things, or whether you are contending for the rights and relations of persons.

What I have tried to say in the lectures is that the reorganizers of society and the conservators of society are at war because they start from the same vicious premises; because they tacitly assume land, goods, money, labor, some subjects of possession, to be the basis of society, and therefore wish to begin by changing or maintaining the conditions of that possession; whereas, the true radical reform and radical conservation must go much deeper and say: "Human relations not only should lie, but do lie beneath all these, and when you substitute—upon one pretext or another—property relations for these, you destroy our English life and English constitution, you introduce hopeless anarchy. . . ."

▶ 80. To Mr. Ludlow, on Maurice's understanding of the function of theology, written from The Keble Beau, Shrewsbury, September 24, 1852

My dear Friend,

. . . And that was nearly what I meant by calling myself a digger merely. If I had not been afraid of your mistaking me, I should have given myself the grand title of a theologian, and said that, leaving other spheres of thought and activity to those who were destined for them, and had been furnished with the gifts appropriate to them, I had taken my ground on that one study in which most people would say that I had a professional interest, but which most regard as hopelessly barren.

But such a statement would have been misleading unless I had impressed you with my own deep conviction that theology is not (as the Schoolmen have represented it) the climax of all studies, the Corinthian capital of a magnificent edifice, composed of physics, politics, economics, and connecting them as parts of a great system with each other—but is the foundation upon which they all stand. And even that language would have left my meaning open to a very great, almost an entire, misunderstanding, unless I could exchange the name "theology" for the name "God," and say that He Himself is the root from which all human life, and human society, and ultimately, through man, nature itself, are derived. I tried to express all in that one phrase that I was a digger, intending distinctly *this*, that I fear all economics, politics, physics, are in danger of becoming atheistic: not when they are worst, but even when they are best . . . that, just so far as we are chiefly constructive, this danger becomes more imminent and tremendous, that the destructive analysis of the last century is not so alarming as the synthesis of our own.

Therefore let people call me merely a philosopher, or merely anything else, or what they will, or what they will not; my business, because I am a theologian, and have no vocation except for theology, is not to build, but to dig, to show that economy and politics . . . must have a ground beneath themselves, that society is not to be made anew by arrangements of ours, but is to be regenerated by finding the law and ground of its order and harmony the only secret of its existence in God. This must seem to you an unpractical and unchristian method; to me it is the only one which makes action possible, and Christianity anything more than an artificial religion for the use of believers. I wish very earnestly to be understood on this point, because all my future course must be regulated on this principle, or on no principle at all. The kingdom of heaven is to me the great practical existing reality which is to renew the earth and make it a habitation for blessed spirits instead of for demons.

To preach the Gospel of that kingdom, the fact that it is among us, and is not to be set up at all, is my calling and business. Be-

161

cause I have preached it so uncertainly—like one beating the air
—I have had an easy, quiet life; far too much of the good opinion
of my friends; merely a few lumps of not hard mud from those
who, now and then, suspect that I have hold of something which
might make me their mischievous enemy. But if ever I do any
good work, and earn any of the hatred, which the godly in Christ
Jesus receive, and have a right to, it must be in the way I have
indicated, by proclaiming society and humanity to be divine realities, *as they stand*, not as they may become, and by calling upon
the priests, kings, prophets of the world to answer for their sin in
having made them unreal by separating them from the living and
eternal God who has established them in Christ for His glory.

This is what I call digging, this is what I oppose to building.
And the more I read the Epistle to the Corinthians, the more I
am convinced that this was St. Paul's work, the one by which he
hoped to undermine and to unite the members of the Apollos,
Cephas, Pauline, and Christian (for those who said "we are of
Christ" were the worst canters and dividers of all) schools. Christ
the actual foundation of the universe; not Christ a Messiah to
those who received Him and shaped Him according to some notion
of theirs; the Head of a body, not the teacher of a religion, was the
Christ of St. Paul. And such a Christ I desire to preach, and to
live in, and die in. Only let us each work in the calling whereto
God has called us, and ask Him to teach us what it is, and we
shall understand one another and work together.

▶ 81. To a person hesitating to take orders because of his difficulties with the Athanasian Creed, November 23, 1852

You remember probably a saying of Dr. Arnold's that the early
Church was utterly wrong and foolish in making the nature of
God, which is so far out of reach, the ground of its belief and confession; whereas some doctrine directly concerning our own human
life ought to be the uniting bond. A more plausible statement was
never made, nor I think one more directly at variance with experience, reason, and Scripture.

Experience shows us that confused and partial notions about
God have been the root of all the divisions, superstitions, plagues

162

of the world. Our highest human reason asks for the knowledge of God as the ground of itself—as that which is to deliver us from the notions, conceits, and imperfect apprehensions which belong to us as individuals. Scripture is either the gradual unveiling of God, or it is nothing.

On the other hand, all experience testifies that what Dr. Arnold would call the religious truths that concern our souls are apprehended by us as *individuals* (e.g., our personal evil, our need of a justifier, the fact of justification), and that whenever they are made the grounds of *fellowship* they lose their meaning and acquire a new and even false character. Reason says that what refers to each man (as *each*) cannot be the foundation for humanity to rest upon; Scripture is addressed to nations, to Churches, to man.

Here then is my justification of the old Church, or rather of that which the history of the Church shows not to have been its work at all, but the necessity of its existence. Because it was for man, and had a Gospel coming from God to man, its creeds were declarations of His nature; they could be nothing else.

Now the key to the life of Athanasius (I am not of course speaking now of the creed which is attributed to him but of the man) is this. He clearly saw that all idolatry lurked in Arianism; that it was a distinct return to creature-worship; that it was the substitution of a pseudo-philosophical dogma for a living God; that it destroyed all basis for union among men. Therefore it was worthwhile to incur all the misery of seeming to fight for a name and a letter; it was worthwhile to be banished from his see, to be hated by five-sixths of the Church, to be the enemy of emperors, to be an outcast among men. He was, I do believe, in the truest, simplest sense of the words, one of the most Catholic of men, who would have quarreled with you about nothing but that which he believed would rob mankind of its greatest treasure.

I am not sure that he would have written the creed; perhaps not. Nor in this day ought anyone to write such a creed, because he would be conveying a false impression of what he meant. But need that creed convey a false impression if we were without it? Is it not a false impression which makes us wish to be rid of it? What it teaches me is this: to know God is eternal life; not to know Him is eternal death. That belief thoroughly and heartily entertained, instead of making us uncharitable, would be the very ground and root of our charity. God is the perfect charity. The Father dwelling with the Son in one Spirit is that absolute and eternal love which is the ground of all things, that upon which we may repose our hopes for ourselves and the universe. Take away any part of this full idea; throw me upon some meager conception of a God—and I fall into idolatry, *first* into the worship of an evil spirit—a mere selfish being at last. This is what I regard with such infinite horror; this is the abyss which I see, not at the feet of some Arian or Unitarian, but at my own; this is what I warn myself and my country and the whole Church of. It is a real, not an imaginary danger. . . .

▶ 82. To Mr. T. Erskine, to whom he wrote a dedicatory letter in his The Prophets and Kings of the Old Testament, written from 21 Queen's Square, December 21, 1852

My dear Friend,

You will see by a book which will reach you by this post that I have taken a great liberty with your name. I was afraid you would refuse me if I asked you beforehand, or that I should make you responsible for what I said. I have longed to do what I have done for many years, when an occasion should offer. I wished to tell others how much I believe they, as well as I, owe to your books; how they seem to me to mark a crisis in the theological movements of this time. I would rather take another less public way of saying what I owe to your personal kindness and your conversation; but you will, I hope, forgive me and believe that I did think it a duty to express what I feel toward you, in connection with the task which God has shown me that I am to perform for His Church, that of testifying that the grace of God has appeared to all men. . . .

▶ 83. To Daniel Macmillan on December 31, 1852

I thank you for sending me Mr. ———'s letter. Whatever he may think of me, it expresses a conviction in which I most cordially sympathize. If I have said in any passage of my books that

164

a man is the author of his own salvation, if I ever had such a thought in my heart, if every word I have spoken with my lips or set down with my pen has not been for the assertion of the doctrine that God is the only source of man's righteousness, holiness, redemption, he has a right to call me heretic, soul-destroyer, anything he pleases, and I will join him in doing so. Instead of regarding Calvinists, so far as they are the assertors of this truth, as monsters, I have always believed them to be the greatest witnesses for the divinest of all principles, and have honored them accordingly. Those lectures on the prophets and kings are from first to last an attempt to ground human life and human acts on that principle. The maxim of them is, "Nothing good in man but what was first in God," and this, "All men are righteous so far as they confess a calling from the righteous God and yield to it." From which I deduce, or rather find in Scripture this further doctrine deduced for me, "that all false religion proceeds from the notion that man is to make his way up to God by certain acts or by a certain faith of his, instead of receiving God's witness of Himself and yielding to His government."

It is just because I find the teaching and the practice of religious men—not Calvinists only, but Calvinists more formally, theoretically, consistently than others—in deadly contradiction with these principles, that I fight against them, and by God's grace will fight against them, for His honor, for the sake of the morality of my country, for the sake of multitudes of young men whom they are driving to Atheism, as well as young women whom they are driving to Rome. Mr. ——— asks what right he or I have to know why God does this or that? I have no right, that is to say, I have no power to penetrate the depth of His *wisdom*; moreover I have no wish to do it; I am content to be lost in it. But that is because He has been pleased to reveal to me in His Son the brightness of His glory, His absolute love; because He has shown me that in Him there is no darkness at all.

On that point I have a right to be certain; he who says I have not, rejects the Bible, and disbelieves the incarnation of our Lord. I will not give up an inch of this ground; it is a matter of life and death. I find as many puzzles in the world as Mr. ——— does; if I thought I could explain them by my experience or my reason, I might be a Calvinist or any other theorist; I cannot; I am baffled,

165

and therefore my heart and reason accept the solution which the incarnation, death, resurrection of Christ offer me. They tell me that whatever else is not certain, God's absolute love is certain. They tell me that if any man pretends to have more love than God, to care more for his fellow men than God cares for them, he lies. For that there can be no love which does not come forth from God's love and is not the image of it. If then there are any persons caring for the shopmen of London, for the workingmen of London, for the prostitutes of London, I say it is absolutely certain that God cares for them, and that I am setting man above God if I think otherwise or fear to say this. And I must proclaim that all protests against slavery or any other abomination have an utterly false and godless ground if they don't proceed from this Gospel of God's love to mankind set forth in the only begotten Son. And again that if we do not accept St. John's explanation of those melancholy facts, which Mr. ——— dwells upon— "This is the condemnation that light is come into the world and men love darkness rather than light because their deeds are evil"; in other words, that though men do not save themselves they do destroy themselves, by yielding to the devil and rejecting their Father in heaven—we deny the Bible, however much we may talk about it.

Will you worship the God and Father of our Lord Jesus Christ, or the devil? Will you acknowledge that Christ is the express image of God's substance? Or, will you say that the Father and the Son are utterly unlike in nature and mind? These are the awful questions which are set before us now, and everyone must answer them. Those who take the answer from the religious newspapers, and those who take it from the Bible, will, I believe, preach on opposite sides in this great controversy.

▶ 84. To Daniel Macmillan on January 27, 1853

Your brother told me that you had some thought of republishing my *Subscription No Bondage*. I have been led to reconsider— though without re-reading—what I said in it, and I believe that it ought not to go forth without a statement to this effect. (1) That

I am more convinced than ever that the Articles are not terms of communion, and that their use for academical education is what I represented it to be in my pamphlet. (2) That I am more convinced than ever that any Articles which are to bear upon general education should be theological. (3) That I am more convinced than ever that the Articles are more comprehensive (being also *less* loose and capricious) than the dogmas of our different parties, and that we should be far more at the mercy of the most intolerant private judgments and public opinion if we lost them. But,

4) That I think I was wrong in deducing from these premises the opinion that subscription ought to be enforced at the universities.

5) That I do not think they are accepted practically or by any great number in the sense in which I urged that they ought to be accepted, but in a different sense, which is dangerous to honesty.

6) That the experience of the last few years has convinced me that the Articles are not likely to be accepted and understood and applied to the purposes for which I believe they are meant, when subscription to them is demanded at the outset of the university course or previous to taking any degree.

7) That on other grounds I object to the Cambridge test of being a *bona fide* member of the Church of England.

8) That though the change of opinion is partly in my own case the result of experiences which I have passed through since I wrote the pamphlet, I believe I ought not to have deduced the conclusion I did from any premises which I then acknowledged, and that I was warned by several friends that I had not proved the doctrine which my title affirmed.

I will make this partial recantation in any form you think best, provided the pamphlet were to appear again. . . .

▶ 85. To his sister Priscilla on Whit-Tuesday, 1853, about his Theological Essays

. . . My mind has been more filled with the *Essays,* by day and sometimes by night, than has been quite good for me. I should like very much if you were able to look at them some day, as they are in fact my letters which express the deepest thoughts that are in me and have been in me, working for a long time, but from a kind of preoccupation, which has made me afraid I should not write of what interested those I was writing to, and especially that I should trouble you on your sickbed with a multitude of things that might worry and wear you.

But I hope now to throw them off, and to be less shut up in my own modes of thinking. I do long to get out of them and to sympathize with everyone, especially my own relations, and with those who are in suffering. But they must pray for me, that I may not be possessed and crushed by my own thoughts. I believe I was to write this book, and could not honestly have put it off. Indeed I have been surprised at the way in which it has grown up under my hands, and have felt it less and yet more my own than any I ever wrote. God will do with it what He sees fit, but I sometimes feel as if the publication of it would be a great crisis in my own life, if it affects no other people. There is more solemnity to me about it than about anything else I have done. Perhaps I have said most of what I have to say in it. . . .

▶ 86. To the Reverend Charles Kingsley, from Clyro, South Wales, July 19, 1853

Your letter came to greet us on my first Sunday here, and right welcome it was. It went ill with me to be obliged to leave London without seeing you, and I longed much to hear how you were all going on. I will not conceal it that I also wanted to know your judgment of my *Essays*, which you have given me so faithfully. I suppose I should generally demur to any such sentence as that the book might make an era in our ecclesiastical history. But on this occasion I don't, though it would not surprise me if it fell flat on its back, and did not rise again.

I also should not be surprised if it did reveal the thoughts of many hearts, if it were for the falling and rising again of many in Israel. If it should lead to a schism, woe to me, should I be the cause of the offense! But I do not know how we are to rise out of schism unless someone proclaims Christ as the center of unity to each man and all men; and voices of the living and of the dead ringing continually in my ears, with, I think, a diviner voice of One that liveth and was dead, tell me that I ought to do that, whether men hear or are deaf.

Many thanks for what you say of the style. I am ashamed of myself for not having spoken more intelligibly; if I did believe what I feign to believe, that Christ is in every man, I am sure I could hold communion by words or signs with every man. So the fault is a moral one. But, indeed, I have tried to overcome it. I have deliberately given up the long sentences which, misled by Coleridge's judgment, I used to approve. And in direct defiance of him, I never talk of objective and subjective, and always give and demand change for technical phrases instead of seeking out a new terminology. Still I have not done what I ought.

. . . I knew when I wrote the sentences about eternal death, that I was writing my own sentence at King's College. And so it will be. Jelf is behaving very fairly, even kindly; but the issue is quite certain. I hope to be shown how I may act, so that my tumble may involve no loss of liberty to any English clergyman, but rather a growth of boldness and conviction. But this must be as God sees it best for us. I know I have done a very serious thing, but I am more than ever convinced that it was necessary.

. . . And, as I have told Dr. Jelf, Scotch Kirk (State and Free) men and orthodox Dissenters and Unitarians are looking with much doubt and misgiving, yet wistfully, toward us, and will find a home with us if we do not make the English Church into an Evangelical Alliance, and call upon the world to fraternize in the belief of everlasting punishment, but in the belief of the Father, Son, and Holy Ghost. Hard fighting is in store for us, dearest friend; but those that are with us are stronger than those who are against us, though we ourselves may be often among the latter. Let us hope mightily for the future. There will be a gathering of Christ's host, as well as the devil's, out of the ranks of Pharisees and Sadducees, of publicans and harlots. We shall not have to choose our own ground, it will be fixed for us; all we shall have to do is to keep it.

Meantime the present with me is agreeable enough. We are

in a comfortable parsonage, a beautiful country, and I hope among a friendly, open-hearted people. Mr. Venables has left us all we can wish in the way of carriages, so that Georgiana is able to get about, without fatigue, in the country round and she trusts she shall be able to make friends in the cottages near. She sends her kind love and hopes to write soon to Mrs. Kingsley. Love to all of you.

▶ 87. To Archdeacon Hare, bringing him up to date on the gathering storm around him, written from Clyro, August 20, 1853

My correspondence with Dr. Jelf is swelling into a volume; and is to be concluded, he tells me, with something almost amounting to a theological essay from him. I have told him that I do not see how argument can now make much difference, as far as my position is concerned. If he, as Principal, disapproves of a professor, and says that he cannot work with him, said professor must be dismissed—the discipline of the college could not otherwise be maintained, and the Council have no choice. But I have said also that I shall not anticipate their decision by resigning, first because I do not want to evade any censure they may see fit to pass upon me; second, because I must have it clearly understood that I do not leave the college because I object to any single Article, doctrine, phrase, to which I have subscribed, but solely because I object to a certain popular construction of a certain theological term, which construction I hold to be *not* the simple, natural, and orthodox one; third, because I demand it as an act of justice from the authorities of the college who have used the *Record* as their organ of communication with the public, that they should say whether they agree with the *Record* in regarding me as a scoundrel, or whether, after their experience of thirteen years, they esteem me an honest man.

This I have the same right to ask as any footman has who is turned off by his master, certain persons having said that he was dismissed for a habit of drunkenness and robbing the pantry. More I do not wish. So I hope to make it clear that an English clergyman has full liberty to maintain every position which I have maintained in my essays, and that a set of new Articles must be framed before he can be deprived of that liberty.

▶ 88. To Archdeacon Hare on September 8, 1853

Could you kindly look over these [Dr. Jelf's notes], sending them back by Sunday's post. I have drawn the sword and thrown away the scabbard, telling Jelf plainly in a note today that I see the differences between us are wider and deeper than even he supposes; that they affect the essence of the Gospel and the whole interpretation of the Bible; that I shall say to the Council: "Do you hold your professors to the Principal's interpretation of our formularies? If you do, *on that ground* our connection is dissolved";—to the bishop: "Do you hold me bound to accept the Principal's interpretation, if I officiate in your diocese? If you do, you silence me." Will you turn to the passages in St. John's Epistle about eternal life, which Jelf affirms—simply as a thing to be taken for granted— concern the *future* state of the blessed. I will send you my answer as soon as it is written. A great deal is at stake, and I feel the responsibility very much.

I hope you will notice the defense of the translators of Matthew XXV—"The rhythm of the passage, and the love of Saxon." This is the morality and reverence for God's word we are to teach our pupils!

▶ 89. To Dr. Colenso, then Bishop-designate of Natal, who had dedicated his book to Maurice, written from 21 Queen's Square, October 7, 1853

My dear Colenso,

When I returned here two days ago my eyes were greeted by the sight of your volume and of the dedication to me. I really do not know what to say to you about that. If I told you that it delighted me beyond any praise I almost ever received, I should express but half the truth. I should convey a very inadequate impression of my own feelings of the generosity and courage which your words manifest, and of the strength and hope which they imparted to me. But I should also not let you see the real fear and distress which your kindness occasioned me. When I consider the great work to which you are called, and the troubles which must, at all events, await you in it, I could not but tremble lest I had been the means of causing you a new and unnecessary hindrance. I am afraid the English bishops—to say nothing of the religious press—will visit upon you the offenses which a large portion of them is willing to charge upon me. And I could have wished that you had stifled all your regard for me rather than run this risk. Nevertheless, I do so thoroughly and inwardly believe that courage is the quality most needed in a bishop, and especially a missionary bishop, that I did at the same time give hearty thanks to God that He had bestowed such a measure of it upon you. . . .

▶ **90. To the Council of King's College after their condemnation of him for "opinions . . . of dangerous tendency . . . calculated to unsettle the minds of the theological students," * written from 21 Queen's Square, Bloomsbury, November 7, 1853**

My Lords and Gentlemen,

I have received from the secretary of King's College a copy of certain resolutions respecting me which were adopted at the last meeting of the Council.

Under ordinary circumstances it would be my duty at once to resign offices which the legislative body of the college has declared that I cannot hold without serious detriment to its usefulness.

But the Council is aware, and the public is now also aware, that certain definite charges have been brought against me by the Principal, upon the strength of which he asked that I should be excluded from my professorship. These charges amounted to a declaration that I had departed from the orthodox faith. He alleged, as his reasons for this grave charge, that I did not accept

* The Council after receiving this letter decided not to proceed any further than to declare the two professorships held by Maurice to be vacant.

172

a meaning of the word "eternal" which he considered to be the only right one, and that I refused to draw certain consequences from that meaning, or to pronounce an opinion upon a subject on which the Articles of the Church of England have not pronounced one.

The decisions of the Council, as it avowedly takes cognizance of the opinions which I expressed on this subject in my *Theological Essays*, and in my correspondence with the Principal, can be understood to amount to nothing less than a condemnation of me upon the grounds which are expressed in the Principal's letter. The Council must be deemed to have accepted the propositions in that letter, and to require that all its professors should accept them likewise.

The Principal evidently shares this opinion. When I wrote to inquire whether my lectures were to be continued till my successors were appointed, he answered that I had better discontinue them from the day on which the resolutions of the Council were passed. He pronounced this decision though he had officially commanded me to be present at the opening of the term and to commence my usual courses, retracting an unofficial letter in which he had recommended me to ask for leave of absence.

I submit that a person ordinarily so courteous to the professors of the college, and so tender of the interests of the students, would not have thus summarily suspended a teacher whom, with a full knowledge of his opinions, he had invited to be a lecturer in the theological department, and who had served the college in the other department for thirteen years—that he would not have interrupted the studies of the term and forced me to break an implicit engagement with those who are taking part in them—if he had not believed that he was executing an ecclesiastical sentence upon a convicted heretic.

I cannot, my lords and gentlemen, believe that, great as are the privileges which the right reverend bench has conceded to the Principal of King's College, their lordships, the bishops, ever intended to give him an authority superior to their own, superior to that of the Articles by which they are bound; I cannot think that they wished to constitute him and the Council arbiters of the theology of the English Church. Such a claim would be

173

alarming, I apprehend, to the public as to our ecclesiastical rulers. If some parents have been suspicious of the influence which I might exercise over their sons, I believe that there are few parents in England who will not complain that the college has departed from its original principle when it gives such a scope to the private judgment of its chief officer, or even to the judgment of the body which manages its affairs.

I think it due, then, to my own character as a clergyman, to the interests of the college, and to the liberties of the English Church, that I should call upon the Council, if they pronounce a theological sentence upon me at all, to declare what Article of our faith condemns my teaching. I conjure them not to use any phrases in condemning me which they would reject as loose and vague if the property or the life of a fellow citizen were in question. Whether I have unsettled the faith of my pupils by giving an interpretation of the word "eternal" which I had maintained to be true—and especially important for students in divinity—before I was asked to join the theological department, the after-lives of those pupils must determine. But if I have violated any law of the Church, that law can be at once pointed out—the nature of the transgression can be defined without any reference to possible tendencies and results. It is this justice, and not any personal favor, my lords and gentlemen, which I now request at your hands.

▶ **91. To his former students at King's College, written from 21 Queen's Square, Bloomsbury, November 3, 1853**

My dear Friends,

I thank you very heartily for your affectionate parting words, which have given me very great pleasure. If I thought they implied the least disrespect to the authorities of the college, I could not have acknowledged them, however personally grateful they might have been. But I know that you have no such feelings, and that you will be as earnest and faithful in all your college duties as you have been in my lecture room. May God bless you each and all and every one with whom I have been connected in this work which is now ended.

▶ 92. In answer to a letter of sympathy to their Rector from members of the congregation of Lincoln's Inn Chapel, written from 4 Grand Parade, St. Leonards, December 30, 1853

Dear Friends,

I received a cordial letter, signed by your names, two days before I left London. I did not like to answer hastily a document which was so gratifying to me, and which touched upon questions that are so interesting to us all. I thought I should show my sense of your kindness better if I entered into some explanation of the principles upon which I have endeavored to act, as the Chaplain of Lincoln's Inn, and in whatever other sphere I have been permitted to work.

You speak of some who have charged me with departing from the "Orthodox Faith." So long as I continue a minister of the Church of England, such an imputation affects not only my theology, but my moral character; it is a direct impeachment of my honesty. Had it been supported by any evidence that I have denied one of the Articles of Faith to which I have subscribed, I should have been bound to treat it with the greatest seriousness, and to demand an examination of its truth before some competent tribunal. But I am bound to pass by with indifference the mere dicta of individuals, however respectable, on such a subject. The Church of England has not made us subject to their judgments. By giving us fixed standards of doctrine, she has done what in her lies to protect us against them.

The other charge, that my teaching is dangerous, and likely to unsettle the minds of those who are brought under my influence, especially of young men, is of a different character. It evades the test of formularies; it must be confirmed or refuted by experience. I can quite understand how much justification good and intelligent men may see for it, in the course which I have followed in my teaching ever since I have taught at all. I merely protest against the assertion that I have in any, even the slightest, degree departed from that course recently, or have spoken or written any words which make me more liable to the imputation than I was seven years ago.

I have the best reason to know that the minds of numbers in all classes of society—of young men especially—*are* unsettled, not on some trifling or secondary questions, but on those which affect their inmost faith and their practical conduct, on those which concern the character of God and their relations to Him. I know that it is counted wisdom by many not to recognize these difficulties at all, or, if they cannot help acknowledging them, to treat them as sinful doubts which must be suppressed, because they interfere with the authority of the Scriptures and of the Church. The ecclesiastical position of those who hold this opinion and act upon it, entitles them to my respect. I should have followed their maxim implicitly, if I had not been thoroughly convinced that by doing so I should foster the infidelity which they desire to check—causing it to break out openly in the more honest, because they feel that that cannot be true which shrinks from the light—tempting the cowardly and self-indulgent to a feigned acquiescence, which involves, it seems to me, the most real and deadly Atheism.

I have maintained, therefore, long before I ministered among you—and in every sermon which I have preached to you—that there is no safety but in looking fairly in the face of all the difficulties which beset ourselves; but in frankly meeting all the difficulties which torment our brethren; that God encourages us to do this; that by doing it we show that we trust Him to give us the help which He has promised us, a help which can deliver us from falsehood and guide us into all truth.

So far as I have been enabled steadily to pursue this method with myself, with you, with all who have in any way been brought under my teaching; so far I have found that the Scriptures and the forms of the Church have unfolded their meaning to me, have shown me a way out of my perplexities, and out of the perplexities of the age; have offered me a deeper theology and a wider humanity than I had ever imagined for myself, or than the age, with its splendid professions—I will not say has ever realized—but has

176

ever dreamed of. So far as I have faltered in this course, and I have often done so, the Bible has become to me a sealed book, the Prayers of the Church have become dull formalities, not the worship of spiritual beings to Him who is a Spirit.

I have, you know, been more anxious that you should learn from the Bible and from the Church than from me. I have endeavored to set them forth as instruments by which God would raise you above your conceits and mine. But I have been as earnest that you should not worship the instruments instead of Him who uses them; that you should receive God's Word as the witness of His love, and what it has effected for us and for mankind, God's Church as the living and continuous witness that that Love is the same yesterday, today, and forever, and that it will put down evil and establish righteousness throughout the universe.

I do not repent of any words in which I have spoken to you of this Love as mightier than all which is opposed to it, or of the triumphs which it is yet to achieve. I believe that, if I had spoken more broadly, strongly, freely on this subject, I should have done more to make you righteous and true. My fear is not of expanding, but of contracting, the Gospel which we are sent to preach; not of seeing too strong a testimony in the Bible to the will of Him in whom is light and no darkness at all, but of limiting its testimonies to meet my narrow conceptions; not of exaggerating the duty of the Church to be a witness against all hard and cruel conceptions of our Father in heaven, which lead to a confusion between Him and the spirit of evil, but of not perceiving how manifold are the ways in which that duty should be fulfilled.

I am sure that if the Gospel is not regarded as a message to all mankind of the redemption which God has effected in His Son; if the Bible is thought to be speaking only of a world to come, and not of a Kingdom of Righteousness and Peace and Truth with which we may be in conformity or in enmity now; if the Church is not felt to be the hallower of all professions and occupations, the bond of all classes, the instrument of reforming abuses, the admonisher of the rich, the friend of the poor, the assertor of the glory of that humanity which Christ bears—*we* are to blame, and God will call *us* to account as unfaithful stewards of His treasures. . . .

▶ 93. To Mr. R. H. Hutton, from Hurstmonceux, January 8, 1854

. . . Perhaps I cannot better introduce what I should wish to say about your remarks on Christ and the Holy Spirit in the *Inquirer,* than by correcting a mistake—a serious one—into which you have fallen respecting my view of the Scriptures. I never supposed that they were to be to the moral student what the outward world is to the physical. I always maintained and have tried to act out the conviction that the whole field of human experience and history lies open to us and requires to be searched and dug into. I have not affirmed *a priori* that the Bible did not merely exhibit one set of phenomena and explanations of phenomena, a few of which were to be accepted, the majority rejected like the stories and explanations of stories in the religious books of the Hindus.

But I have said *a posteriori* that I believed the Bible did serve as a key book which enabled us to understand the histories and legends of various nations, to justify the true beliefs which were in them, to show what false beliefs or unbeliefs had mingled with these, to explain how they had become confounded. I have called for the application of this most severe test to its records; I have said that they ought to bear it if the book is what it assumes to be, and that Christians have wronged and degraded it by severing it from all other books instead of manfully evincing their own confidence in its veracity and its strength by trying whether it will not throw light upon all.

You seem to treat the question whether there may not be just as well twenty, or thirty, or a hundred, or thirty thousand mediators between God and man as merely a question between you and me turning upon philosophical experience.

Now I—holding as you do that the whole experience of the world is intended for the moralist and theologian, not a particular portion of it which has been gone through in Judea or England in the first century or the nineteenth—find all religions of the world so many attempts to produce these twenty or thirty or a hundred or thirty thousand mediators. I find them bearing the most harmonious unanimous testimony to the necessity of some uniting point between the absolute Godhead and the voluntary worshiping creature. I find them broken, divided, superstitious

178

schemes for propitiating an unwilling and ungracious Being, because they have not been able to perceive the uniting point, because they have been obliged to create it, somewhere in the material or the spiritual world. And I accept the Bible explanation of this difficulty—the Bible proclamation of the One Person in whom God is at one with His creatures, in whom He can meet them and they can meet Him—as perfectly satisfying to my own individual conscience, and also to that reason of mankind which I trace in all these diverse and warring experiences.

I have attempted to explain in my Boyle Lectures [*The Religions of the World*] why I think the experiences of mankind respecting a divine Spirit who awakens the thoughts, faculties, faith, hope, love in us, and directs them to an object above themselves, to a common object, in whom they find that which satisfies them, and which they are created to behold and enjoy, are altogether *distinct* from those respecting a Mediator—why, when they are *separated* from them or substituted for them, the result is either a priestcraft such as we see in Hinduism, or a self-worship such as we see in Buddhism, the two never being able to coalesce, each continually becoming more degraded, more superstitious, more exclusive. I will not go over the evidence here. I merely refer to it that you may see I have not been so heedless of the difficulty you have started as you suppose.

I do not attach any extravagant value to any arguments of mine or to any course of thought through which I have been led. . . . I do hope and trust that I should be glad to see every notion of mine exposed and annihilated if it blocks up the way to truth. To exhibit that truth, not in notions but in a Person, has been and is the object of my life. I believe that so it will unite us all to each other, that while we behold it split into opinions, it must separate us more and more from each other. . . .

▶ 94. To his sister Esther, Mrs. Julius Hare, in September, 1854

I am much more desirous to learn than to teach upon the subject of the future state and its occupations. I feel that I have been driven by the necessities of my own being to seek so much more for a present deliverance from cruel and pressing enemies, than for any future bliss, that the vision of the latter has often been almost entirely obscure to me. I am sure that this has been a grievous loss to myself, and has put me at a distance from many with whom I should wish to be in sympathy. But I am sure, also, that there is a deep reason why to particular persons, particular portions of truth should be, for a while, in shadow. They may miss great comfort, but they are thereby shown what they especially are appointed to understand and proclaim. The blindness and ignorance is their own, but the illumination in the other direction is God's.

The necessity of confessing a kingdom of heaven within—a kingdom of heaven ever present with us now; different in kind from the visible world, but affecting it, and swaying its movements continually—has been with me an overwhelming one. At times I have seen clearly, and even felt how little it could avail to talk of such a kingdom in a corrupt and evil world, to men oppressed with plagues, and tormented with devils, unless one could give them a much fuller and brighter prospect of that which is to come, than I have ever done. I have perceived that sometime or other I must either hold my tongue, or that it must be unloosed to speak of the better things which shall one day be manifested.

But the hindrance has been great, partly from the feeling that the future state, as we are wont to hear it described, is so vague, so selfish, so much a denial of that truth concerning the redeemed state of man, which I have been sent to bear witness of; partly from the dreariness and coldness of my own heart and imagination, and from the hollow in my head where the organ of hope should be. Since we are *saved by hope*, the consciousness of being without any natural tendency to it, or capacity for it, has been more crushing to me than anyone knows. But how deeply does one learn by this very misery, that it is hope which purifies, hope which delivers! How is one obliged to feel the force of the words, "the God of Hope!" How thoroughly one knows that the Devil is the spirit of despair!

But the result is, that the words of the Apostle, "Looking for the revelation of our Lord Jesus Christ," have seemed to me the only words that gave me any glimpse into the future state, or into

180

the use which we are to make of it, in urging ourselves and others to fight. I think the millenarians are altogether right, and have done an infinite service to the Church, in fixing our minds upon these words, and so turning them away from the expectations of mere personal felicity apart from the establishment of Christ's kingdom; from the notion of heaven which makes us indifferent to the future condition of the earth. I think they have done good, also, in urging the hope of Christ's coming, as a duty upon the Church, and in denouncing the want of it as a sin.

But it seems to me that a preparation was needed for these statements and exhortations, which they have not given us. Their preaching, I fear, has been false and mischievous, because they have not begun with acknowledging Christ as the King over men's spirits, as their Redeemer from the evil spirit, as the Ruler over the universe now, and therefore have substituted for the revelation or unveiling of Him, which the apostles speak of, the notion of an external advent or descent, which instead of carrying out the work which He came upon earth to do—instead of being the fulfillment of His spiritual redemption, instead of affirming that triumph of mankind over all its oppressors which was implied in His cross and resurrection and ascension—reverses the order of His government and redemption, sets the visible again above the invisible, lays the world at the feet of the same selfish tyrants, who under religious pretexts—boasting the name of saints—have trampled it down already and obstructed its intercourse with its just and lawful Ruler.

If this is their truth and their error, then it must be our duty and privilege to believe constantly that Christ the Redeemer of mankind, who has been manifesting Himself in all ages for the deliverance of the earth from its tyrants, and for the assertion of right and truth against wrong and falsehood, will be manifested completely for that end, that every eye shall see Him, that every thing shall be brought to light by Him, that every creature shall be unveiled in its true character and condition by the revelation of Him, who is the first born of every creature; that all who have exercised any dominion or influence under Him, and for Him, shall give account of that dominion and influence, and shall confess all that was right in it to have been His; all that was oppressive

181

and blighting and hurtful, to have been from their resistance to His will; all that was feeble and ineffectual in it, to have been from distrust of His power.

I think, as I have said already, that the millenarians are right, and practical, and in harmony with Scripture when they bid us think more of Christ's victory over the earth and redemption of it to its true purposes, than of any new condition into which we may be brought when we go out of the earth. By doing so, they make all our feelings and interests social, they connect everything we do and feel and suffer, with our kind; they give us Christ as the object of our thoughts, and not ourselves. . . .

The great thing, I suspect, is to assure ourselves not that these things *may be*, but that they *shall be*; that Christ's appearing is as certain as the sun's rising, or as our deaths; that we do not make it certain by our faith, but that its certainty is the warrant of our faith, and that which is to cure us of its sluggishness. And if this is so, we may encourage all persons always to expect Christ's manifestation; the more they do expect it, the better they will be, the more they will rise out of their sloth, their scorn, their confusions, their selfishness; the more they will work on manfully in their own appointed tasks, whatever they be, the more they will work with each other; the more they will fight against the temptations which will recur in a thousand different shapes, and will come again and again, as angels of light, to separate themselves from others under any pretense whatever, in faith, in hope, in worship; the more they will prize common thanksgivings, common prayers, and will rejoice to meet in using them, that they may pray against the devil, who is leading them, and all the people about them, to set up themselves, that they may not trust Christ, and glorify God; the more they will endure all stupid preaching as one of God's appointed trials of our faith and patience, and as a strong reason for asking Him to send true pastors, or else to stop all our mouths, and speak Himself, which I take it He is doing, and that in very wonderful and terrible thunders, as well as in very soft whispers.

And this has much to do with the recognition of friends in a future state. I have always said, with what sorrow and sincerity God is my witness: Have we ever yet recognized our friends in

182

this state? Is it not just the poorest beginning of recognition, the occasional exchange of a smile or signal of freemasonry, followed by hours and days of misconception and estrangement? Is not this the thing of all others to strive for, and therefore to expect? Is not the want of it that which most makes us ashamed, and therefore which we are sure God reproves in us, and desires to correct in us? If in spite of all reluctance, we determine not to go out in search of Christ into the deserts, not to shut ourselves in the secret chambers that we may have Him to ourselves there, if we will expect Him among the knaves and blackguards and hypocrites of the world, and will act as if we believed they had the same right in Him as we have, seeing we are knaves, blackguards, and hypocrites without Him, and they will be delivered from their stupidity, knavery, and hypocrisy, if they acknowledge Him as the Truth and the Life—we shall be acquiring by degrees the power of recognition, the human sympathies which He is seeking to cultivate in us; we shall be winning a victory over the vanity and conceit which shut us up in our own little circles and lesser selves; we shall be preparing for the gathering together of all in Christ. Which gathering together cannot, as I think, the least interfere with the development of all the special, individual faculties with which it has pleased God to endow us, but must be the means of educating them to their highest point, and of directing them to their highest purposes.

Here the great hindrance to all work is that it is not fellow work. The philologer cannot understand for what the chemist spends nights and days in his laboratory; the painter and the musician scarcely know what the other is about; how little does either care for the jurist or the moralist! Each is seeking after some precious stone, some elixir, some uniting law which would explain contradictory facts, or other laws which he cannot doubt, yet which seem at variance. Each pursues long trains of thought, often finds them ending where they began, weeps in secret, and dies disappointed, and the preacher gets up and declares that he has spent his years in vanity.

It has not been so! it is not true! There has been vanity in all his work, for there has been selfishness in all. There has been disappointment, for God has been leading him, in a way he knew not, to find that truth is deeper than all his trowings about it. But nothing has been in vain, no threads have been begun to be unwound which shall not be altogether unwound. We want but the discovery of *the* center that all men and all thoughts should fall into their proper orbits and accomplish their complete revolutions. The revelation of Christ must be the revelation, however gradually, of all these hidden principles and secret powers, and directing laws, which men in all directions have been seeking after; must be the revelation of all the relations in which they stand to each other and to God's universe.

But the majority of the world are not seeking for these, but are engaged in hard physical toils. And shall not the purpose and meaning of all these be revealed also? Shall not the benefits which they have been procuring to those who have been engaged in them, while they have seemed only to be ministering to the luxury and corruption of other men; the victories which they have won over the curse of the earth; the powers which they have awakened and cultivated, be all made manifest before men and angels; the principalities and powers, which have tried to make men's labors the means of crushing and enslaving them, being made a show of, openly, and the Son of God vindicating the name of the carpenter's son which He bore upon earth by asserting every energy of man's bodily frame, every natural machine as His?

To speak of the revelation of all the blessings which have been wrought out in the hearts of men and women through sickness and sufferings; to say how all the powers and energies which disease has cramped, will attain the freedom which Christ's word gave to the palsied man and leper; to say how the whole creation, which has groaned and travailed, shall enter into the liberty of the Son of God, is not for me. The Gospels and the eighth chapter of the Romans have said it all, and I only throw out this hint to show how much more we are actually told of the effects of the manifestation of Christ in Scripture than we commonly fancy, how much the history of His incarnation is the foretaste and prophecy of them.

So far, then, as I have at present been taught—and I must repeat again how little I feel I have been taught—respecting the future state, I would try (1) always to connect it with the unveiling or manifestation of Jesus Christ, as St. Paul and St. John do; (2) to connect it, as they do, with the restoration of the earth, and its deliverance from whatever hinders it from being the kingdom of God, and of His Christ; (3) to connect it with the manifestation of Christ in the flesh as the Lord of man, as his deliverer from all that degrades him from being the image of God, and the member of a kind, into the slave of the world he is set to rule, and a self-seeker; (4) to connect it with all our actual and present pursuits, occupations, duties, enjoyments, sufferings, so that the full fruit and result and consummation of these shall be what we look forward to, as the effect of their being restored to their obedience to Christ, and saved from all that is base or merely accidental; (5) to connect it with continuous, though free and joyful labor, so that no redeemed spirit shall ever be imagined to be the possessor of a certain felicity, and not the warrior with Christ's enemies, so long as there are any to be put down; the ruler and judge of some province of His empire, the seeker and discoverer of the secrets of God's truth and glory, which He has hidden, that His children may search them out.

►95. To the Reverend Charles Kingsley on August 4, 1855

. . . God has given you infinite faculties of enjoyment. But He has given you with these the higher trust of being manly and of caring for your fellow men and their miseries and sins. What I fear (perhaps most unreasonably) for you is that the first gift should devour the second, that your sympathy with what is beautiful in nature and human society should make you less able to stand out against them, more tolerant of that which is eating into the hearts of individuals and nations.

Godliness, I am certain, is the true support of manliness. The belief that the Son of God has interfered for His creatures, and has grappled with their sin and death, is the one protection of nations and men against sloth, effeminacy, baseness, tyranny. Oh, don't think it is a vulgar thing to be a preacher or even a priest, and a fine thing to be an artist. If you do, you will not be a true artist, but an artificer to please the world. And do not think that the way of resisting Devil's worship is to deny any of the great facts and laws of humanity, which have been turned to the Devil's use, but to claim them from him.

A finished reconciliation and atonement is the one answer to the scheme of men for making atonement; if you part with it, all superstitions, all Moloch cruelties, will reproduce themselves; and you will try your natural incantations against them in vain. If you knew what bitter repentances I have had to suffer for hard words spoken in former days, to friends whom I might have helped if I had been wiser and gentler, you would believe that I do not write these words to you without tremblings. I have well deserved to alienate all whom I love, and with many I have succeeded rather too well. But I have such confidence in your truthfulness that, if I had none in your affection, I think I should still have run the risk of seeming to send you a lecture rather than a letter. I do so the more boldly because I know that I am not pleading my own cause, except as it is yours, for I repeat what I said before, that the time is come when you ought to feel yourself, and to make the people understand, that you are not tied to any maxims of mine, and that if you have received anything from me, it has been in the way of honest merchandise, the balance of trade, if accounts were fairly examined, being all on my side.

96. To the Reverend S. Hansard on the significance of the Lord's Day, June 5, 1856

. . . This objection to the acts of the Lord's Day Society, and the terrible suspicion which it involves that there must be something in our religious condition which is very like that of the Jews when they made the Sabbath day the main excuse for denying the Son of man, and the Son of God, and seeking to kill Him—has weighed so much upon my mind that I have not dared, nay, that I have scarcely been able to dwell upon those arguments, often of a very opposite kind, which are resorted to by the defenders of Sunday amusements.

I do feel the force of some of those arguments, such as those drawn from the present condition of the people, and from the possible hope of withdrawing them from the gin palace, very keenly; but they are balanced by others of nearly equal weight, and they are mixed with statements, mischievous I think, from the half truth which is in them, to which I am less and less able to subscribe. When it is said that the Christian Sabbath is not a Jewish Sabbath, I admit the assertion altogether; but that is because I think it much higher and finer than the Jewish Sabbath, not poorer or of less perfect obligation.

When it is said that it does not rest upon a formal law, I admit it, just as I hold that baptism and the Communion of the Lord's Supper belong to the Gospel and not to the law, to the New Testament, and not to the Old, to the spirit and not to the flesh, and consider them more precious and more binding for that reason. And just as I seek for the groundwork of baptism in circumcision, and for the Lord's Supper in the Passover, just as I could not understand the one without the other, or see what we have gained if we had not the divine seed out of which the flower has developed itself to compare with it, so I could not understand the Christian Sabbath if I did not find the first form of it, and the statement of its permanent significance in the Fourth Commandment.

I look upon it as still expressing that union of rest and work which is implied in the constitution of the universe, and in the constitution of man; as still affirming that man's rest has its foundation in God's rest, man's work in God's work; as still proclaiming a common blessing to the master and the servant, and the cattle. I look upon it as still an ordinance connected with the nation and its holiness, declaring our nation, as it did the Jewish, to be holy and chosen, and consecrated to God. I look upon it in its Christian form as declaring that the union of God and man, which was set forth in the law, has been accomplished by the resurrection of our Lord, and that God can now rest in man and man in God.

Holding this to be so, I regard the Christian Sabbath or Lord's Day as the great message to human beings—the great silent message which is mightier than words, but which words ought to interpret—concerning this reconciliation. I think the early Reformers were indifferent to it, in part at least, because they did not heartily acknowledge a reconciliation of God with human beings, but only with believers or the elect. I think those who call themselves the successors of these Reformers are teaching people to regard the Sabbath as a day of penance and sackcloth because they do not believe in this reconciliation of God with mankind, and would not have it preached either silently or by the lips of God's heralds. But I think there is a sense in our people that the Sabbath has some profound blessing for them which is latent under all the perversions of it; and that hence we may explain much of the passive as well as of the active opposition to what looks like an attempt to treat it as a day only or chiefly of bodily recreation.

If you ask me what seems to me our duty as clergymen, I should say, first of all to preach continually that reconciliation of God to man, and to take every opportunity of affirming that the Sabbath is a witness of it. Second, to vindicate by all possible ways the force of our Lord's words respecting the Sabbath day, as not proclaiming certain allowable exceptions from the severe observation of it, but as asserting the essential meaning and character of it. He chose that day for healing the sick, surely to testify that the bodies of men are dear to Him, and that this day is especially to assert how dear they are. Third, to combat vehemently the doctrine which is openly proclaimed both by laymen and by clergymen, that our Lord's words were suitable to His time, when Pharisaism was rampant, and are not suitable to ours, which are Latitudinarian; an accursed doctrine, to the application of which there are no limits, and which must subject the whole Gospel to our caprice. Fourth, to combat as vehemently the doctrine that He spent so many of His precious words and acts in merely vindicating a special exception to law, instead of declaring its essential force and meaning. Fifth, on the strength of His teaching and example, to consider how we may best claim the Sabbath day as a practical instrument for benefiting men's physical as well as their spiritual condition, always endeavoring to show how one is related to the other, making all our acts not concessions or exceptions, but parts of one Gospel, and carefully adapting ourselves to English habits and local circumstances; neither condemning foreign practices, nor desiring the least to imitate them. . . .

188

97. To Mr. Solly, September 20, 1856, on the sect principle

. . . I think the Church of England is the witness in our land against the sect principle of "forming churches" which is destroying us and the Americans too (see on the latter point Mrs. Stowe's testimony in *Dred*). As long as we think we can form churches we cannot be witnesses for a Humanity and for a Son of man. We cannot believe that we do not choose Him, but that He chooses us and sends us to bear witness of His Father and of Him. Everything seems to me involved in this difference. I admit that the English Church is in a very corrupt, very evil condition. I am not afraid to own that, because I believe it is a Church and not a sect.

The sect feeling, the sect habit is undermining it. The business of us who belong to it is to repent of our sectarianism and to call our brothers to repent, to show that we have a ground on which all may stand with us. If we do that business well we shall have as many kicks, I fancy, as we shall get anywhere, kicks from all sides. Of all temptations, that of putting oneself at the head of anything, that of getting up a mere sect which must be worse and more devilish than the old—and that is saying a good deal—is the one which I would strive against most. I know only God can enable me wholly to overcome it. . . .

▶ 98. To Miss Williams Wynn, on May 11, 1858, from East-bourne where he was recovering from a breakdown in health

. . . I think we clergy are bitterly estranged from all classes of our people, high and low, wise and unwise. I think we have ourselves to blame for this estrangement. But I do not believe it would be removed or materially lessened if we were able to talk ever so glibly in a philosophical dialect, and to translate the New Testament into phrases about the subject-object. It seems to me that the heart and flesh of the intellectual man, as much as of the clodhoppers, are crying out for the living God; and that it is just this cry we have not understood, and have been unable to

189

answer. The God we have preached has not been the God who was manifested in His Son Jesus Christ; but another altogether different Being in whom we mingle strangely the Siva and the Vishnu—the first being the ground of the character, the other its ornamental and graceful vesture. It is fearful to say so; if I spoke of what good people actually and in their heart of hearts believe, I should use no such language, but the very opposite.

When I am describing what we have made of the Gospel of God's redemption of the world, I cannot soften my expression. I do therefore anticipate a very deep and searching reformation, one which cannot be attended with less trials, one which I trust is to issue in greater blessings than the Reformation of the sixteenth century. How or when it is to begin, what Tetzel is to evoke what Luther, I know not, I dare not conjecture.

I feel very strongly that the ascension of our Lord into the heavens, and the glorification of our nature in Him with the corresponding truth that the Church exists to witness of Him, not only as her Head, but as the Head of every man, will be the battle cry that will rally Protestants and Romanists, hungry seekers after wisdom, lonely tatterdemalions without bread, about the one standard; and that opposition to this proclamation, a resolute clinging to the Fall as determining man's condition, a practical acknowledging of the Devil as the arbiter of it, will be the characteristic of the opposing host, gathered also from all sects, schools, churches. . . .

▶ 99. To Mr. J. N. Langley on Scotland, Calvinism, and the episcopate, May 11, 1858

Any Arminian protest against modern Calvinism must fail anywhere, but especially in Scotland. The Scotch are too logical, yes, and with all their faults, too *godly* for that poor feeble mixture. The strength of Calvinism lay of old in the proclamation of God as the originator of all faith and righteousness in man. The reformation of Calvinism must come from the steadfast grasp of that truth. Resolve not to let it go or dilute it with any philosophical explanations or theories, and you must come to a gospel that God is seeking after men to bring them back to His fold, that He has redeemed the race, that there is no good of any kind in any creature which must not be referred to Him, which it is not a sin to claim for the creature, under any miserable subterfuges, such as that "this only means the natural conscience" or "only means some beautiful relic of the Fall"—as if these phrases meant anything at all!

I believe fully that Scotch godliness and Scotch logic may both conspire to these results. And then the idea of the episcopal constitution of the Church as a fatherly constitution, as a universal constitution, will come all in good time. If it comes too soon before the other belief, it will be an unhealthy exotic which must be kept alive by hot airs and regulated houses; if it follows that free and manly development of the old Calvinism, it may strike its roots into the national soil and bear worthy fruits hereafter.

100. To Mr. Hutton, on August 23, 1858, from Tunbridge Wells

I do not wonder that you should have been struck by an apparent contradiction in my doctrine respecting men as members of a body, and my eagerness that in their writings they should throw off the symbol of a corporation and each present himself as an *I*. To me the one position seems a consequence of the other. Because I desire that all men should regard themselves as forming one fellowship in a real and living Head, the formation of sects and corporations, grounded upon mere similarity of opinions, is that which I most dread. Believing our union to be as much a law of moral science as gravitation is a law of physical science, I must, indeed, see in all these formations and combinations the illustration of an eternal principle. I must desire that every sect, be it the narrowest and most exclusive in the world, should yet not disperse into its elements till it has realized the meaning of its union, and till its members are thus prepared to understand what place they have to occupy, what special duties they have to fulfill in the human commonwealth.

With respect to the English Church I have felt and do feel

191

bitterly how it is always on the point of drifting into mere sectarianism; and I know that it may make itself the most proud and self-exalting of sects. I rejoice that the parties within it do not suffer it to become a mere huge negation of Romanism and Calvinism. I rejoice that they compel us by their narrowness and savagery to feel after some ground in which Romanists and Calvinists may meet with the preservation of all that is distinctive (distinction being opposed to separation as life to death) and positive in each, not after a ground which both are forbidden to approach. To make Churchmen feel therefore that they are not members of a corporation bound together by certain professions of opinion, but that they exist to testify of a body to which men as men belong, has been the aim which I have tried to keep before me and which I have, with shameful feebleness, pursued. . . .

▶ 101. To Erskine of Linlathen, on February 10, 1859, commenting on Maurice's controversy with Mansel

. . . That the Bible should be defended expressly on the ground that the knowledge of God is impossible, and that this defense should be hailed in so many quarters as triumphant, gives me a kind of staggering sensation as if everything was turned upside down, and as if we were approaching a day in which the most utter denial would take the shape of unquestioning acquiescence. I feel as if one must lift up a voice against this, if it was only for the sake of the young men in Oxford, who must be tremendously shaken by such words coming from high quarters. But I tremble while I undertake the task, so many bad feelings mingle themselves with every controversy.

▶ 102. To Mr. J. M. Ludlow, on July 3, 1859, on the nature of evil

I do not differ from you about the existence of evil being the great crux of all. I learned many years ago, from Augustine, that it must, by its very nature, be the unintelligible thing, that to attempt to reduce it to a law or principle is to commit a contradiction. The question is not that at all. It is whether the unintelligibility of evil or the omnipotence of God is a reason for not regarding Him as carrying on a war against evil and for not expecting that in that war evil will be vanquished. I know that there are some who think so. For God to make war instead of crushing evil, if it can be crushed at all, by a simple fiat, is for them a simple absurdity. What I say is that if it be, the Bible is from beginning to end an absurdity. For it is the book of the wars of the Lord. It does not define evil, but it assumes evil; it assumes evil to be in a will; it assumes evil not to be vanquishable by an Omnipotent fiat; it sets forth a process by which it has been overcome in a number of wills; it teaches us to pray, *"Thy will be done on earth as it is in Heaven,"* where it is done perfectly; it says that if we pray according to God's will He hears us and we shall have the petition which we ask of Him.

Whether these assertions accord with Mr. Mansel's Carlton Club and Oxford commonroom yawn, " 'Pon my soul, I can't see why evil should not last forever if it exists now," I leave simple people to judge. I do not see why he should think otherwise, for evil to him is like everything else—a notion. But it is not a notion for you; you feel that you must fight with it to the death. And if you do not frankly confess what in your heart you believe, that God is fighting against it, you will be obliged to feel that you are fighting against Him. Your attempt to escape from this doctrine which goes through the whole of the Bible—that being nothing else than the book of the wars of the Lord—convinces me that I was right in the strong language I used, and that there is a skepticism in all our hearts—I am sure there is a deep skepticism in mine—on the subject which can only be removed by earnestly thinking what the agony and bloody sweat of Christ must mean, whether that was not the battle of God with that which is resisting His nature.

I think I am also right in speaking of eternal death. I know no other language which will bring as strongly before our minds the principle which Scripture assumes, that death is not the departure of the breath out of the body, but the loss of the life which must be the eternal life of God. At all events, what is done is

193

done. If I had taken advice, I should have let Mr. Mansel alone altogether; but there are monitors within which must be obeyed, whatever voices without contradict them.

▶ 103. To the Reverend D. J. Vaughan, on September 3, 1859, in answer to a letter concerning the distinctions of persons of the Trinity and their action upon man

There cannot, I think, be any subject so important for us at one time or other, but especially at this time, as that with which your mind has been exercised. I am well convinced that it is God and not man who sets such problems before us, and that it is He who shows us the way of solving them.

No passage, perhaps, on the whole is so helpful for this purpose as that in the third chapter of the Epistle to the Ephesians, "For this cause I bow my knees," etc., chiefly because it does not give us a formal result, but explains the process, the continual process, by which the Apostle himself arrived at a living result. He bowed his knees to a Father, not of himself but of a whole family in heaven and earth. He asked not for himself apart from the Ephesians, but with them, that they might be strengthened with might by the Spirit in the inner man. But this involved the next step: Christ would dwell in their hearts by faith. And that would lead to the next. They would find the ground on which they and all creation stood: "Being rooted and grounded in love." And so they would know the height and length and breadth of the love of God which passeth knowledge.

Here, I conceive, is the doctrine of the Trinity in its most practical form, yet with all its most delicate distinctions; no confounding of the Persons, no division of the substance. And thus is it received and has it been received in all ages by thousands of men and women in weakness and suffering, who were as utterly unable to enter into scholastic subtleties as they were to fly over the moon. They arrived, in the act and exercise of prayer, at the root of all these distinctions. The habit of looking up to a Father hindered them from ever thinking that the Spirit who drew their hearts to Him was their own spirit. He must be a universal Spirit,

194

a Spirit working in others as well as themselves; working to unite them. He must have proceeded from the Father, but He leads them not directly to the Father, but to One who has come from Him to redeem them, in whom only they are redeemed or righteous or sanctified, to whom they refer themselves, in whom they find themselves, through whom only they can see what the Father is. And perceiving in Christ that He is the infinite and eternal Love, they are certain that the Spirit who worketh in them, the Spirit of Love, is the eternal bond of unity between the Father and the Son, as He is between them on earth. As He is their guide and comforter, and the guide and comforter of myriads besides them, as they have resisted Him and He has overcome them, they cannot regard Him otherwise than as a person.

All the acts and qualities which they attribute to any present friend dwell supremely in Him. Yet because He is in them, speaking to them, they must distinguish, though they can never separate, Him from that Lord whom they must always think of as the common Lord of all, as the Mediator between man and God, as standing at the right hand of God, as their way to the Father. Just as likewise they must always distinguish the Son from the Father, whom He trusts and loves and obeys, whose will He does, whose perfect image He is.

I should not have dwelt so much upon this text if I had not known, in my own small experience, that it is one which is very dear to simple people, and one upon which some of them meditate day and night. It seems to me to contain the resolution of that difficulty which you feel so strongly—and not more strongly than a multitude of laymen and clergymen—about the Christ in us and the Spirit in us. We should never forget that Christ is the Anointed of the Spirit; that St. Paul, the great witness for Christ as made unto us wisdom, righteousness, sanctification, says, "If we have not the spirit of Christ we are none of His."

Those chapters in the Epistle to the Romans contain, it seems to me, the most skillful and profound exposition of that relation between the subject and the object which our formal schoolmen make into such a hard crust for the understanding to bite through. It is not a school formula, it is a living principle in the very nature of things and of man. And it is in the nature of man because its prototype is in the nature of God. We realize it in that distinction and union of the Spirit in us, with Christ in and over all, which St. Paul sets forth. That distinction and union imply a Father from whom the Son comes, of whom the Spirit testifies. That unity of the Father and the Son and the Spirit, one God of Love blessed forever, is beneath all.

It seems to me that we may in this way ascend from the Pauline theology, which is that of the Reformation, that of our Evangelicals, to the truth which, as you hint, modern Evangelicals, and in some, though not in the same, degree, their fathers, have converted into a mere explanation of our justification and sanctification, and so have grievously imperiled. They will, I trust, be led through their own wonderful teacher to look at the Gospel less selfishly, to regard it as a Gospel for mankind; then the full meaning of the old Creeds will come out of them. If not, they will be distanced by the Unitarians, many of whom are rising, through their old confession of a Father and their new apprehension of a Spirit working in them—not without many plunges down into a Pantheistic abyss—to that real and profound belief in the "divine Unity," which they were groping after through what Coleridge called their "Worship of Unity."

Having been bred amongst them, I must needs sympathize much in struggles to which I owe everything. Nor have I any greater cause for thankfulness than this, that God did not suffer me, in the fierce reaction against their denials, and what appeared to me their feebleness, to lose sight of the truth which is implied in their name; although in the pursuit of it I have been led to the very opposite point of the compass from theirs.

With respect to your remarks that the Old Testament was the preparation for the Son, as the New may be the preparation for the Spirit, I would observe:

1. That the New Testament opens with the announcement, "He shall baptize with the Spirit"; that the baptism of Jesus Himself with the Spirit is inseparable from the account of Him as the Son; that He goes by the Spirit into the wilderness to be tempted by the evil spirit; that the whole battle of His life on earth as described in the Gospels is with evil spirits; that the gift

196

of the Spirit at Pentecost opens the New Kingdom of which the declaration, "He whom you crucified is both Lord and Christ," was the formal proclamation; that the distinction between the Old and New is always expressed in the words, "That which was hidden before, God has now revealed to His holy apostles and prophets by the Spirit." I think, then, that the old opinion is right. We are *in* the age of the Spirit; not looking forward to it.

2. The Old Testament revealed neither the Father nor the Son *as such*. What strikes me most in opening the Gospels—say, at the Sermon on the Mount—is this new name of Father. One has had the hint of it in the heathen world, in the old "mythologies"; at first one is inclined to say, "Scarcely a hint in the Law and the Prophets." Look again, and you see not hints, but an orderly preparation for this revelation; or, to speak more correctly, the commencement of it. The revelation of an unseen guide and protector is the foundation of the Abrahamic family. The revelation of the guide as the "*I am*," the absolute Lord and Lawgiver, is the foundation of the Jewish commonwealth and code. The revelation of the King sitting on the holy hill of Zion, of *my* Lord, to whom the Lord says, "Sit at my right hand," is the foundation of the Jewish royalty. The revelation of the Word speaking to and in the holy men is the foundation of the Jewish prophecy. Everywhere is the proclamation of a One God; in the law the formal curse and denunciation of the worship of any god but the One. Yet all the wonderful defense against idolatry and the experiences of the slavery to which it leads, are not discoveries of the divine Unity. The impulse to human and to animal worship is tremendous; the best men are most agitated with the question, "How can He whose glory is above the heavens care for us worms upon earth?" The Israelite felt the deep necessity of believing in the Protector, Friend, Lawgiver, King, Inspirer. That necessity drew him to prayer. In prayer he attained a sense of unity which in the world he could never find.

That one should stand forth and say, "I am that King of whom David spoke, the King who has been reigning over you so long: I was with Abraham; I know the innermost meaning of the Law that was given on Sinai; I am the Word who spoke to the prophets," would not have satisfied the wants and cravings that had been awakened in Israelites, unless He could have said also, "I came from a Father; I will baptize you with the Holy Ghost." He was expected; He was the desire of that nation and of all nations. But He would not have accomplished the expectation and desire; they must still have looked for another if He had not been able to say this, and to do what He said.

3. And so, I think, we arrive at the explanation of St. John's words, "The Spirit was not yet, because that Jesus was not yet glorified." The baptism with the Spirit is the recognition of men, of men of every nation, and kindred, and tribe, as the sons of God in the only-begotten Son; the acknowledgment of men as spirits capable of holding communion with the divine Spirit, capable of falling under the dominion of evil spirits, redeemed from that dominion by God Himself, consecrated to be His ministers. The baptism of the Spirit was thus the formation, out of a particular nation, of a universal society capable of adopting all nations into itself, a society having its home both in earth and heaven; witnessing of God's love and gracious purposes to all the kindreds of earth; witnessing that they are, as spiritual beings, under the direct government of God Himself. Nothing like this had been or could be in the former days. Till Christ was glorified, till it was fully declared that the Son of man is the Son of God by the resurrection from the dead, till it was shown that the barrier of death does not separate the two worlds, there could not be this manifestation of a personal Spirit dwelling in a Universal Church.

But though I differ from you in thinking that we are to wait in any sense for the Spirit as the gift of a future dispensation, I fully agree with what I take to be the meaning of the observation, that we have much to learn, perhaps a tremendous crisis to pass through before we learn, respecting our own position as baptized with the Spirit and so made Children of God. I foresee a terrible breaking down of notions, opinions, even of most precious beliefs, an overthrow of what we call our religion—a convulsion far greater than that of the sixteenth century—in our way to reformation and unity.

Still I believe they will come, and that they will come through an unveiling to our hearts of the old mystery of the Trinity, in which our fathers believed, but which they made an excuse for exclusion and persecution, not a bond of fellowship, a message of peace and deliverance to mankind. The preaching of the Trinity in its fullness will, I conceive, be the everlasting Gospel to the nations, which will involve the overthrow of the Babel polity, and the brutal tyrannies as well as the foul superstitions of the earth. So long as we substitute for it the preaching of God as the destroyer, not the righteous Judge of men, so long as we deny that He has revealed Himself in the Lamb that was slain from the foundation of the world; so long I believe the inhabitants of the world will not fall before us, and that it is not good for them that they should.

These last hints belong to another part of the Bible than the Pauline Epistles. I believe the Apocalypse to be the book which will at last be found to remove most veils from this mystery, as well as from the meaning of all the previous Bible history, and from the course of God's government of the world from the beginning to the end. But on that subject I must not enter now.

▶ 104. To the Reverend Isaac Taylor, on April 10, 1860, about liturgical revision

Your kind and friendly treatment of an article which might easily and excusably have annoyed you, deserves my warm thanks. That you should remember any former instructions of mine with pleasure and should still regard me as a fellow laborer, is a sincere satisfaction to me. But it is a much greater satisfaction that you should accept so cordially the doctrine that God has claimed us all in Christ as His sons, which seems to me the "Article on which the Church stands or falls"; where I use the *Article* not in its vulgar sense as importing that which is formal and dogmatic, but that which is necessary to the vitality and coherency of the body of Christ. *Individuals* may hold fast the faith of their own adoption while they rather rejoice to think that mankind are accursed; but the Church must either fulfill its witness of a redemption for mankind, or be cut off. And I cannot help thinking that a time is at hand when we shall awaken to this conviction, and when we shall perceive that what we call our individual salvation means nothing, and that our faith in it becomes untenable when we separate it from the salvation which Christ wrought out for the world by His incarnation and sacrifice, resurrection and ascension.

When you add to the assurance of your own belief the statement that the Dissenters embody the idea of the divine Fatherhood in all the forms of prayer which they approve (though I should like more specific illustrations of it that I might know what exactly it amounts to), I yet take it with all thankfulness and joy. But it strengthens me in my conviction that such changes as the Evangelical clergy of our own communion are likely to desire and recommend cannot meet the wants of the Dissenters. For certainly they assent with manifest reluctance to the broad language of the Catechism and of our prayers; and when that language is transferred from the Liturgy into any unauthorized forms, they pronounce it heretical.

A friend and old pupil of mine sent me, only a fortnight ago, some family prayers of his, which he said his friends and neighbors among the clergy had declared to be very objectionable solely on this ground. I have been listening during the last week to sermons in this place, which are, I apprehend, good average specimens of watering-place divinity. The tone in them is uniform. *In a certain sense* all men being created by God are His children; *in a somewhat more enlarged sense* that name may be given to the baptized, in the *only true and important sense* it is restricted to the true believers; to those who are conscious of having Christ as their personal Savior. In this way the Gospel of God to man is emptied of its power; faith, not God, is made the source of every good and perfect gift.

Now, can one, who regards this inversion as one which is as much undermining the faith and morality of this generation as the glorification of works undermined the faith and morality of the sixteenth century, patiently consent that the Liturgy should be remodeled by the hands of those who are sanctioning it? I am convinced that they are sanctioning it against their higher and diviner instincts; that the opposition to it comes from the striving of the Spirit of God in them; that when they adopt the words of the Liturgy *as it is*, they are not affronting their consciences but only the opinions of their school. The distinction, I own, is a perilous one. I do not wish that they should be forced to make it.

200

I would abolish the Act of Uniformity that they may not be forced to make it. I would do this with my eyes open; knowing their power; knowing the influence they possess with the bench of bishops; knowing that I and others who think with me are far safer under the protection of an Act of Parliament than we should be if left to the mercy of an ecclesiastical public opinion, dictated by the journals, executed by the episcopate. But such considerations ought not, I conceive, to move us in the least. Let us have an honest clergy at all hazards, or as honest a one as we can get. But do not let us surrender the one great witness which we possess, that a nation consists of redeemed men, sons of God, that mankind stands not in Adam but in Christ. Give up the Prayer Book to an Evangelical or semi-Evangelical commission, and this witness will be eliminated from it by a thousand little alterations, which will be counted insignificant; but which will in fact render the English Church another Church altogether.

"But the Broad Church will have its representatives in such a commission!" I do not know well what the Broad Church is. I always took it to be a fiction of Conybeare's. If it means anything, I suppose it is a representation, under different modifications, of that creed which is contained in Whately's books, or of that which has arisen at Oxford out of the reaction against Tractarianism. Now I must say that I would rather trust a living Book to the lowest Churchman who had imbibed any of his lore from Newton or Romaine, than to these accomplished and tolerant persons. Personally I have the greatest respect for them; so far as they protest against any cowardice and deceit in handling the Word of God, . . . so far I am willing to bear any disgrace with them. But that which seems to me the great disease of our time, that we talk about God and about our religion, and do not confess Him as a living God; Himself the redeemer of men in His Son; Himself the inspirer of all right thoughts, the guide into all truth by His Spirit, is characteristic of no school so much as of this (I mean when it resolves to be a school).

The Liturgy has been to me a great theological teacher; a perpetual testimony that the Father, the Son, and the Spirit, the one God blessed forever, is the author of all life, freedom, unity to men; that our prayers are nothing but responses to His voice speaking to us and in us. Why do I hear nothing of this from those who profess to reform it? Why do they appear only to treat it as an old praying machine, which in the course of centuries gets out of order like other machines, and which should be altered according to the improved mechanical notions of our time? . . .

▶ 105. To "Q" from Newport Salop, August 23, 1860

. . . Every year and day convinces me more that our preaching will be good for nothing if the main subject of it is not the atonement of God with man in Christ—if we may not proclaim His sacrifice as a finished work; if we may not ground all our sacrifices upon it; if we stop short of the Eucharistic proclamation that God of His tender mercy hath given us His Son to be a full, perfect, and sufficient sacrifice, oblation, and satisfaction for the sins of the whole world. Any notions, theories, practices, which interfere with the fullness of this Gospel deprive men, it seems to me, of a blessing which has been bestowed upon them and to which they have a right—deprive them of the only effectual foundation for social and individual reformation.

What I say of preaching, I say also of prayers. If they are separated from the confession and presentation of the perfect Sacrifice, once made—if they are not petitions that the will which is expressed in that sacrifice may be done on earth as it is in heaven, if they are not presented through the High Priest and Mediator within the veil—they are, in my judgment, not Christian prayers. I say not that they are ineffectual; for it is He who makes prayers effectual which are very dark and ignorant (otherwise what would become of us?); but I say that they are anticipations of a Gospel—attempts to reach an unknown, unrevealed God—not derived from the Gospel of God, from the revelation of the perfectly righteous and loving Being in the perfect Mediator.

Starting from these premises, I am bound to say that I do look upon many of the most popular statements respecting the Atonement, as interfering with the fullness of this Gospel, as interfering with the finished work of Christ, as robbing an immense portion of mankind of the blessing which the Bible declares to be theirs,

202

as having the effect of inverting prayers, of divorcing them from Christ's sacrifice, of changing them into petitions that God's will should not be done, but should be changed.

I look upon these popular notions as exceedingly natural, as embodying thoughts and feelings which every man ought to be acquainted with in himself, and to deal most tenderly with in others, as containing elements of old pre-Evangelical philosophy which all students and divines ought to be familiar with; but as forming no part of the message from God to man, except so far as that message meets all the confused speculations and anticipations of the human heart, and satisfies its inner craving after God, and its secret testimonies respecting Him, by sweeping away the dark imaginations which it must form of Him when it creates Him after its own likeness.

All notions respecting a conflict in the divine mind between the claims of justice and mercy; all notions of the Son winning from the Father that which did not proceed from His own free, gracious will; all notions which substitute the deliverance from punishment for the deliverance from sin; all notions which weaken the force of the words, or make them anything less than the classical words on this matter, "Lo, I come to do thy will, oh God," are, it seems to me, of this kind, subversive of the divine revelation, rationalistic in the worst sense of that word, not to be countenanced or tolerated.

[These notions] are to be avoided even at the risk of parting with words in themselves innocent and (provided they are not scriptural words, which will always be found safe and sufficient) not to be played with or tampered with from any worldly calculation that the humble and meek cannot afford to dispense with them, seeing that the humble and meek crave for the pure milk of God's word that they may grow thereby, and are cruelly treated when those whom they reverence introduce any adulterations into it; or from any equally worldly calculations that those who doubt or deny the Atonement will take courage from the effort to separate the Gospel and the Church message concerning it from the elements which have defiled it, seeing that these elements are the great justification of their unbelief to the consciences of the sincere, seeing that those who merely cultivate unbelief as a profession, hate nothing so much as these efforts to distinguish, and as those who make them.

These are my convictions, which have grown stronger and stronger in me in every day, so far as the grandeur and necessity of the divine Atonement has been more manifested to me; weaker and weaker so far as I have lost sight of it, or have not given thanks for it. They have been accompanied by an ever deepening feeling that the danger of this age as of all previous ages—of the age in which our Lord dwelt on earth in human flesh most conspicuously—is not chiefly from those who consciously or unconsciously depart from orthodoxy; but from those who make orthodoxy an excuse for denying the Union of the Father with the Son, the perfect Manifestation of the Father in the Son; the desire of the Father and the Son by the Spirit to bring all men into the obedience of the Truth. I have therefore been found, and by God's grace I hope still to be found (when I am obliged to fight), fighting always against the popular, not the unpopular, men of the day. . . .

▶ **106. To the Reverend A. P. Stanley, February 12, 1861, about the stir caused by the publication of Essays and Reviews**

I am greatly distressed at the Episcopal movement about the *Essays and Reviews*. As my only hope of resisting the devil worship of the religious world lies in preaching the full revelation of God in Christ set forth in the Bible, I cannot have much sympathy with the book generally. But I look upon the efforts to suppress it as mere struggles to keep off the question, "What dost thou believe? dost thou believe in anything?" which must be forced upon each of us, the bishops included. The orthodoxy which covers our Atheism must be broken through, and whether it is done by the *Essays and Reviews* or in any other way, seems to me a matter of indifference, though it is not a matter of indifference whether the Church shall be committed to a new persecution which must make the new reformation, when it comes, more complicated and terrible. . . .

107. To Mr. J. M. Ludlow on the Trinity, March 15, 1861

. . . Your language respecting the doctrine of the Trinity that it "expresses certain profound relations in the Divine nature" is perhaps as skillfully chosen as any language could be to describe a certain contemplative belief of ours *ab-extra*. If I could put my thoughts about my own opinion about the Trinity into a phrase I could not find any that I should like much better. But it is precisely this which I feel myself unable to do. The name of the Father, the Son, and the Holy Ghost is for me the name of the God in whom I am living and moving, and having my being. It is the name into which I baptize little children, which is about them as they grow up into men, which is to reveal itself to them in all their conflicts and hopes, their sorrows and joys, which their doubts and their infidelity, like their faith, are instruments in making known to them.

So I have felt it to be myself, having been brought up a Unitarian, and having learned by every fresh experience that in the fullest and best sense of the word I can be nothing else than a Unitarian—the pursuit of unity being the end which God has set before me from my cradle upward, the confession of unity as infinite, embracing, sustaining, being the confession which I make in the Creed that I have accepted in my mature years. I cannot ask anyone else to understand this experience or force the utterance of the results of it upon any. But I do perceive that if I have any work in the world it is to bear witness of this Name, not as expressing certain relations, however profound, in the divine nature, but as the underground of all fellowship among men and angels, as that which will at last bind all into one, satisfying all the craving of the reason as well as of the heart, meeting the desires and intuitions that are scattered through all the religions of the world. A phrase like that of yours, it seems to me, might be a fine scholastical meeting point for men who were content to sink their strongest convictions upon the subject of which they were speaking, for the sake of a compromise, but would only mislead our readers respecting the object which we all have at heart. . . .

▶ 108. To Mr. J. M. Ludlow, May 23, 1861

I do as I would be done by. I should like everything I write to be criticized in like manner, and to appear with the criticisms unanswered, unless what I have said answers them. Nothing you have said alters my opinion that we can do the world most good by setting forth our beliefs in our different modes, by fairly exposing the difference and the conflict of those modes, and by expressing or manifesting our conviction that they are reconciled in a Truth of which we have a strong and vital, though an imperfect perception. This is my idea of criticism, and of what you and [the Reverend C. K.] Paul name compromise. Criticism, it seems to me, will be always negative, cruel, *Saturday Review*-ish, unless it becomes an interchange of thoughts between men who care much for each other and more for Truth.

Compromise must always tend to the impairing of moral vigor, and to the perplexing of the conscience, if it is anything else than a confession of the completeness of Truth, and of the incompleteness of our apprehension of it. I accept the Articles as a witness of truths which I cannot comprehend in my little system, and which my neighbor cannot comprehend in his little system. But God forbid that I should accept them if they compel me to give up any portion of that which I believe to him, or him to give up any portion of that which he believes to me. These are the compromises of politicians, which have no place in the kingdom of God, seeing that they are based on calculations of self-interest and fear, not on mutual sacrifice. . . .

▶ 109. To a lady, on August 3, 1861, about Holy Communion

If I did not believe that you and I and all people whatsoever have actually been redeemed by the sacrifice of the eternal Son of God, and that in His flesh and blood there is a new and living way consecrated for us into the presence of God, I would not urge you to frequent the Communion table. Because I do believe this and am sure that such a redemption goes beneath all thoughts, dreams, apprehensions, and that we only approach God because

He has drawn us to Him, therefore I say, "No thought about our feelings or qualifications, the amount of our faith, the consistency of our lives, the sincerity of our repentance, ought to keep us back." We go to confess the want of feelings and qualifications, the inconsistency of our lives, and the insincerity of our repentance; we go to ask that God will give us what we have need of out of His fullness.

But above all we want the witness and pledge of a common salvation, of a God who cares for all in Christ as much as for us. We want the plainest testimonies, those that are least dependent upon our temperament or state of mind, that He is the same yesterday and today and forever. The Sacrifice is His; He gives up His Son for us all. The Son went with the Father fulfilling His will. We can but come, recollecting that perfect Sacrifice, giving God thanks that He is perfectly satisfied with us in His Son, asking to have the Spirit of Sacrifice, and that that Spirit, who is within us convincing us of righteousness, of judgment, may dwell in us and quicken us to all the good works which God has prepared for us to walk in.

You will be tormented, as all are in this day, with thoughts about the meaning and extent and necessity of Christ's sacrifice. The more you connect it with Communion, the more you interpret its meaning, its extent, its necessity by the fellowship it establishes between you and God, between you and your brother, by the only not infinite resistance which there is to that fellowship in yourself and in your brother—the more will you overcome these difficulties practically if not theoretically; and the practical conquest of this is what we need, the other will come so far as we require it. The very words which indicate the Lord's Supper— "Eucharist" and "Communion"—are explanatory of the whole Gospel, of our necessities, of the way in which God has satisfied them.

▶ 110. To the Reverend E. Philips, on April 20, 1862, about the New Testament conception of the devil

I am afraid I shall never succeed in persuading you that I mean what I say, and have not some esoteric doctrine which I wish to hide. I do not *talk* about the personality of the devil or the spirits of whom I read in the New Testament, because I do not find the writers of the New Testament talking about it, and because I believe I should convey a very confused impression to my hearers if I did. They might fancy that by personality I intend some bodily form, of which I hear nothing and know nothing; though if I did hear or know anything, the hearing or the knowledge would give me no trouble and no satisfaction. A spirit and only a spirit is to me personal. I do not call a frog or a flea a person, for it is not spiritual. Whenever I am told of a spirit, evil or good, I at once assume that that is like me, can hold converse with me, can tempt me to wrong, can encourage me to right.

The Holy Spirit is the inspirer, as I believe, of all the energies by which my personal life manifests itself. He gives me the sense that I am a person; how can He be impersonal? The evil spirit speaks to me as a person, tempts me to think that I am not a person, tries to reduce me into a thing. I never should dream of calling him a thing. What then do you require of me? I believe in nations not in nationalities, in persons not in personalities. I avoid these popular newspaper phrases, not because I covet abstractions, but because I hate them.

Mr. Hall, the Baptist preacher, was once accosted by one of his confrères: "Sir, do not you believe in the devil?" "No, Sir," he answered. "I believe in God. Do not you?" Now he had an intense feeling of the Devil as his personal and constant enemy; but he kept his *belief* for his everlasting friend.

▶ *111. An autobiographical part of a letter (probably 1830-34) to Mr. Hutton describing Maurice's incarnational theology of Christ as the Head of the race; published in* Tracts for Priests and People *(1862)*

. . . It led me to ask myself, "What does that unfallen nature of Adam mean? Did not Adam stand by God's grace, by trust in Him? Did he not fall by trying to be something in himself? Could he have had a nature which was good, independent of

God, more than we? Is not such a notion a subversion of Christian belief? But *did* the race ever stand in him? Old theology taught quite a different doctrine."

Our own Articles set forth Christ very God and very man—not Adam—as now and always the Head of the race. They teach us of an infection of nature which exists in every son of Adam. They call that a departure from original righteousness. This original righteousness stands, and has always stood, in Christ the Son of God, and in Him only. Here, it seemed to me, was the true practical solution of the difficulty. I could believe that the Head of man had entered fully into the condition of every man, had suffered the temptations of every man, had wrestled with the enemy of every man; and that He had brought *our* humanity untainted and perfect through that struggle. And this because He had never lost his trust in His Father, His obedience to His Father—had never asserted independence as Adam did, as each one of us is continually doing.

His temptations become, then, real in the most tremendous sense. They were more fierce than any mere individual can ever undergo. He did, in truth, feel the sins—bear the sins—of the whole world. And every man may turn to Him as knowing his own special danger, his easily besetting sins, as having felt the power of them. And no man has a right to say, "My race is a sinful, fallen race," even when he most confesses the greatness of his own sin and fall; because he is bound to contemplate his race in the Son of God, and to claim by faith in Him his share of its redemption and its glory. I can therefore do justice to the Unitarian protest against the language in which many who call themselves orthodox describe the condition of mankind, just because I adopt the belief in the perfect divinity and the perfect manhood of the Son of God. I can, with the inmost conviction, assert that in me—that is, in my flesh—dwelleth no good thing, just because I feel that all good which is in me, or in anyone, is derived from the perfect humanity of Christ, and that, apart from that, I am merely evil. Just so far as I have been able to grasp this belief in a Head of humanity—just so far the greatest problems of ethics seem to me to find a solution; just so far do I see a light in the midst of the deepest darkness, a hope rising out of the

209

depths of despair, a unity which is mightier than all sects and divisions.

112. To his son Edmund at Oxford, who had written about Mr. Jowett in June (or July), 1862

. . . Nevertheless, I do not undervalue legends. They contain man's attempts to feel after God's ideas; they bear witness that no idea can be presented to us without some vesture. But the vesture of God's own ideas must be facts. If He reveals His ideas to us, the revelation must be through facts. I accept the revelation recorded in the Scriptures as a revelation of the divine mind through facts. I accept all History as revelation of some portion of the divine mind through facts. I believe the modern process of idealizing tends to destroy ideas and facts both, and to leave nothing but a certain deposit of both. The sensation novel is the appropriate sink or cesspool for this deposit.

All historical criticism is good, it seems to me, just so far as it tests facts in love and reverence for facts, and for what facts contain; all is bad and immoral which introduces the notion that it signifies little whether they turn out to be facts or no, or the notion that their reality as facts depends upon certain accidents in the narration of them. I do not believe Mr. Jowett would ever encourage either notion, though both are encouraged by men called orthodox and called liberal.

▶ 113. To his son Frederick in the army and about to leave for India, August, 1862

. . . I prize the words of our ordination service. I may have entered very imperfectly into them when I used them first, though I did not use them dishonestly. But every year has made it clearer to me that I have no right and no power to speak a word if the Spirit of God is not really with me, and that I was to say so once and am to say so still, that other men who need His presence as much as I do may be confident that He is also with them and may ask for His guidance continually.

I know how many there are who would tell me that I might apply this language to any occupation more properly than to yours. They will say that your calling cannot be a godly one, that I am profaning what is holy when I am daring to talk of a Spirit of love and peace as dwelling with the soldier and prompting his deeds. I have considered the arguments of those who speak thus— I was brought up to regard them as almost self-evident; I have deliberately rejected them.

The Bible has convinced me, history has convinced me, personal experience has convinced me, that they are not true. I find the expression "Lord of Hosts" everywhere in the Scriptures, and I accept it as a right and honest expression of a great truth. I find that the leaders of armies and that armies themselves have done nobly works which I recognize as God's works. I find a spirit of order and obedience in them which I scarcely find elsewhere, and which I wish civilians could imitate. I find justice, gentleness, tenderness not merely mixing with such qualities in military men, but eminently characteristic of some among them. This being the case, I have solemnly and with my whole heart and soul refused to make an exception from the maxim which I think governs all offices and undertakings in the case of the office and undertaking of the soldier.

I recognize him in battles and in the preparation for battle, as the servant of the living God. I believe the Spirit of God as really calls him to his duties and fits him for them as He calls me to mine. And having this faith—without which it would be anguish to think of you in India or anywhere—I feel more bound to insist upon this principle when I discourse about soldiers than in almost any other case.

For I see how terrible have been, how far more terrible must be, the effects of a loss of this faith, in the mind of armies generally, and of the individuals who compose them. The sense of power which armies give is something so tremendous—the illustrations of it in the history of the Roman armies, which had prevailed through discipline and obedience, when they began to think they could govern the state and make emperors, are so

211

palpable—that every true citizen must ask himself, "Who will guard our guardians, who will keep them from being our destroyers?" The question is serious at all times, it was never so serious as now, when the faith in mere constitutional arrangements is growing faint, when so many are crying out for that organization of forces which they say is only to be attained under a military despot.

If while this temper is appearing among civilians, the soldier parts with the feeling, which has never been extinct yet in the Englishman, though at times desperately weak, of a vocation, if he accepts the statement of pious men that he is only a devil's instrument, the prospect for this land and for all lands is darker than one dares to contemplate. But a mere vague impression of there being something good, gentlemanlike, patriotic in your profession will not avail to counteract this temptation, which will become greater every day, which many of the circumstances of such a country as India are likely to foster.

Nothing, I believe, short of a firm conviction, growing with the experience of personal weakness, that you have a calling, that it cannot be fulfilled unless you are just, manly, gentle in all your doings to all the people with whom you converse, and that there is a divine Overseer of your thoughts and purposes who is inspiring you with justice, manliness, gentleness, who is fighting in you against what is false, inhuman, ungracious, and that your Guide, Teacher, Restrainer, is the Guide and Teacher and Restrainer, whether they heed Him or not, of all your superiors, equals, dependents, of your own countrymen, and of the natives— nothing but this will stand you in stead when savage impulses get hold of you, and there are motives which seem to justify them, and the public opinion of your class is in favor of them, and you have the power of indulging them.

▶ 114. To the Reverend J. L. Davis about Bishop Colenso's book on the Pentateuch, September 23, 1862

The pain which Colenso's book has caused me is more than I can tell you. I used nearly your words, "It is the most purely negative criticism I ever read," in writing to him. Our correspondence has been frequent but perfectly unavailing. He seems to imagine himself a great critic and discoverer, and I am afraid he has met with an encouragement which will do him unspeakable mischief. He says I have only appealed to his pride in my argument. I fancy I wounded his pride even more than I ought. I appealed to his love of truth. I asked him whether he did not think Samuel must have been a horrid scoundrel if he forged a story about the I AM speaking to Moses, and to my unspeakable surprise and terror he said, "No. Many good men had done such things. He might not mean more than Milton meant." He even threw out the notion that the Pentateuch might be a poem; and when I said that to a person who had ever asked himself what a poem is, the notion was simply ridiculous, he showed that his idea of poetry was that it is something which is not historical. And his idea of history is that it is a branch of arithmetic. . . .

But I cannot forget his exceeding generosity to me at a very great risk to himself. If I am bound by my duty to the Church, and to him as a friend, to remonstrate on the course he is now pursuing, I am also bound not to let anyone suppose I desert him for the sake of preserving my own position. These considerations make my course somewhat embarrassing. I do, however, begin to see clearly at least what is demanded of me. That is one of the points on which I should like to talk to you; though I would rather have been here than in London.

▶ **115. To Mr. Hughes concerning a proposed meeting at Exeter Hall to rally sentiment against slavery with respect to the Civil War in the United States, January 26, 1863**

I have not seen any notice of the Exeter Hall meeting at which you said you should appear, and I don't know what is its definite object. I feel very strongly, as I told the congregation at Vere Street yesterday afternoon, that the invitation to sympathize with those who declare slavery to be the cornerstone of their institutions should be resisted by all who believe in another cornerstone than that. The attempt of the American divines and English

213

newspapers to enlist St. Paul and the New Testament on their side are to be exposed as ridiculous and denounced as hypocritical. I tried in my own place as a clergyman to do this. And I would go to Exeter Hall at least as one of the audience for the same purpose, if I did not feel that the cause was too sacred a one to connect with the faith, the policy, or the success of the North. A wrong move in that direction may, it seems to me, prove very mischievous and throw the game into the hands of the *Times* and *Saturday Review*.

I think *they* have made a false move, they have presumed on the dislike of the English people to the Federals, and on their liking for any vigorous insurgency, and are thrusting forward their pro-slavery arguments rashly and in a way that will not be borne. I should say, do not cut the rope short with which they may hang themselves. Let them fairly and thoroughly commit themselves to the cause which they have in their hearts, let them not have an excuse for confusing it with criticisms upon the blunders of the North or of the English supporters of the North. . . .

▶ 116. To the Reverend J. De la Touche who was considering resignation because of doubts about his faith, written from Holder House, Dorking, April 14, 1863

I do not know whether you will think me less or more fitted to enter into that tremendous difficulty of which you speak in your last letter, when I tell you that I was brought up a Unitarian, and that I have distinctly and deliberately accepted the belief which is expressed in the Nicene Creed as the only satisfaction of the infinite want which Unitarianism awakened in me, yes, and as the only vindication of the truth which Unitarianism taught me.

You feel that our Lord is a man in the most perfect sense of the word. You cannot convince yourself that He is more. No, nor will any arguments convince you that He is more. For what do you mean by that *more*? Is it a *Jupiter Tonans* whom you are investing with the name of God? Is it to him you pray when you say, "Our Father which art in heaven"? *Is* God a Father, really and actually a Father? Is He in heaven far away from our con-

214

ceptions and confusions, One whom we cannot make in the likeness of anything above, around, beneath us? Or is all this a dream? Is there no God, no Father? Has He never made Himself known, never come near to men? Can men never come near to Him?

Are you startled that I put *these* questions to you? Do they seem more terrible than any that have yet presented themselves to you? Oh, they are the way back to the faith of the little child; and to the faith of the grown man. It is not Christ about whom our doubts are. We are feeling after God if haply we may find Him. We cannot find Him in Nature. Paley [in his *Natural Theology*] will not reveal Him to us. But He is very near us; very near to those creatures whom He has formed in His own image; seeking after them; speaking to them in a thousand ways.

The belief of a Son who was with Him before all worlds, in whom He created and loves the world; who for us men and for our salvation came down from heaven and became incarnate, and died, and was buried, and rose again for us and ascended on high to be the High Priest of the universe; this belief is what? Something that I can prove by texts of Scripture or by cunning arguments of logic? God forbid! I simply commend it to you. I know that you want it. I know that it meets exactly what your spirit is looking after and cannot meet with in any books of divinity. For we have to find out that God is not in a book, that He *is*, that He must reveal Himself to us, that He is revealing Himself to us.

I am *not* distressed that you should be brought to feel that these deep and infinite questions—not questions about the arithmetic of the Bible—are what are really haunting and tormenting you. I believe that the clergy must make this discovery. We have been repeating phrases and formulas. We have not entered into them, but only have accepted certain reasonings and proofs about them. Now they are starting up and looking at us as if they were alive, and we are frightened at the sight. It is good for us to be frightened, only let us not turn away from them and find fault with them, but ask God, if we believe that He can hear us, to search us and show us what is true and to bring us out of our Atheism.

How, you ask, can I use the prayers of the Church which assume Christ's divinity when I cannot see sufficient proof that He is divine? That is a question, it seems to me, which no man can answer for you; nay, which you cannot answer for yourself. If I am right, it is in prayer you must find the answer. Yes, in prayer to be able to pray; in prayer to know what prayer is; in prayer to know whether, without a mediator, prayer is not a dream and an impossibility for you, me, everyone. I cannot solve this doubt. I can but show you how to get it solved. I can but say, the doubt itself may be the greatest blessing you ever had, may be the greatest striving of God's Spirit within you that you have ever known, may be the means of making every duty more real to you.

I do not know who your bishop is. If he is a person with whom it is possible to communicate freely, I should tell him that I had perplexities which made the use of the Prayer Book not as true to me as it once was, that I wanted time for quiet thought; that I should like to be silent for a little while—I would ask him to let me commit my charge to a curate till I could see my way more clearly. That would be better, surely, than a resignation, painful not merely to your friends but injurious to the Church, and perhaps a reason for severe repentance afterward. But I may be only increasing your puzzles by this suggestion. Of the fathers in God on earth I have no certainty. Of the Father in Heaven I can be quite certain. Therefore one of my hints may be worth nothing. The other is worth everything.

▶ 117. To a clergyman, on commerce and theology, July 1, 1863

I acknowledge as fully as anyone can that commerce is an instrument in the divine education and that if there is, lying at the root of Society, the recognition of the unity of men in Christ, the actual intercourse of men in different countries will bring out that belief into clearness and fullness, and remove the limitation and narrowness which arise from the confusion between Christ Himself and our notions about Him. But that commerce is in itself apart from this principle any bond of brotherhood whatever—that it does not rather lead to the denial of all brotherhood, to murderous conflicts between labor and capital, to slavery and slave trade—I know not how in the face of the most patent and recent facts it is possible to maintain. In the sixth century there were mobs in Constantinople partly to uphold blue or green in the circus, partly to put down Monophysite or Nestorian opinions. In Boston, in the nineteenth century, there were mobs to put down Mr. Garrison and the supporters of the Negroes. You may if you please say that Theodora and her mobs were working in the supposed interests of theology, you must say also that the New England mobs were working in the supposed interest of commerce. That both were mistaken on their own grounds we are agreed; but that admission does not prove commerce to be a more uniting principle than theology.

On the contrary, I am thoroughly convinced that all the scandals and falsehoods which are most reasonably complained of in modern theology result from its mixture with commerce and the adoption of commercial principles as the groundwork of it. Mr. Bright said most truly at the meeting on Saturday that from the time the slave states adopted the doctrine that slavery was a divine institution the question became a religious one, and a religious war was inevitable. That is the most conspicuous and flagrant instance of the adoption in a money-worshiping community of a religion based on the acknowledgment of a God who is the enemy of Mammon into its service. But it is only an instance.

Our English theology, popular as well as systematic, has been gradually reconstructing itself on the commercial or material bases; I find it the hardest thing possible not to adopt phrases in the pulpit and in writing which assume its habits and motives. The creeds have been the perpetual witnesses to me against this commercial theology, which is, I believe, helping to destroy our commercial as well as our personal morality. I agree with you that St. John's words are in direct opposition to the inferences which have been deduced from the Athanasian Creed, and indeed from all the creeds. But St. John's words have been made intelligible to me in their length and breadth by the creeds. The limitation of God's favor to Christians arises, it seems to me, from the notion that a Christ who came into existence eighteen hundred years ago is the Head of a sect, not the Light of Light, the very God of very God.

217

A simply humanitarian Christianity, whatever largeness it may affect in theory, will practically shut up humanity within the conceptions of the person who professes it. Humanitarians will therefore try to throw off Christianity as a restraint. But the vagueness and hollowness of a mere worship of abstract humanity will soon be palpable to them. What must follow, Comte has admirably illustrated in his own practice, though of course he could not foresee the developments of his scheme or his example. . . .

▶ *118. To Miss Williams Wynn about Renan's* Life of Jesus, *December 22, 1863*

. . . I can *hope* for good from it abroad in this way. I think the image of an actual living Christ has been so hidden under earthly disguises, that I can imagine Renan himself and many of his readers awaking up for the first time to the conviction, "There actually was such a Person as the Evangelists speak of! He did live in Palestine 1,800 years ago. He is not merely a picture of our fancy." I think this; and I think also that some earnest priests may begin to say to themselves, "Why is this so? What have we done to earn that this should be so? How can we begin from henceforth to declare a Christ who was born and died, but who rose and liveth evermore?"

If the first thought—still more if the last—should be aroused, we may give God thanks that such a book has been permitted to come forth. We may perceive that He is justified even now in His doings as we know He will be hereafter. But when I look at the book itself, I can see nothing but plausible and graceful falsehood. M. Renan's Jesus is not the one whom your friend or you have reverenced. He is a charming Galilean with a certain sympathy for beautiful scenery and an affectionate tenderness for the peasants who follow him; but he is provoked to violence, impatience, base trickery, as soon as he finds his mission as a reformer unsuccessful.

The Frenchman bred amidst pious frauds calls him the most delightful and wonderful of men, who practices innocent artifices, resorts to thaumaturgy unwillingly, but when he does resort to it is guilty of willful imposture beside the grave of his friend. We in England should say he was a horrible liar and audacious blasphemer. We should pronounce the Jews right in the judgment which they passed upon him.

To me the book is detestable, morally as well as theologically. It has brought to my mind, as I have said in my paper on it, that wonderful dream of Richter's in which Jesus tells the universe, "Children, you have no Father." For the God whom He calls His Father is one who cannot exist, or how would He dare to trifle with His name? Jesus is, for M. Renan, one of the highest of mortal creatures, though far below our standard in the nineteenth century. He only pretended to be the Son of God, though he had better right to the name than most. He has been dead for 1,800 years. What God have we but Necessity or Nothingness? "Children, you have no Father," is the message which Renan is sending from one end of Europe to the other. How ought he to stir us up to ask on what ground we may proclaim the opposite tiding to all human beings in all corners of the earth.

▶ **119. To Sir E. Strachey, on September 18, 1864, about Bishop Colenso**

Your proposal is most kind, and your way of putting it kinder still. I will answer with the frankness you desired. There has been an estrangement between Colenso and me since he came to England. I think that the Bible is the great deliverer from ecclesiastical bondage—the great protestor for human freedom. That is the maxim I have always tried to maintain. When he took up exactly the opposite maxim, when he treated the Bible as itself the instrument of our slavery, and seemed to think that to throw it off would be the great step to emancipation, I felt that he was giving up the ground to the Bishop of Oxford and Dr. Pusey. I saw nothing before us but that fanaticism against criticism, that effort to bind a human tyranny upon us, which these last few years have developed.

I do not say that I may not have been faithless, that I may not often have been unkind. But I had a deliberate conviction that I owed this duty to the Church and to the cause of liberty. If I identified myself with those who were called liberal thinkers, who seemed to be, and, in many respects were, pleading for the rights of the clergy and the rights of conscience, I must have abandoned my own position, a position difficult enough to maintain—full of sorrow, involving an isolation from all parties; but, as I think, necessary for the good of all parties.

To make Colenso understand why I do this—that I am not a traitor to freedom and friendship also—is impossible at present. If I met him at your house I suspect we should only embarrass each other and embarrass you. We should either preserve a forced silence on all questions which were most interesting to us, or impose upon each other by words of doubtful signification. I hope hereafter we may understand each other better; but I should be sorry to lose the pleasure of free intercourse with you by making this effort. Still I leave this question wholly to you. I have met the Bishop several times, and there is, I hope, not the least unkindness between us.

▶ 120. To the Reverend Charles Kingsley on May 18, 1865

If I cannot see you I wish very much to see your sermon. I quite agree with you that theology is what our age is crying for, even when it thinks that it is crying to be rid of theology. To be free from every theodicy—from every attempt to construct a divinity out of the notions of divines or philosophers, or an Exeter Hall conception of what a Mighty Being must do or ought to do with a rebellious universe—is a great necessity for us.

But those who talk of leaving men to their religious instincts or their perceptions of morality are preparing a fresh succession of such burdens for us and our children. It is the incubus of morbid religious instincts, of partial apprehensions about justice and mercy and their inevitable hostility, under which we have been so long groaning. What but a revelation of God in the Living Word (i.e., theology) ever has emancipated in any degree, or ever can emancipate, the nations thoroughly from that oppression? The Name into which we are baptized, the Name which was to bind together all nations, comes out to me more and more as that which must at last break these fetters. I can find none of my liberal friends to whom that language does not sound utterly wild and incomprehensible, while the orthodox would give me for the eternal Name the dry dogma of the Trinity—an opinion which I may brag of as *mine*, given me by I know not what councils of noisy doctors and to be retained in spite of the reason, which it is said to contradict—lest I should be cast into hell for rejecting it. I am sure this Name is the infinite all-embracing charity which I may proclaim to publicans and harlots as that in which they are living and moving and having their being, in which they may believe, and by which they may be raised to the freedom and righteousness and fellowship for which they were created.

Will not our lips be some day opened to say that this is even so, and that the kingdom of heaven is not a possession for those who would shut it up, but for those who would open it, as the apostles did, to all kindreds and tongues and tribes? All perplexities and contradictions of human opinion and practice seem to me preparing the way for this discovery; otherwise they would drive me to despair.

► **121. To the Reverend Charles Kingsley, on May 20, 1865, about Maurice's view of Baptism as a sacrament**

I thank you for wishing to have an explanation, and version into English, of my queer phraseology about baptism. It must have sounded to you and to many as pedantical and grotesque, especially as after once adopting it I have pertinaciously adhered to it, and have seemed incapable of giving any tolerable equivalent for it in nineteenth-century speech. I will try to account for both of these eccentricities.

That sacraments must be the *organon* of a revelation, if it fulfill its pretensions, that they have been actually so to Christendom, is *the* lesson which I owe to our Tractarian school, and to the Romanist teachers from whom they have received their lore; the one which history has confirmed in my mind; the one which has been my great deliverance from the dogmatism of Dr. Pusey and of the popes. For if sacraments express the purpose, and the relation of God to man, dogmas *cannot* express it. To dogmatize about sacraments is to destroy their nature. To dogmatize about God is to assume that man does not receive the knowledge of

God from Him, but imputes the forms of his own intellect to Him.

Sacraments are, as I think, the necessary form of a revelation, precisely because they discover the divine nature in its union with the human, and do not make the human the standard and measure of the divine. Suppose then I find this baptism into the divine Name as the form which has been recognized by Greeks, Romanists, Protestants of all classes and opinions, for these twelve or thirteen hundred years (to go back no further and to involve oneself in no antiquarian discussions), that seems to me as complete a declaration to all these Greek, Romanist, Protestant nations as I can imagine, of Him in whom they are living, moving, having their being; a far graver protest than it is possible to invent against their divisions and hatreds, against the pretensions by which their priests have exalted themselves into the throne of Omnipotence, against the oppressions which have assumed the Devil to be the real Lord of the Universe. . . .

The *Name* must, according to the logician, be an *attribute*; I attribute it to God. If He has a name and can reveal it, the notion of it as an attribute given by men is a contradiction. Upon this the whole question turns; the question debated through all the Middle Ages, debated with the alternative of Godliness or Atheism now; "Is logic the mistress of theology or only one of its handmaids?"

To me it seems that baptism into the Name contains that Gospel to all nations which St. Paul preached to the Athenians, and that if we abandon it for any other we shall not declare Christ to man, but only proselytize a few of them to our Christianity, so making them twofold more the children of hell than ourselves, which, as I remember you once observed, must be a very difficult process indeed. . . .

▶ 122. To Mr. Ludlow in May, 1865, on Lincoln's Second Inaugural Address

As to democracy, I regard Lincoln's inauguration speech as the grandest return from the democracy of the Declaration of Independence to the theocracy of the Pilgrim Fathers that I have seen anywhere. I always hoped that might be the effect of the war on the best Americans. I never dreamed of seeing it expressed officially in such language as that. And it was not merely the old Calvinistic theocracy—the divinity minus humanity. Insofar as it recognized the divine vengeance for the wrongs of the colored race, it implied a Christ as Head of the human race. I should count it a treason to Lincoln's memory to relapse into the other kind of speech, as we must do if we call the people to sympathize with him as a democrat. The horror of democracy which you impute to me is a horror in the interest of the people.

I believe the Sovereign has been great so far as he or she has confessed a ministry—ignominious so far as he or she has merely clutched at a dominion; that the nobles have been great so far as they have confessed a ministry—ignominious so far as they have been aristocrats or oligarchs. I apply the same maxim to the larger class. If they will accept the franchise as a ministry, as an obligation—if any one of them, like Lincoln, accepts any function, be it as high as it may, as a calling—I shall rejoice. If they grasp at any power merely as a power, I believe the voice of Demos will be the devil's voice and not God's. I apply no different rule to one set of men from that which I apply to another. I look on the tyranny of the one, the few, or the majority with like abhorrence. And I am confident, as the Emperor of the French is, that the tyranny of the majority is the surest step to the tyranny of the one.

▶ **123. To Mr. John Hodgkin on the Word of God, July 31, 1865**

When 11,000 clergymen declared eighteen months ago that the Bible not only contains, but *is*, the Word of God, the position struck me not as an exaggeration, but as a perilous *denial* of the truth. *The* Word of God, I believe, as St. John taught and as George Fox taught, to be very much above the Scriptures, however He may speak by and in the Scriptures. . . . And if it is true, as the Bible says, that by the Word of the Lord were the heavens framed, and the earth by the breath of His mouth, may not this be the true way to the removal of scientific perplexities? Nay, is it not possible that the scientific men may have been led by a higher teaching than they knew, to break through certain apparent constructions of the letter that they may lead us to a deeper theology, that they may bring us to confess the presence of Him in whom is life, and whose life is the Light of men? God's ways are not as our ways. What we dread most as signs of unbelief may be His method of scattering unbelief. Theologians and scientific men may both wake up with awe, and say, "He was in the place, and we knew it not." . . .

The Bible becomes dearer and more sacred to me the more I read it; I have no sympathy with its arraigners, even too little with its critics. Yet I feel compelled often to stand with both against those who turn it into a god, and so deny the living God of whom it bears witness. That idolatry is so fearful, and the numbers who are rushing into it so great and respectable, that I feel we ought to bear any reproaches and any suspicions, rather than be the instruments of promoting it. . . .

▶ **124. To his son Edmund traveling in Germany, August 15, 1865**

. . . I am much delighted by the interest you take in the pictures at Dresden. I am sure the right way to admire any great work of art is to know it thoroughly, to let it speak to you, and not to be in a hurry to form an opinion about it. What you say about the religion of the old Catholic pictures and the difficulty of receiving it in our day has much truth in it. I used to mourn at the thought and to be pained by it. Now it gives me hope.

I look upon Protestantism as unfriendly to Art, favorable to Science. But out of it, I believe, will arise a faith deeper and broader, warmer than Romanism, more devoted to Truth than anti-Romanism, under which Science and Art will flourish as sisters. Over all the visions of the past in which the old artists indulged, there is a dark shadow; it hangs often more heavily still over our study of the present. There will come a time when the future will be presented to us in colors grand and awful, but full of brightness, when the Revelation of the Son of man and His judgment, instead [of] being [a] gloomy spectacle, such as they appeared to Michelangelo and Tintoretto, will be contemplated as the true accomplishment of the mystery of the Birth and the Cross and Resurrection, which were all that could give them any sense of reconciliation. The new heaven and new earth, wherein dwells Righteousness, will be regarded as the satisfaction of the poet's and the patriot's dreams, not as blessings which are to reward the few, and from which the multitude are to be shut out. . . .

▶ **125. To Dean Stanley,* on December 27, 1865, concerning Lecture XXXVI in Stanley's Jewish Church**

The one subject upon which I have not yielded to your arguments is that of the priesthood. I do not dispute any of your facts, or their value: I should go further than you go in speaking of the sins of the Jewish priests, and of those who, rightly or wrongly, have borne that name in all countries and all ages. . . .

If you introduce the other idea—that of the Epistle to the Hebrews—if you consider the offering of animal sacrifices to be no longer the priest's duty, because the Elder Brother of the Human Race has offered that perfect sacrifice of the will which can alone be satisfactory to God, I entirely accept the change. But it seems to me to involve the principle that those who set forth this Elder Brother to men should be themselves perpetually commemorating His complete sacrifice by claiming the right to offer up themselves and all human creatures to the living and true God; which oblation must include the consecration of all animal and vegetable life, of all things as well as of all persons, of all offices and tasks, and therefore be inseparably connected with the Old Dispensation, taking up its fundamental maxim into itself, and explaining why its mere accidents have passed away.

* This letter of Maurice's (not in the son's biography) may be consulted in *Life and Letters of Dean Stanley* edited by R. E. Prothers (1894), II, 250-252.

In this sense I do not see how you can show that the prophetical office has more of an enduring character than the priestly. I admit the permanence of the first, but certainly with as manifest an alteration of its outward appearances as it is possible to conceive. I fully believe that the prophet will be always wanted to reprove the abominations of the priest—that Savonarola was to Alexander the Sixth what Samuel was to Hophni and Phineas. But I think the true prophet will always have to rebuke prophets who speak a lie in the name of the Lord, as well as priests who cause His offering to be abhorred.

Each of those offices, like the royal, subsists, I think, in its original purpose and significance, Christ being the real interpreter of each, embodying them all in Himself, who is the same yesterday, today, and forever. And I cannot but feel that in the southern nations of Europe, where the priest has extinguished the prophet, in England, where the prophet has extinguished the priest, in the United States of America, where there has been an obliteration of the king, there is a peril to that which has exalted itself, even more than to that which has been depressed.

Nevertheless, I look for the revival of each land through that which it has, in a measure, reverenced: the priesthood will, I trust, rise up for the deliverance of France and Spain and Italy; the preachers (lay and clerical) may yet do something for England. The American people may assert the majesty of Christ's kingdom above their own sovereignty. I do not, therefore, consider you unpatriotic for giving what appears to me an exaggerated and exclusive prominence to the prophet. It is a genuine English belief. But if England is to serve humanity, I ask of it justice to what has been so sacred in the eyes of the other nations.

▶ **126. To Dr. Ewing, the Bishop of Argyll and the Isles, March 1, 1866**

. . . I have been reading Pusey's *Eirenicon* and Newman's *Letter*, and am more and more convinced that the want of both is that they look elsewhere for peace than to the center of peace, for something else to hold the building together than the cornerstone. It must be healing the wounds of the daughter of my people, which have been opened so long, *very* slightly, to propose certain explanations of the Thirty-nine Articles which may make them tolerable to Romanists, or certain explanations of the decrees of the Council of Trent which may make them condemn (or not sanction) certain practices that are offensive to Anglicans.

And evidently Pusey and Newman equally—or the first rather more than the second—look not to the Christ ascended into the heavens that He may fill all things as the bond of communion, but to some kind of descent into the elements. What that is must always be a subject of debate; it can never by a pledge of fellowship. Curiously enough, Newman defends Mariolatry because we want the idea of an ascended humanity as well as of a descended Godhead. A remarkable testimony to that which we do indeed want, the belief that He that descended is the same that ascended.

▶ *127. To the Bishop of Argyll, April 10, 1866*

It seems to me that the words, "That they all may be one as thou Father art in Me and I in thee," denote the only ground of Catholic unity; and that so long as any mortal bishop or prince assumes the place of Him in whom all things were created and by whom all things consist, so long there must be need of a protest to maintain this Catholic unity. I certainly find no *explicit* acknowledgment either of this Catholic or of this Protestant principle in Stanley's comments on the *Eirenicon*. I find an *implicit* denial of both in the *Eirenicon* itself, insofar as it assumes that a union between divided churches may be effected by mere arrangements about dogmatic articles, whether the Thirty-nine or those of the Council of Trent; or by an agreement of these churches to persecute and exclude certain persons or schools; insofar as it hints that the English Church may ally itself with a church which tries to fraternize in a Latin vicar of Christ, and not in Christ Himself, the ascended High Priest and Bishop and King of the universe. And I am much more inclined to hold with you that these and other indications foretell the approach of a great conflict and crisis in the Church, than with Stanley's notion that the improved temper of the age promises a quiet and happy solution of all controversies.

Nevertheless I do accept the *Eirenicon* in its barest and driest form as a sign that the question of our day is the question how the broken limbs of Christendom may be united; as a sign that all movements toward reformation *now* must be directly and consciously movements toward unity. And I do think that Stanley has very ably and beautifully indicated the inevitable departures from Pusey's approved and darling maxims, into which he has been forced by the effort to become in any form or under any limitations a minister of peace to hostile churches. Whatever therefore may be the immediate consequences from the High Church or the Broad Church manifesto, I am inclined to look upon both as divine messages which may help us in tracing the will of God concerning us.

And it has occurred to me that perhaps you might derive from an observation of these signs of the times, a hint as to the nature of the work which you have contemplated. Instead of a volume of essays, might it not take the form of a volume of confessions?

To such a volume, of course without any name, I think I might contribute; for I have had glimpses at times of the ways in which we Churchmen are striving against the Spirit of Truth and Charity; of the injuries which we have inflicted upon the world, while we charge our evils upon it, and suppose that it must be lost, while we are saved; of the restoration which God, who raiseth the dead, would effect for the world by quickening and uniting the Church; glimpses that have appalled me, and that seemed to demand humiliation and confessions, lest they should be forgotten and God's grace in sending them be set at nought.

Others doubtless have had many more of such discoveries of God's purposes to us, and of our rebellions against them, and they may also find that method of expressing their shame and their hopes the safest and most reasonable.

If you, as one of our fathers, would gather together a few of such confessions with any of your own and with any words of introduction or comment, it might be an Eirenicon such as no scheme of concord and adjustment is ever likely to be. I submit the thought to you with diffidence, but with some hope that you may entertain it and improve it.

▶ **128. To the Bishop of Argyll, who had hesitated to sign the Pastoral Letter of the First Lambeth Conference because of its phrase that Christ reconciled the Father to us (Article II), October 6, 1867**

I have thought earnestly about the subject of your letter, and I will try to tell you why I am very thankful that you did not refuse to sign the Pastoral Letter, on the grounds which you mention, and why I hope and trust that you will not make the second Article a reason for separating from the English Church.

I confess that I was not struck by the sentence or clause of the letter to which you refer. I read it over twice without even noticing that there was such a one. I *was* struck and pained by the omission in such a document of any allusion to the Living Word; by the want of any recognition of the principle which *the* Theologian regarded as the ground of his theology, while there was so laborious a statement respecting the claim of the Scriptures to a title which they so rarely claim for themselves. But you were right, I think, in not protesting against language which, interpreted by the Articles and the history of the Reformation, means an assertion of the *Lex-Scripta* in opposition to oral traditions and ecclesiastical decrees; and (interpreted by the same Articles and the same history) cannot be intended to disparage or ignore Him who is One with the Father and the Light of men.

And here comes in the other point. There is no assertion, in all our dogmatic formularies, of the Living Word, as the root contained in the second Article. I have always turned to that Article, occurring where it does, as the great witness for a theology constructed not like that of Knox or the Westminster Assembly, on the basis of the Fall, but on the Basis of Redemption; or rather on the original constitution of men in the Only-Begotten Son by which the Redemption itself must be interpreted. If anyone separates the words "reconciled the Father to us" from the context of the Article and grafts them on another scheme of divinity— one which supposes Christ to have suffered and been crucified, to have died and been buried, that He might persuade the Father not to *punish* men, or a certain portion of men, for their original guilt or their actual sins—he simply changes the whole meaning of the language to which we have subscribed; *he* ought to recall *his* subscription; there is the most utter and entire avoidance of that vile notion in this Article and in every one which succeeds it.

Christ has died and been buried to take away sin, not to exempt any from the punishment of sin. And what is *sin?* Separation from God, a breach between the creature and Him in whose image he is made, a division between the child and the Father. In *this* sense (which is the sense of the Article) it is as true that Christ reconciles the Father to us as that He reconciles us to the Father. In His own person He destroys the barrier between us and Him, and till that is removed there can be no *Atonement;* the Father may seek reconciliation with us, but He is not reconciled to us. I wish you would seriously consider the Article in this light—not only dismissing the other notion, but regarding the Article as the most effectual protest against it—and then I think you will see that you not only have gained much by inducing the bishops to refer you to this Article as the explanation and justification of their phraseology; but that the Article fills up that omission in the Pastoral of which I complain. . . .

▶ *129. To the Bishop of Argyll on December 10, 1867*

The assumption in most men's minds is that the Prayer Book, as such, is exclusive, and that all passages like those your friend has quoted are splendid inconsistencies. I am thoroughly convinced that this is not so. I came to the Prayer Book out of a Dissenting school, and it was the largeness and freedom of its declarations which struck me as the great escape from their narrowness and sectarianism, from the narrowness and sectarianism of those who, like the Unitarians, utterly severed God from His creatures, as much as from the pseudo-Calvinism which made Him the Savior of the elect, the destroyer of mankind.

I believe the Catholic faith—the faith in a Father who so loved the world as to give His Son for it—in a Son, who, because He is one with the Father, and came into the world to do the will of His Father, offered Himself freely as a sacrifice to redeem men from sin and to bind them to God—of a Spirit who proceeds from the Father and the Son to bind all kindreds of men into a divine Unity—has been underlying Christendom, expressing itself in the Universal Baptism, in the Holy Communion, in prayers that carried men above all their notions and dogmas. I believe that this faith has been struggling against a huge mass of sacerdotal and popular opinions in every age, and that there is in our age a wonderful gathering of Romanist and Protestant dogmatists, of Spiritualists and Comtists, of Conservatives and Democrats to overthrow it. One always suspects that every Synod in Rome or in London will aim some blow at it, will subvert it by its own decrees. At the same time out of Romanism and Protestantism, out of every form of philosophy, out of every political school, there are coming forth such witnesses of it as a real foundation upon which honest men can stand, though the earth should be removed, and the mountains carried into the depths of the sea, as there never have been in any previous age, and as gather the testimonies of all previous ages into themselves. . . .

▶ *130. To Mr. T. Erskine of Linlathen to whom Maurice had paid a visit soon after Christmas, January 13, 1868*

My dear Friend,

I do indeed look back with much wonder and thankfulness to the intercourse with you which inaugurated the beginning of this year for me. There is so much in the interchange of convictions even if one receives nothing fresh; but you gave me what was the quickening and renewal of thought and life, that had been in me doubtless, but that were not clearly or consciously in me, so that I felt you to be truly an instrument of the Spirit doing and fulfilling His work.

I have especially recurred to all that you said about faith. It seems to me that all my teaching here ought to be affected by it. I cannot help perceiving that we have been trying to build social life and personal life upon distrust and suspicion of each other, and of God; and that the human ethos is, as you said, that of trust; *the* man, the divine Man being the Truster Himself and the source of Trust in all the race. I quite feel with you that Christ's trust in the Father is the sign and witness of His divine nature, that which corresponds and shows forth the righteousness of God, that which is the basis of righteousness for man. And I cannot doubt that in Him God justified the trust of every man, Jew and Gentile, since the foundation of the world, and pronounced sentence upon all the distrust and self-exaltation of every Jew and Gentile.

All polities and societies grew up, I conceive, through the trust of men in each other and through trust in someone whom they could not see and could not name, but who, they felt, was not far from any one of them. And, as clearly and obviously, all polities and societies perished through distrust of the members in each other, and through distrust of their Father in heaven; through the establishment of some dark power to be dreaded and hated, not trusted, in His place. The Revelation of the Father, by the Son, as well as of the Son by the Father, was in truth that which men in all different ways, in their social acts and theories, had been showing that they needed.

Christ came, in the fullness of the time, to bring to light the mystery that had been about all ages and generations, though hidden from all. And in all ages since, the trust of men in every work they have engaged in, as thinkers, discoverers, martyrs, has had no other root than that faith of Jesus Christ, that confidence of Him in His Father which sustained Him in life and death, and to which he appealed in every leper and blind and palsied man, as well as in everyone whom he raised from the tomb. That I understood to be your meaning, and my conscience thoroughly responded to it.

I wish I had read more of your book [on the Epistle to the Romans] and talked more about it with you. The part I read interested me deeply. And I think when you come to the third chapter, of which you speak, you will be able to show how much its sense has been perverted by the effort to make out a charge of universal depravity from it as *the reason for the necessity of faith*; whereas, if I read him right, he is teaching us that the Psalmist found among the Jews of his age—those Jews who were in the covenant, and had every call to exercise faith—an utter want of it, and therefore great moral corruption. "What the law speaks it speaks to those who are under the law"—the Jew is proved to have no better standing ground in himself or in his national privileges than another man, that he and all might know that they have a standing ground in God's righteousness; that no trust in that can be wrong or can fail. "All are concluded under sin," are found to be sinners in themselves that they might be all righteous in God; that they might, Gentiles as well as Jews, believe that Christ had been manifested for their justification.

Justification by faith is surely a most wholesome and complete doctrine when it means faith in a Justifier, in One who is righteous, and who makes righteous; but is it not a pestilent doctrine if it means that we are justified by faith in our difference from those who are not justified? That is the very faith which St. Paul is tearing to pieces as the essential unbelief. . . .

▶ *131. To Miss Williams Wynn, written from 3 St. Peter's Terrace, Cambridge, February 17, 1868*

My dear Friend,

Your very kind letter to Georgina of this morning must, I am grieved to say, be answered by another hand than hers. She has had threatenings of rheumatic gout for many days, and now she is fixed to her bed by sciatica. She sends you her dearest love, and begs me to tell you how fully she had intended to write to you all last week. She has been making herself unnecessarily anxious about me, merely because I have yielded to the doctor's wishes, and for a time given up duty in London. But I am, as she allows, and bids me tell you, very much better for the holiday, and quite equal to the modicum of work I have allowed myself here. I

233

find that both lectures and sermons take more out of me than they did; but I think it is better they should. They are less of intellectual exercises, and more parts of my life, than they were in earlier days. Those lectures which I am now delivering on National Morality seem to me more personal, more like confessions, than anything I ever wrote. . . .

▶ 132. To Mr. T. Erskine of Linlathen on July 23, 1868

My dear Friend,

I have wished much that you should read some lectures which I have written, "On the Conscience." They approach from the opposite side that great question which you approach in your *Commentary* on the Romans from the divine side. The righteousness of God speaks, as I think and you think, in Christ directly to that in each man which God has created to recognize His voice. It seems to me that the conscience with its mysterious duplicity is the very self in each man; that which is feeling after God if haply it may find him, that which, if it does not find him, must sink into selfishness and brutality and make gods after its own likeness. That is the state which I find described so wonderfully in the first chapter of the Epistle. All the rest of it develops, it seems to me, most clearly and delicately the twofold principle of the conscience till the crisis of its agony and of its deliverance is reached in the seventh chapter.

I have not alluded to the Epistle in my lectures. Nor do I think that any commentary upon it ought to treat the conscience as St. Paul's *primary* subject. The manifestation of righteousness as you have set it forth, in connection with the Union of the Father and the Son, is undoubtedly that which has first to be exhibited. But I have been so much impressed with the truth of St. Paul's statement when it is looked at as a lesson in moral and human philosophy, that I could not but speak of it to you. My endeavor has been to get rid of what is called psychology and to bring each of my students to say: The conscience is not a part of my soul, but is I myself. Parting with it, I lose not like Chamisso's hero my shadow, but the substance from which my shadow is cast.

234

► *133. To one whose son was about to join the Roman Catholic Church; written from Tenby, September 15, 1868*

Your interesting letter only reached me last night, having traveled from London to Cambridge, where I am now living, and thence to this place where I am spending a few weeks for Mrs. Maurice's health. But for this cause you may be sure that I should not have delayed to thank you for your kind confidence in me, and to try—though with a deep sense of my inadequacy to treat those diseases of the spirit which I am encountering continually—if I could say anything which might help you or your son.

His statement of the case for Protestantism and of that for Romanism shows that his mind is argumentative and logical, and (I should say) that he has read quite as much as is good for him in support of the anti-Papal side. I am much more afraid of the effect which may be produced on any thoughtful and skeptical man by the defenders of the Protestant position than by its assailants. And this not because I have the least doubt that we have a firm and impregnable ground to stand upon, if we will claim it, but because we are so much inclined to rest upon negations, and to trust in the skill with which we can maintain them.

Your son thinks—Protestant and Romanist disputants alike teach him to think—that what he wants is some security for his *opinions.* "Can you obtain," the Romanists say to him, "any tolerable certainty for right belief unless you have an infallible dictator as to what you should believe?" "Yes," replies the opponent. "If I read the Scriptures and pray, I can get at least a fair probability of going right or not very wrong." Now I would venture to ask, "Does either the Church suppose that it speaks orally, by St. Peter and his successors; or does the Bible set this problem before me?" One as little as the other.

The Church preaches to me in its creeds a Gospel of a Son of God and a Son of man, the Head and Lord of every man, in whom I may believe and trust, who is the Deliverer from death and the grave and hell, to whom I may commit my body and soul and spirit, who has come from the Father of the whole Family in

235

heaven and earth, who is with me forever, who gives us His Spirit that He may make us members of His family, sharers of His nature. Is not that the "oral" teaching? If not, the Romanist is at issue with his own creeds. If he puts any person between us and the Son of God and the Son of man, if he says that the Son of God and the Son of man is *not* the Head of every man, and that He is *not* calling every man to trust in Him for life and death— he is at war, not with Protestantism, but with the message of St. Peter, and I presume of the successors of St. Peter if they call themselves Vicars or Ministers of Christ. On the other hand, if the Protestant puts the Bible between human beings and the Son of man; if he bids any human being engage in a long train of biblical study or comparison of arguments respecting texts of Scripture before he believes in Christ as his Prince and Deliverer, he sets at naught the Bible, he makes it a dead, nay, a killing letter.

To a man in the business and work of the world like your son, the message of an actual Lord and Friend and Helper is worth all the opinions that were ever held and all the debates that were ever debated by all the Protestants and Romanists in the world. And what a bond that faith is between them! What need is there to decide if four-fifths are Romanists and one-fifth Protestants; if it be indeed true, as they both profess to hold, that Jew, Greek, Barbarian, Scythian, bond and free are all one in Christ?

Your son knows, doubtless, how people who disbelieve in Christianity are talking of Humanity, are making that an object of worship. He will find, I think, that the old faith of Romanists and Protestants in a Son of God, who has exhibited the perfect image of God in a perfect Humanity, is the satisfaction of these longings. Christ is now as He was before He came in the flesh the desire of nations. When Romanists and Protestants understand this, they will cease to wrangle about opinions. The first will feel that there is another and higher center than any Latin Bishop to whom they may turn; higher and yet how much nearer, how much more capable of understanding each one of us as well as of binding us all into one. The other will protest against the authority of the Latin Bishop, only because he hides Christ from those to whom He has united Himself, and therefore will be aware of his own tendency, to make the books of the Bible, or his notions about the Bible, into barriers of the same kind.

Your son thinks that the mistakes and blunders into which we have fallen are reasons for doubting the promise of Christ that His Spirit shall guide us into all truth. I can say, after sixty-three years of mistakes and blunders, that I cling to that promise all the more confidently on account of them; that I believe they have been instruments, in God's hands, of giving me glimpses of the Truth, that I have the certainty that there is One who is absolute Truth. During the threescore years and ten of our earthly pilgrimage, we are just spelling out our primers. Through ages upon ages the divine lessons will be unfolding themselves. To own the height and depth, the length and breadth, of the love which is revealing itself in all God's works and ways, to trace it in a few of its manifestations toward human beings, is better work than to discuss any opinions. So best we learn what opinions have meant to those who have striven about them most earnestly.

▶ **134. To the Bishop of Argyll, on June 3, 1869, about the Eucharist as the sacrament of unity**

I have never read any writing of Hutton's which would lead me to suspect him of any Romanist conceptions about the Eucharist. When any of us try to *conceive* a sacrament we do, in the admirable language of our Article, "destroy the nature of it." The idea of a sacrament must involve a paradox—*the* paradox of theology, *the* paradox of our human life. To bring it under the terms of a definition, to set it forth as a formula, is simply to take the sacramental essence out of it. Protestants perform *this* process of transubstantiation as much as Romanists. And there are times when the consciousness of the contradiction becomes so strong in our mind, when we are so disgusted with our intellectual experiments, that we plunge back into sensualism as the only possible escape from notions which we feel to be cold and dreary, and which we suspect are untenable.

The bread and wine, are they not actual food? are they not better than mere theories? But surely they cannot be *only* bread and wine if they are better. What else? There, no doubt, is all Romanism close at hand. And then there must be a new theory to explain the difference between *these* elements and all others. What or who has descended into them? Who brought about the change? Who, but the priest and his wonderful invocation? It is true, as you say, that these thoughts connect themselves with the belief of the Incarnation; that is to say, with the belief of Christ's *descent* into flesh and mortal condition, severed from the belief of His *ascent* into the glory which He had with the Father before all worlds. Restore that belief to the Church, which has nearly departed from it, and all dream that priestly intercession brings Christ back into these more than earthly limitations becomes hateful. The Eucharist, the communion with Christ where He is, with the Son of man as the Head of humanity, as the perfect Image of the Father, scatters that dream far more effectually than all arguments. In fact, no arguments *can* scatter it, till we labor, instead of defining the Eucharist, to give it an honor which it has never had. Till we accept it as the very *organon* of scientific theology and of social life, we shall never get rid of the abuse which has clung to it. Nay, it will still continue to be the symbol of all the divisions of Christendom, when it is meant to be the expression of our unity.

▶ **135. To the Rev. F. J. A. Hort on the education question, April 5, 1870**

I could cheerfully, even thankfully, give up the Catechism if it were, or I had ever treated it as being, a summary of the doctrines whereby the Church of England is distinguished from Dissenters. Since they consider it to be such, since so many of us adopt the same opinion, I cannot suppose that it will hold its ground. But I have always contended that by its form as much as its spirit such a notion of it is shown to be untenable; that the "What is thy name" gives the hint of the most personal as well as the most Catholic, or, to use the modern phrase, the most "unsectarian" education. I should be very loath to give up this testimony just at a time when it seems most needed, when we want most to show that secularism is narrow and exclusive, faith comprehensive. I do not know whether this can be shown by any legislative measure—whether the effort of the state to educate must not ultimately involve the loss of all personality, of all Catholicity in our teachings. . . .

. . . under the name of Progress we seem drifting back into the old Bell and Lancaster notion of cramming a number of children into a schoolroom and cramming them with a number of fragments of information—part labeled religious, part secular—which, if they should be able to digest this hard morsel, was to be their education. All our training schools have been experiments for getting out of this rut. It may be that we can only be effectually delivered from it by sinking more deeply into it. . . . Here I think it is important to show that our formularies enable us to embrace the people; that sects and secularists alike ignore their necessities, even their insatiable cravings; that the state can only bring them to the water without the least power of giving them drink. . . .

▶ 136. To the Bishop of Argyll, April 29, 1870

. . . If we do not set forth the ascended Christ as the object of trust and hope to mankind, as Him who by ascending has led captivity captive and received gifts for men, as the center to whom all may turn, and in whom all are one, the desire to bring Him down from heaven—to see Him in the elements on the table— will be, as it has been, irresistible. Priests will be believed to possess the power, because the power must be conceived to reside somewhere; the denial of the Ascension will be called faith in the Incarnation. And it is absurd to say that if we wot not what is become of Him who is gone into the mount we shall not make a calf and bid men worship it; there must be a priest-king in Rome if the Priest-King at the right hand of the Majesty of heaven is not reverenced there, but is sought to be brought back to His mortal conditions or to an image of His mortal conditions here. If these men are right we must give up saying the Lord's Prayer. Our Father is *not* in heaven; there is no heaven; all is of the earth, earthly. I have felt this feebly for a long time; now it comes to me with a tremendous demonstration. . . .

▶ 137. To the Bishop of Argyll, written from Cambridge, May 26, 1870

My dear Bishop,

Your kind remarks on my article in the *Contemporary* [on Newman's *Grammar of Assent*] have given me great pleasure. I am not accustomed to meet with such sympathy with what I write.

I should have quite expected Mr. Wace's criticism. But whatever he may say, Luther "tilted at propositions" much more vehemently than I have done. His assertion of the right and duty to believe in God who justifies was the great blow, the deadly blow, to those who make faith consist in assent to propositions. Dr. Newman's bitter dislike of Luther is due much more to his revolt from Aristotle and Aquinas than to his revolt from the Pope. When Luther, and still more Melanchthon, succumbed to propositions in their later days, when assent to the doctrine of justification was substituted for belief in the Justifier, Protestantism went into the lean, sickly, and yet contentious stage of its existence, only to emerge from that into indifference—a mere denial of Romanism. The reformation that we want is the same rise out of assents into faith as in the sixteenth century; only it must be into faith in a God who has redeemed mankind, in whom I may trust because I am a man, and that I may vindicate my rights as a man. . . .

▶ 138. To a lady who wrote to Maurice after her father's death as to whether he believed the departed have a knowledge of those who remain behind; written from Cambridge, November 17, 1870

My dear Madam,

. . . You will not doubt, I think, though you may not know as bitterly as I know, that there is a Cainlike going out of the presence of God: a flight from Him as if He were an enemy because He knows what we are and what we have done. And there is surely a Gospel inviting us back into that presence, bidding us arise and go to our Father, telling us that a new and living way has been opened for us by which our spirits may ascend to Him. To do that, is, I conceive, what St. John meant by *coming to the light that our deeds may be made manifest*. It is accepting as a comfort, not a curse, the belief, *Thou hast searched me out and known me. Thou art about my bed and board. Thou spiest out all my ways. Thou understandest my thoughts afar off.* To be known thoroughly, known altogether, is the blessing of blessings, for it imports that we are right. God cannot behold iniquity. He sees us as we truly are in Christ. He looks upon us, and regards our evil as far from us. St. John extends this principle a step further. He says, *If we walk in the light as He is in the light, then have we fellowship one with another, and the blood of Jesus Christ cleanseth us from all sin*. It is high teaching, yet it is confirmed by our commonest experience. We have not fellowship one with another, not with the nearest relations, not with the dearest friends, whilst we are indulging vain selfish thoughts; by their own nature they cast us off from fellowship. And the effort of those who care most for us is to bring us out of those selfish, unreal thoughts; to bring us back into intercourse with them, to make us trust them. They recognize us as meant for the fellowship; they deem it a strange anomalous state that we should be out of it. Our absence from it is what causes them their bitterest pain— our return to it is their joy. And when we return to it we become healthy, simple, free from fancies. The law then under which we are placed is the law of fellowship; to be out of fellowship with God and man is to be in a wrong, disordered condition; the more we enter into it, the more we become reasonable human beings, what we were meant to be. . . .

I dare say you know about disembodied spirits. I know nothing. They seem to me to belong to the realm of fancy and not of fact. Our Lord took all pains while He was on earth to show how much He cared for bodies; He was constantly raising them out of disease, and making them healthy. He bade the body of Lazarus

241

come forth. He gave that as a sign that *All who were in their graves should hear the voice of the Son of man and that those who hear should live.* He brought His own body from the grave. His Apostle, who knew most of the redemption of the will from its chains, looked forward to a redemption of the body and of all creation, from the travail to which they were subjected not willingly. He said that *if the Spirit of Christ dwells in us He shall also quicken our mortal bodies.* Why not believe that those words are spoken simply and sincerely; that they represent facts which have been accomplished, which are accomplishing themselves every hour? You are weary of words which you have heard from me and others about some final deliverance of the human spirit from its sin and woe. You cannot be too weary of them if they interfere in the least degree with the message, *I am the resurrection and the life,* which was spoken once to a woman sorrowing for her brother, which is spoken now by the same voice to every woman sorrowing for brother, father, husband, child; an ever present resurrection an ever present life; that is the pledge and warrant for all hope of a future resurrection, of a future life. Not a future but an eternal life, the life of God, the life of love, is what Christ tells us of. . . .

Index

Dissenter, 44, 70, 205
Doctrine of Sacrifice, 27

Ecumenism, 9, 32 ff.
Education, 14 ff., 238 ff.
Election, 28, 35, 199 f.
English Church, 69, 92, 97, 100, 169, 189, 191
English Reformation, 34
Episcopacy, 89 f., 135
Episcopate, 31
Epistle to the Hebrews, 11
Erskine (Thomas) of Linlathen, 7, 76, 97, 164, 191, 231, 234
Essays and Reviews, 17, 204
Eternal death, 169, 193
Eternal life, 13 f., 143, 145 ff.
Eternal punishment, 13, 143 ff.
Eternity, 145
Eucharist, 9, 30, 202, 238 (*See* Holy Communion, Lord's Supper)
Eustace Conway, 7, 66
Evangelicalism, 105
Evangelicals, 36, 76, 83, 85, 117, 121, 200
Evans, W. J., *v*
"Evidences of Christianity," 152
Evil, 192 ff.

Faith, 144, 232; ground of, 61, 88
Fall of man, 22, 27, 76, 77, 229
Feuerbach, Ludwig, 104
Forms of worship, 9, 30
Forsyth, P. T., 5
Froude, J. A., 5
Future state, 171, 179 ff.

Gladstone, W. E., 73
God, 9, 28 f., 106, 112, 117, 149, 161, 162, 190, 214, 234; absence of in religious systems, 122; as deliverer, 143; as Father, 214; as living person, 55; as perfect love, 49, 63, 145; as source of righteousness, 165, 191; knowledge of, 16, 24, 54 f., 56 f., 63, 64, 109, 129, 145; name of, 220, 222
Goethe, 135
Gospel, 76, 84, 145, 177, 190, 235

Hare, Georgina, 10, 117, 121, 130, 131, 137, 138, 139, 140, 141

Hare, Julius, 7, 46 ff., 52, 70, 127, 150, 156, 170, 171
Has the Church or the state the power to educate nations?, 14
Headlam, Arthur C., 13
Hell, 112
High Churchman, 105
Hinduism, 112, 179
Hocking, W. E., 10
Hodgkin, John, 223
Holland, Henry Scott, 5
Holy Communion, 206 (*See* Eucharist, Lord's Supper)
Holy Spirit, 89, 115, 179, 194 ff., 198, 208
Hope, 82, 104
Hort, F. J. A., 5, 13, 14, 143, 151, 238
Hughes, Thomas, 213
Hurry, Anne, 45
Hurry, Edmund, 45
Hutton, R. H., 18, 175, 191

Incarnation, 22, 26, 57, 112, 214 ff.

Jelf, R. W., 117, 133, 137, 154, 157, 169, 170, 171
Jerusalem, Bishopric, 99
Justification by faith, 28, 63, 233, 240

Keble, John, 64, 75
Kierkegaard, S. K., 20
Kingdom of Christ, The, 8, 29, 32, 34, 82, 85, 101
Kingdom of God, 145
Kingdom of Heaven, 180
Kingsley, Charles, 11, 107, 121, 128, 129, 132, 150, 154, 158, 168, 185, 220, 221
Kraemer, Hendrik, 10

Lambeth Quadrilateral, 34
Learning and Working, 14
Liberals, 36, 65, 76
Lightfoot, J. B., 13
Lincoln, Abraham, 222
Liturgical Movement, 30
Liturgics, 30, 199 ff.
Liturgy, 136, 148
Lord's Supper, 29 (*See* Eucharist, Holy Communion)

244

Ludlow, J. M., 11 f., 122, 128, 150, 151, 160, 192, 205, 206, 222
Luther, Martin, 28, 240
Lutheranism, 9, 35
Lux Mundi, 13

MacMillan, Daniel, 101, 104, 106, 164, 166
Man, 9, 26 ff., 60, 208 ff., 229
Mansel, Henry L., 16, 191
Maurice, Anna Barton, 87, 96, 100, 113, 114
Maurice, Edmund, 8, 210, 224
Maurice, Elizabeth, 6
Maurice, Emma, 7, 43, 72
Maurice, Esther, 7, 10, 179
Maurice, Frederick, 8, 40, 210
Maurice, Frederick B., *v*
Maurice, Frederick Barton, 8, 14
Maurice, Frederick Denison: autobiographical letters, 40-46; biographical account by editors, 5-17; chaplain of Lincoln's Inn, 119; controversy with Colenso, 212, 219; controversy with Mansel, 192; enters Oxford, 52; first wife's death, 114; King's College—154 ff., storm, 170, leaves, 174; ordination, 62; religious press attacks him, 133; remarries, 142; sickness, 233
Maurice, Michael, 5, 6, 43, 44, 49, 54
Maurice, Priscilla, 43, 53, 115, 116, 167
Maurice, Priscilla Hurry, 41 f., 44, 46, 59, 114, 142
Mediator, 58, 178, 179, 195
Method, 19; as a preacher, 175 ff.
Millenarians, 181 ff.
Ministry, 9, 31, 37, 62
Moral and Metaphysical Philosophy, 8

New Testament, 90, 148
Newman, John Henry, 11, 65, 75, 76, 85, 117, 121, 240
Niebuhr, H. Richard, 5, 22
Niebuhr, Rheinhold, 13

Oxford Movement, 7, 64 ff.
Oxford Tracts, 81, 84, 101
Oxford University, 53, 73

Paley, Wm., 47
Palmer, W., 100
Parker, Esther, 41
Parties in the Church of England, 36, 65, 75, 86 ff., 135, 150
Paul, St., 59, 110, 196
Phillips, E., 207
Phillips, G. L., 16
Plato, 24, 48, 124, 152
Platonism, 24
Prayer, 62, 202
Prayer Book, 131 f., 180, 230
Predestination, 28
Presbyterian, 84, 89, 135
Priest, priesthood, 225, 237, 239
Protestantism, 8, 9, 28, 100, 102, 224, 235, 240
Pusey, Edward, 7, 75, 76, 84, 221

Quakers, Quakerism, 9, 82, 85
Queen's College, London, 13

Ramsey, Arthur Michael, *v*, 5, 23
Rationalism, 105
Reason, 25, 113
Reasons for not joining a party, 83, 85
Redemption, 24, 77, 144, 199, 229, 241
Reform Bill of 1830, 72, 73
Religion, 106, 109
Religions of the World, 10, 179
Renan, Joseph E., 218
Resurrection, 140, 242
Revelation, 23 ff., 56, 57, 64, 103, 112, 197, 220, 221, 232
Roman Catholicism, 11, 32 (*See* Catholic Church)
Rome, Romanism, 117, 118, 235
Rose, Hugh, 73, 75

Sabbath, 185 ff.
Sacrament, 221, 237
Sacrifice, 27, 28, 30, 202, 207, 225
Sanders, C. R., 13
Scott, A. J., 92
Scripture, Scriptures, 23 ff., 108, 144, 148, 178
Second Vatican Council, 25
Sect, 32 ff., 93, 189, 191
Sequel to What Is Revelation, The, 16

245